SAP ABAP Objects

A Practical Guide to the Basics and Beyond

Rehan Zaidi

Apress®

SAP ABAP Objects: A Practical Guide to the Basics and Beyond

Rehan Zaidi
Dubai, United Arab Emirates

ISBN-13 (pbk): 978-1-4842-4963-5
https://doi.org/10.1007/978-1-4842-4964-2

ISBN-13 (electronic): 978-1-4842-4964-2

Managing Director, Apress Media LLC: Welmoed Spahr
Acquisitions Editor: Susan McDermott
Development Editor: Laura Berendson
Coordinating Editor: Rita Fernando

Cover designed by eStudioCalamar

Distributed to the book trade worldwide by Springer Science+Business Media New York, 233 Spring Street, 6th Floor, New York, NY 10013. Phone 1-800-SPRINGER, fax (201) 348-4505, e-mail orders-ny@springer-sbm.com, or visit www.springeronline.com. Apress Media, LLC is a California LLC and the sole member (owner) is Springer Science + Business Media Finance Inc (SSBM Finance Inc). SSBM Finance Inc is a **Delaware** corporation.

For information on translations, please e-mail rights@apress.com, or visit http://www.apress.com/rights-permissions.

Apress titles may be purchased in bulk for academic, corporate, or promotional use. eBook versions and licenses are also available for most titles. For more information, reference our Print and eBook Bulk Sales web page at http://www.apress.com/bulk-sales.

Any source code or other supplementary material referenced by the author in this book is available to readers on GitHub via the book's product page, located at www.apress.com/9781484249635. For more detailed information, please visit http://www.apress.com/source-code.

Printed on acid-free paper

Another book dedicated to my mother....

Table of Contents

About the Author

Rehan Zaidi is a consultant for several international SAP clients. He started working with SAP in 1999 and writing about his experiences in 2001. He has written several articles for both *SAP Professional Journal* and *HR Expert*, and he also has a number of popular SAP- and ABAP-related books to his credit.

He provides SAP consulting to companies and helps clients (both on-site and remote) with their SAP technical requirements (ABAP, Workflow, Quick development of Fiori apps, and S/4 HANA-related requirements). Rehan also creates documentation and training manuals for a number of companies based in the United States.

Rehan is interested in providing publicity options to ERP consulting firms. His clients are located in a number of countries and continents, including the Middle East (GCC region) as well as North America and Europe. He is currently working on a new ERP programmer magazine. He can be reached at erpdomain@gmail.com.

About the Technical Reviewer

Farhan Ullah started his career in SAP as an ABAP developer in 2002. He is a certified ABAP developer and a successful SAP ABAP trainer. He has also moved toward providing functional consultancy and fulfilling the business analysis role. However, he remains vested in ABAP development and keeps abreast on the latest ABAP tools and technologies. With more than 15 years of experience in various roles, Farhan has broad expertise in solution design, project management, support of long-term customer relationships, and strategic business development.

CHAPTER 1

Creating Classes and Objects

Within ABAP object-oriented programming, classes are defined which encapsulate data as well as functions. Objects (also known as instances) can then be created based on the class in question. Classes can be created locally (within a program) or globally (available to all programs in a system). ABAP also supports polymorphism via simple inheritance interfaces.

In this chapter, we start by defining the key terms used in the ABAP Objects arena. Then, we look at the various components of a typical class in ABAP Objects and walk through the steps required to create a local class in an ABAP program. In the next section, we look at the global Class Builder transaction SE24 and review the steps required to create a global class that can be accessed by all ABAP programs. We also discuss the constructor concept, the creation of objects, and the syntax for calling the methods of the created class. We also demonstrate the importance of defining static components in the class concept. We wrap this chapter up by creating a full-fledged coding demo of the PLAYER class by printing a list of football players (via the usage of a static attribute and method).

The following topics will be covered in this chapter:

- Classes and their various components

- Object creation and instance-method calls

- Static components

- The predicate expression IS INSTANCE OF

- Deferred class definition

1

© Rehan Zaidi 2019
R. Zaidi, *SAP ABAP Objects*, https://doi.org/10.1007/978-1-4842-4964-2_1

Technical requirements include:

- Access to a SAP NetWeaver 7.5X system with ABAP authorization

- Basic knowledge of ABAP programming

Classes and Their Components

A *class* is simply defined as a general representation of a real-world thing. Typical examples include a factory, a purchase order, and a player. There may be none, one, or a number of instances for this class at any given time. These instances are known as *objects*. The creation or generation of these objects is called *instantiation*. For example, a purchase order class may have two objects—purchase orders 620000022 and 6200000023.

Within ABAP, classes can be local or global. A local class is defined in a program, whereas the global class is defined via the Class Builder transaction SE24. (A global class can be addressed by all the programs within a given SAP system.) An ABAP class (whether local or global) may have the following components:

- **Attributes**: Attributes are the data of a given class or object. They may store important information like the unique key or they may uniquely identify the object. They may also store characteristics of the object or may even help you determine the current state or status of the object. For example, the PURCHASE ORDER class may have the Purchase Order Number attribute. Likewise, the PLAYER class may have the Player Weight and Height attributes. The attributes may be based on any data type. It is also possible to define an attribute based on the reference to any other global or local class. (This means that a given class will have an attribute that is another class' object.) An attribute may also be read-only, i.e., defined as constants.

- **Methods**: These are actions or operations that can be done on objects of a given class. For example, the PURCHASE ORDER class may have a number of methods, such as PurchaseOrder_Change or PurchaseOrder_Delete.

- **Events**: These are signals generated as a result of changes in an object's state. Typical examples include `SalesOrder_Changed` and `Player_Transferred`. The events that are triggered for a given object can be linked to special handler methods. (The coding within such methods is executed when the relevant event occurs.)

In addition to class components, visibility sections are also important. Within a class definition, there may be three visibility sections (at the global Class Builder level, these are known as *visibility* levels). These are Public, Private, and Protected. You may have any number of events, attributes, and methods within these visibility sections.

Let's consider these components in a little more detail:

- **Public components**: These are defined within the public section of a class and can be accessed from anywhere—from the class itself, outside the class, or from a subclass of the class in question.

- **Private components**: These are only accessible from within the class in question. For example, the `EMPLOYEE_NO` attribute may be accessed via a method of the class called `WRITE_EMPLOYEE_NO`. Private section components can be accessed by the class only, and not by its subclasses or by users outside the class. (An exception to this is the *Friend Class* concept, which we will discuss in Chapter 6.)

- **Protected components**: These are defined within the protected section of a class. These components are only accessible within the class itself or from any of its subclasses (either immediate or their subclasses).

The components of a class can be static (instance-independent) or instance (instance-dependent). Static components, such as static attributes, are for the entire class (for all objects of the class) and not specific to any one object instance. These are defined via the addition of the `CLASS` prefix . For example, `CLASS-DATA` is used to define static attributes, whereas `CLASS-METHODS` specifies static methods of a given class. For example, we may have a static attribute called `TOTAL_EMPLOYEES` that's used to store the total number of employee objects. Likewise, to find the total list of employees, a static method (`GET_TOTAL_EMPLOYEES`) may be contained within a class.

A class (known in this context as a *subclass*) can be inherited from another class (called a *superclass*). The inherited class may then have additional methods of its own as well as contain redefinitions of methods derived from its superclass. It is also possible to define a class as *final*, meaning no subclasses may be created for it. A final class may not be inherited. Also, a particular class may be defined as abstract, meaning that no objects may be created for the class. However, abstract classes may be inherited and subclasses may be defined. For example, consider the PLAYER class. We may define this class as an abstract class, since we cannot have just a player. It should either be a cricket player or a football player, which are derived classes of PLAYER. So, PLAYER is an abstract class that cannot be instantiated but only derived in the form of a subclass.

Local Classes

As mentioned previously, classes may be defined as global or local. Local classes are defined within a given program and are local (only accessible) to the program in which they are created. These may be defined in programs using the transactions SE38 and SE80. In this section, we look at how to define a simple local class in a program.

We first create a definition of the class. We define the class by the name of PLAYER. This class has two sections—public and private. The private section has three attributes with type STRING, including NAME, COUNTRY, and CLUB, as follows:

```
public section.
   methods write_player_details.
   methods constructor importing
                     name type string
                     country type string
                     club type string.

 private section.
    data name type string.
    data country type string.
    data club type string.
endclass.
```

Within the public section, there are two methods, constructor and WRITE_PLAYER_DETAILS. The constructor method has three importing parameters for name, country, and club, as shown. The actual code of the constructor and WRITE_PLAYER_DETAILS methods is written in the implementation of the class, as follows:

```
class player implementation.
 method write_player_details.
    skip.
    write :/ 'Name :', me->name.
    write :/ 'Country :', me->country.
    write :/ 'Club :', me->club.
 endmethod.

 method constructor.
   me->name = name.
   me->country = country.
   me->club = club.
 endmethod.
endclass.
```

In the constructor, we assign the imported values of name, country, and club to the corresponding attributes of the object in question (the one being created at the time of the constructor call). The special variable called me is used for this purpose. The constructor is called automatically when new objects are created for the class (we will see this in detail in the next section).

Tip   A special variable called me is provided for accessing the components within a class from within the class. This is the self-reference variable. These refer to the instance of the class under consideration at the time of program execution or object method. This refers to the attribute of the current object in question.

The implementation of the WRITE_PLAYER_DETAILS method writes the values contained in the three attributes—name, country, and club.

It is worth noting that the sequence of the three sections is important. The sections should be ordered as public, followed by protected (if any), and then finally private. If this sequence is not followed, an error occurs, as shown in Figure 1-1.

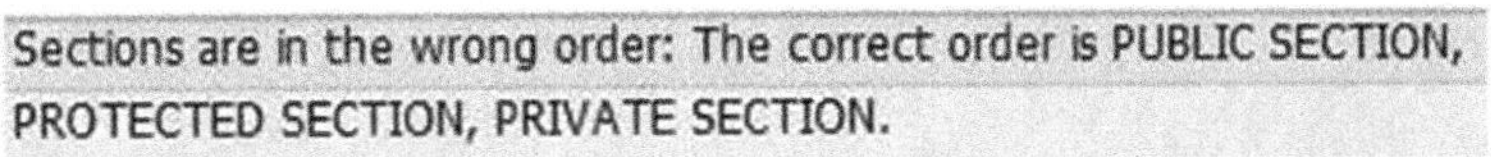

Sections are in the wrong order: The correct order is PUBLIC SECTION, PROTECTED SECTION, PRIVATE SECTION.

Figure 1-1. *Misplaced section error*

We will now create the same class using transaction SE24, i.e. as a global class. Defining a class within the Class Builder allows it to be accessed from all programs (and even workflows). Moreover, the Class Builder provides a number of tools and features that the developer may use. Alternatively to transaction SE24, you can also define global classes using transaction SE80. These will be discussed in detail in Chapter 3.

Global Classes

In this section, we define a global class using the transaction SE24 from the Class Builder. This class will have the same components as the local class defined in the previous section. Follow these steps:

1. Call transaction SE24. The screen shown in Figure 1-2 appears.

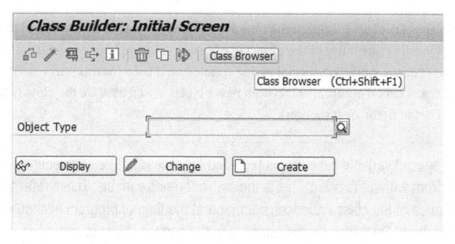

Figure 1-2. *Class Builder transaction*

2. Enter the name of the class in the field provided. We will create a class called ZST6_PLAYER_CLASS. Then click the Create button. The popup shown in Figure 1-3 appears.

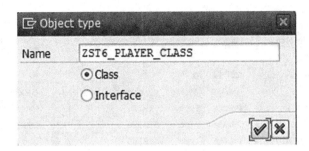

Figure 1-3. *Object type*

3. Make sure the Class radio button is selected.

4. Click the Continue button. The dialog shown in Figure 1-4 appears.

5. Enter a suitable description (in our case PLAYER Class) in the field provided.

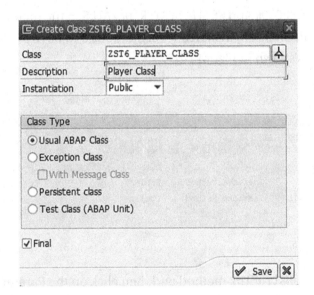

Figure 1-4. *Create the class*

6. Do not change any of the other values shown in the dialog box. Click the Save button. This takes us to the screen shown in Figure 1-5.

Class Interface		ZST6_PLAYER_CLASS			Implemented / Active	

Properties   Interfaces   Friends   Attributes   Methods   Events   Types   Aliases

☐ Filter

Attribute	Level	Visibility	Typing	Associated Type		Description
NAME	Instance Attribute	Private	Type	STRING	⇨	Name of Player
COUNTRY	Instance Attribute	Private	Type	STRING	⇨	Country of Player
CLUB	Instance Attribute	Private	Type	STRING	⇨	Club of Player

Figure 1-5. *Class components*

7. Note that there are a number of tabs on the screen, including
    Interface, Friends, Attributes, and Methods. Click on the
    Attributes tab and enter the three attributes—NAME, COUNTRY, and
    CLUB—as instance-level attributes.

8. Choose the type as STRING and visibility as Private.

9. Enter CONSTRUCTOR and WRITE_PLAYER_DETAILS in the method
    list. Both methods are instance-level methods and have public
    visibility, as shown in Figure 1-6.

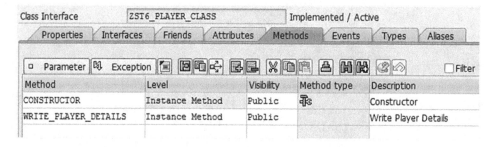

Class Interface		ZST6_PLAYER_CLASS			Implemented / Active	

Properties   Interfaces   Friends   Attributes   Methods   Events   Types   Aliases

☐ Parameter   ☐ Exception   ☐ Filter

Method	Level	Visibility	Method type	Description
CONSTRUCTOR	Instance Method	Public	⛏	Constructor
WRITE_PLAYER_DETAILS	Instance Method	Public		Write Player Details

Figure 1-6. *Methods*

10. Select the Constructor method and then click on the Parameter
     button. This will take you to the parameter specification screen of
     the Constructor method, as shown in Figure 1-7.

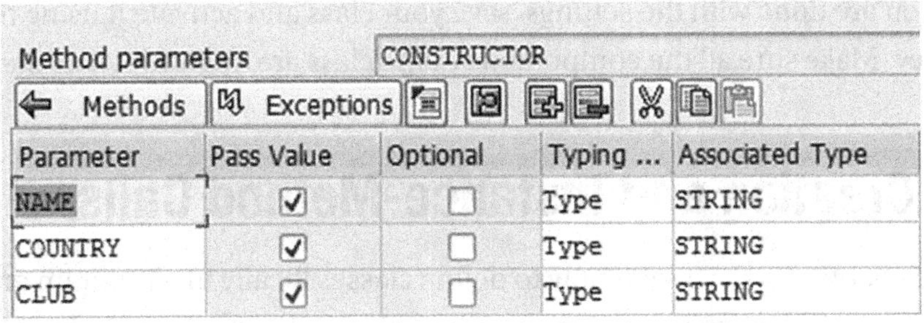

Method parameters		CONSTRUCTOR			
← Methods ▯ Exceptions ▤ ▣ ▤ ▤ ✂ ▢ ▨					
Parameter	Pass Value	Optional	Typing ...	Associated Type
NAME	☑	☐	Type	STRING
COUNTRY	☑	☐	Type	STRING
CLUB	☑	☐	Type	STRING

Figure 1-7. *Constructor method*

11. Here we will specify the three parameters of the constructor—
NAME, COUNTRY, and CLUB—as shown. Double-click the name of
Constructor method to open the method code editor, as shown in
Figure 1-8.

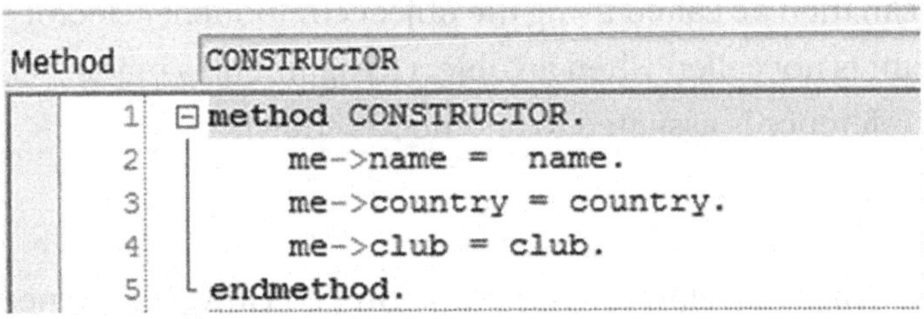

Method	CONSTRUCTOR

```
1  ⊟ method CONSTRUCTOR.
2        me->name  =   name.
3        me->country = country.
4        me->club = club.
5   └ endmethod.
```

Figure 1-8. *Method code editor*

12. We can now write the constructor code. The three values
imported into the method are assigned to the corresponding
components of the class attributes using the self-reference
variable me. Similarly, we will enter the WRITE_PLAYER_DETAILS
method code, as shown in Figure 1-9.

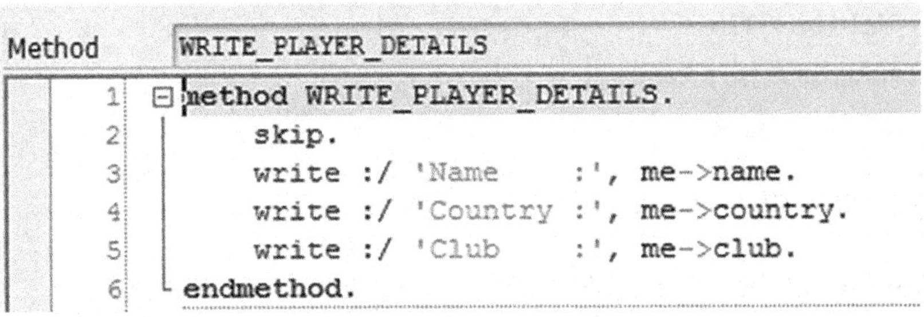

Method	WRITE_PLAYER_DETAILS

```
1  ⊟ method WRITE_PLAYER_DETAILS.
2        skip.
3        write :/ 'Name     :', me->name.
4        write :/ 'Country :', me->country.
5        write :/ 'Club     :', me->club.
6   └ endmethod.
```

Figure 1-9. *write_player_details method*

When you are done with the settings, save your class and activate it using the CTRL+F3 key. Make sure all the components in the class are in an activated state.

Object Creation and Instance-Method Calls

So far in the chapter we have seen how to define classes locally in a program and within the global Class Builder. In this section, we learn what is involved in creating objects based on the local and global classes created in the previous sections. One or more objects can be created for a particular class within a program. Let's see how this is done.

The first step is to define the reference variable for the defined class. This can be either the local class or the global class.

We then call the CREATE OBJECT statement in order to generate an object (instance) for the given class. For the object, the constructor is automatically called.

The method can then be called using the object component selector ->.

The constructor is not called when an object assignment is made, i.e., when one particular object reference is assigned to another, as shown:

```
: OBJ2 = OBJ1.
```

To call methods of global classes, the code is similar. However, we need to call the respective global class. For global classes, we have an additional shortcut available.

For example, to add the CREATE OBJECT statement, follow these steps:

1. Click the Pattern button. The dialog box appears as shown in Figure 1-10.

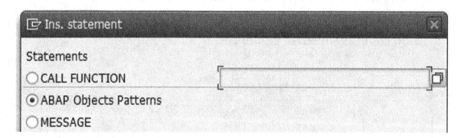

Figure 1-10. *Ins. statement*

2. Then select the ABAP Objects Patterns option and click the Continue button. This will display the object-oriented statement pattern popup, as shown in Figure 1-11.

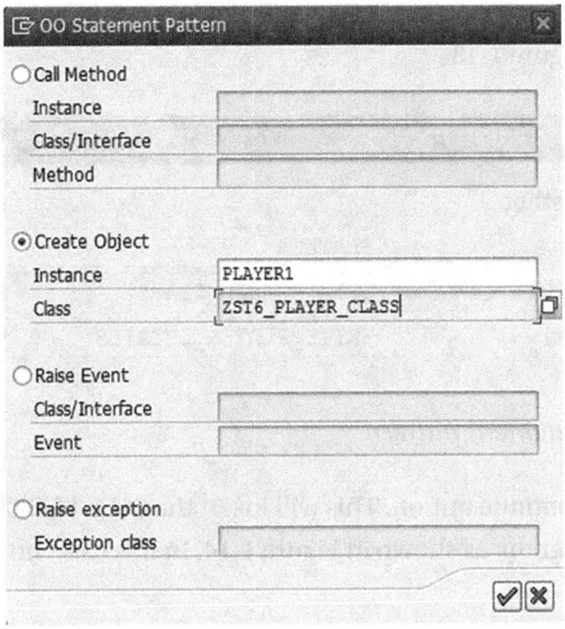

Figure 1-11. *Statement pattern*

3. Choose Create Object. We also need to enter the instance name and the global class to be used. Then click the Continue button.

This will add the code shown in Figure 1-12 to your ABAP program.

```
CREATE OBJECT PLAYER1
    EXPORTING
        NAME    =
        COUNTRY =
        CLUB    =
        .
```

Figure 1-12. *Create Object statement added*

Similarly, to add a CALL method statement to the OO statement pattern dialog, follow these steps:

1. Enter the instance name in the field provided (in our case, PLAYER4).

2. Enter the name of the global class (ZT6_PLAYER_CLASS) in the field provided. When the f4 help for the method is taken, all methods of the specified class (other than the Constructor) are displayed in the Hit list.

3. Fill in the Instance name, Class name, and the Method name, as shown in Figure 1-13.

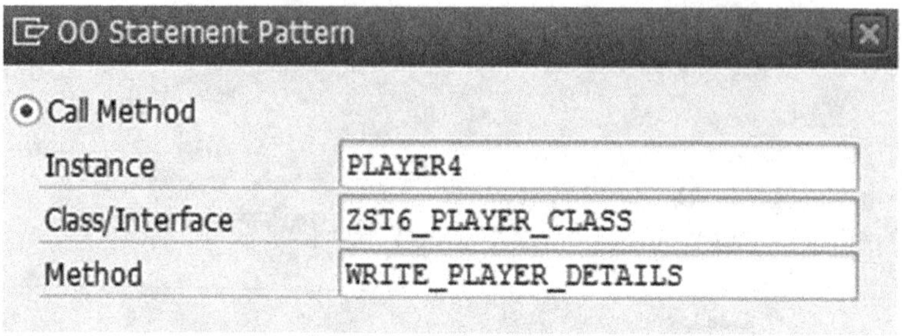

Figure 1-13. *OO statement pattern*

4. Click the Continue button. This will insert the CALL METHOD code into the program, as shown in Figure 1-14. In this case, no method parameters exist.

```
CALL METHOD PLAYER4->WRITE_PLAYER_DETAILS
```

Figure 1-14. *Call method*

Methods and Method Calls

We have already seen methods in action. In this section, we look at methods in greater depth.

A method can have importing parameters and exporting parameters. A method can create an object of another class, or the same class to which the method belongs. Constructors are special methods that are called at the time of object creation or instantiation. They may or may not have an importing parameter.

There are various ways of calling a method.

Suppose we have a method called WRITE_PLAYER_DETAILS that has no importing or exporting parameters. In that case, the following two forms of method calls are permissible:

- CALL METHOD player1->write_player_details.

- player2->write_player_details( ).

There are certain methods that have one RETURNING parameter and any number of IMPORTING parameters. These are known as *functional methods* and the RETURNING parameter corresponds to the RESULT value returned by the method.

There are various ways of calling a functional method:

- When there are no parameters for the functional method, the call may be like this one:

```
result = func_meth( )
```

- If one value is passed as a parameter (this may correspond to a non-optional IMPORTING parameter), the call may look like this:

```
result = func_meth(VAL1 )
```

- When two values are supplied for importing parameters, the call may look like this:

```
result = func_meth( par1 = VAL1 par2 = VAL2 ).

CALL METHOD func_meth
exporting   par1 =  VAL1
            par2 =  VAL2
            receiving   result =  result.
```

Here we saw some of the examples of methods and method calls. In the newer releases, a number of other forms of functional methods are possible. We will see these in more detail in the next chapter.

In the next section, we cover another important topic related to ABAP Objects—static components.

Static Components

So far, we have been working with instance-level components (methods and attributes). Now we will look at static components. Unlike instance components, static components belong to the entire class and not to any given object of the class. All of the objects in a class can access its static attributes. If you change a static attribute in an object, the change is visible to all other objects in the class.

There are three kinds of static components:

- Static attributes

- Static methods

- Static events

If a class is composed of only static components and no instance components, the class is called a *static class*.

In this section, we will see how to define static components in our local class.

Note   We also have static constructor in a class. This is called only once for a class (and internal session), prior to the first access made to the class.

The class (static) constructor is defined in the class definition, as shown here:

```
CLASS myclass DEFINITION.
 PUBLIC SECTION.
 CLASS-METHODS class_constructor.
 """ static constructor
 PRIVATE SECTION.
 ............
 ENDCLASS.
```

To add static components to the local class definition, we use the CLASS prefix, such as CLASS-METHODS or CLASS-DATA.

For example, within the class definition, we may define a static internal table called PLAYERS_LIST based on the TY_PLAYER type, as shown:

```
class-data: players_list type STANDARD
 TABLE OF ty_player.
```

Similarly, we may have a static method called DISPLAY_LIST_OF_PLAYERS (also in the class definition) as shown:

```
class-methods display_list_of_players
```

The method code in the implementation section of the class method is written similarly to the instance method.

Accessing static components is a little different from that of instance components. Unlike the instance component access, we use the class component selector => to refer to static components. For example, suppose we need to call the static method DISPLAY_ LIST_OF_PLAYERS of the PLAYER class from outside the class. We may do so as follows:

```
player=>display_list_of_players( )
```

The class name is used in this case and not the name of any object of the class. Similarly, if a static attribute called MYATTR of a class called MYCLASS has been defined as public, this attribute may be accessed outside the class as shown:

```
write : MYCLASS=>MYATTR
```

So far, we have seen how to define and access static components within a local class. Depending on the scenario, static components such as attributes and methods may be used in your classes. We will see more uses of static components in the next chapter.

A Full-Fledged Demo

In this section, we create a local class that will contain static components. We make a copy of the local class created earlier. We then add the static components in order to create and print a list of football players.

In the copy of the class, we will make these changes. We will first create a DEFERRED definition of the PLAYER class. Next, we will create a type TY_PLAYER based on the reference type TY_PLAYER, which in turn is based on the PLAYER class.

```
CLASS PLAYER DEFINITION DEFERRED.
 TYPES: TY_PLAYER TYPE REF TO PLAYER
```

The DEFERRED variant of the class is used to make the existence of the class known, irrespective of where the class is defined in the program. For example, in the following example, the PLAYER class has a deferred definition, which means the reference type definition for TY_PLAYER does not give an error. The actual definition of the PLAYER class comes later.

```
class player DEFINITION DEFERRED.
 types: ty_player type ref to player.
 class player DEFINITION.
 ......
 endclass.
```

Within the PLAYER class, we add a static attribute called PLAYERS_LIST. This is a standard internal table of players. We used the TY_PLAYER type created in the previous step.

```
PRIVATE SECTION.
 DATA NAME TYPE STRING.
 DATA COUNTRY TYPE STRING.
 DATA CLUB TYPE STRING.
 CLASS-DATA: PLAYERS_LIST TYPE STANDARD
 TABLE OF TY_PLAYER.
```

We add a static method called DISPLAY_LIST_OF_PLAYERS to the class definition. This will later be used to print the list of players stored in the PLAYERS_LIST internal table.

```
CLASS PLAYER DEFINITION.
 PUBLIC SECTION.
 METHODS WRITE_PLAYER_DETAILS.
 METHODS CONSTRUCTOR IMPORTING
 NAME TYPE STRING
 COUNTRY TYPE STRING
 CLUB TYPE STRING.
 CLASS-METHODS DISPLAY_LIST_OF_PLAYERS.
```

Next, we make a small change to the class constructor. We append the object currently being created to the internal table PLAYERS_LIST (using the self-reference variable me). Our constructor will look like the one shown here:

```
METHOD CONSTRUCTOR.
 ME->NAME = NAME.
 ME->COUNTRY = COUNTRY.
 ME->CLUB = CLUB.
 APPEND ME TO PLAYERS_LIST.
 ENDMETHOD.
```

Finally, we write the method to display the list of players. Within this method, we first define a TEMP_PLAYER reference variable to hold the reference to the PLAYER class.

We then loop at the PLAYERS_LIST internal table. Within the loop, we call the WRITE_ PLAYER_DETAILS method for each object reference contained in the internal table.

```
METHOD DISPLAY_LIST_OF_PLAYERS
 DATA : TEMP_PLAYER TYPE REF TO PLAYER.
 WRITE :/ '------------PLAYERS LIST------------'.
 LOOP AT PLAYERS_LIST INTO TEMP_PLAYER.
 TEMP_PLAYER->WRITE_PLAYER_DETAILS( ) .
 ENDLOOP.
 WRITE :/ '----------------------------------'.
 ENDMETHOD.
```

Next, we write the code to create the two objects based on the PLAYER class and then call the static method DISPLAY_LIST_PLAYERS. This is shown here:

```
data: player1 type ref to player.
data: player2 type ref to player.

CREATE OBJECT player1
EXPORTING
name = 'John Mann'
country = 'Germany'
club = 'Bayern Munich'.

CREATE OBJECT player2
EXPORTING
name = 'Paul Goldberg'
country = 'Britain'
club = 'Liverpool'.
player=>display_list_of_players( ) .
```

We created two objects (PLAYER1 and PLAYER2) based on the PLAYER class. (The constructor is automatically called twice, once for each object, and each time the respective player details are appended to the internal table called PLAYERS_LIST.)

Finally, we print the list of players by calling the static method DISPLAY_LIST_OF_ PLAYERS. This will generate the output shown in Figure 1-15.

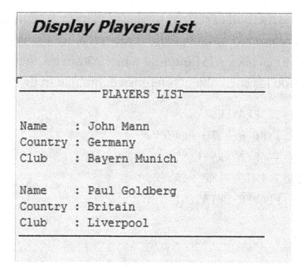

Figure 1-15. *Players list displayed*

The full code listing of this example is shown next:

```
class player DEFINITION DEFERRED.
 types: ty_player type ref to player.

 class player DEFINITION.
 public section.
 methods write_player_details.
 methods constructor importing name type string
 country type string
 club type string.
 class-methods display_list_of_players.

 private section.
 data name type string.
 data country type string.
 data club type string.
 class-DATA: players_list type STANDARD TABLE OF ty_player.
 ENDCLASS.

 class player IMPLEMENTATION .
 method write_player_details.
 skip.
```

```
write :/ 'Name :', me->name.
write :/ 'Country :', me->country.
write :/ 'Club :', me->club.
endmethod.
method constructor.
me->name = name.
me->country = country.
me->club = club.
append me to players_list.
ENDMETHOD.

method display_list_of_players.
data : temp_player type ref to player.
write :/ '------------PLAYERS LIST------------'.
loop at players_list into temp_player.
temp_player->write_player_details( ) .
endloop.
write :/ '-----------------------------------'.
endmethod.
ENDCLASS.

start-OF-SELECTION.
data : player1 type ref to player.
data : player2 type ref to player.

CREATE OBJECT player1
EXPORTING
name = 'John Mann'
country = 'Germany'
club = 'Bayern Munich'.

CREATE OBJECT player2
EXPORTING
name = 'Paul Goldberg'
country = 'Britain'
club = 'Liverpool'.
player=>display_list_of_players( ) .
end-OF-selection.
```

The IS INSTANCE OF Predicate Expression

In newer releases, SAP supports a new predicate expression called IS INSTANCE OF. It allows you to check whether a particular reference variable is based on a given class or not. This may be used in an if statement to program a check and then execute appropriate code. The predicate expression checks if a given reference variable refers to an object of the specified class (or any of its subclasses—not emphasized here for simplicity's sake). In this case, however, it must be ensured that the reference variable is not initial. This may be used to check the reference of local and global classes.

The generic syntax of this predicate expression is:

```
IF MYREF is instance of class_name.
 ENDIF.
```

Here the expression is true when MYREF is a reference variable based on the class_name class. The comparison must be done with an object type (i.e., a class or an interface). The MYREF statement expects a reference variable pointing to the type of class compared in question. Now consider the following example:

```
class player DEFINITION.
 public section.
 methods write_player_details.
 methods constructor importing name type string
 country type string
 club type string.
 private section.
 data name type string.
 data country type string.
 data club type string.
 ENDCLASS.
 class player IMPLEMENTATION .
 method write_player_details.
 skip.
 write :/ 'Name :', me->name.
 write :/ 'Country :', me->country.
 write :/ 'Club :', me->club.
 endmethod.
```

```
method constructor.
me->name = name.
me->country = country.
me->club = club.
ENDMETHOD.
ENDCLASS.

START-OF-SELECTION.
data player1 type ref to player.
CREATE OBJECT player1
EXPORTING
name = 'John Mann'
country = 'Germany'
club = 'Bayern Munich'.

if player1 is instance of player .
write :/ ' Object of Player class '.
endif.
```

We can also use the IS INSTANCE OF expression to compare interface references. This will be discussed later in the book.

Here, we have defined a class and implemented its methods. We then defined a reference variable pointing to the PLAYER class, and then created an object using the player1 variable. Finally, we use the IS INSTANCE OF predicate to determine the type of the player1 object. The if statement returns true.

When the program is executed, the output is as follows:

Object of Player 1

Consider another example:

```
data player1 type ref to player.
 CREATE OBJECT player1
 EXPORTING
 name = 'John Mann'
 country = 'Germany'
 club = 'Bayern Munich'.
```

```
if player1 is instance of cl_salv_table .
write :/ ' Object of Player class '.
endif.
```

Here, we are using the IS INSTANCE OF expression in order to find out if the reference variable MYREF points to a reference in the CL_SALV_TABLE class. In this case, the program does not compile correctly and results in a syntax error.

Apart from the IS INSTANCE OF expression, during the past few releases there have been a number of changes in ABAP as far as the ABAP Objects are concerned (in particular in NetWeaver 7.52). One change is that we can define functional methods with both exporting and receiving parameters. We will see this in a later part of the book.

Deferred Class Specification

It is now time to discuss an important variant of class declaration—the DEFERRED variant. This form of the CLASS statement allows you to make the class known to the program, irrespective of the location of the addressed class' definition. Using this form, you do not need to specify a definition part. It must also be noted that you do not need to specify the ENDCLASS while making a DEFERRED specification. The complete definition of the class must be included later in the program. Typically, this is required when you need to address a local class before it is defined.

Consider for example the following case:

```
CLASS myclass1 DEFINITION.
 PUBLIC SECTION.
 DATA object_of_2 TYPE REF TO myclass2.
 ENDCLASS.
 CLASS myclass2 DEFINITION.
 PUBLIC SECTION.
 DATA object_of_1 TYPE REF TO myclass1.
ENDCLASS.
```

Suppose we have this program and try to include in myclass1 a reference to an object of the myclass2 class. The code would give us a syntax error.

This is because we tried to address myclass2 (within the declaration of myclass1) before defining it. (The program then tries to find this class in the global class library.) The myclass2 class does not give an error since myclass1 has already been defined.

To solve the issue, we need to include the following line before the definition of myclass2:

```
CLASS myclass2 DEFINITION DEFERRED.
```

The complete code is:

```
CLASS myclass2 DEFINITION DEFERRED.

 CLASS myclass1 DEFINITION.
 PUBLIC SECTION.
 DATA object_of_2 TYPE REF TO myclass2.
 ENDCLASS.
 CLASS myclass2 DEFINITION.
 PUBLIC SECTION.
 DATA object_of_1 TYPE REF TO myclass1.

ENDCLASS.
```

Note that the words DEFERRED and DEFINITION are used together. As you will see, no error occurs now.

It must be noted that the components of the class may not be specified within a DEFERRED DEFINITION.

When PUBLIC is used as well, this variant makes a global class visible but defers its load until the end of respective program unit.

Summary

We learned the basics of ABAP object-oriented programming. We saw how to define local classes and global classes. We also discussed the ways of creating objects of these classes and calling their methods.

Let's proceed to Chapter 2 in which we will move one step forward in ABAP Objects. We will see more examples on object creation and method usage, as well as events creation and generation.

CHAPTER 2

Class Components in Detail

The first chapter introduced you to the basic concepts of object-oriented ABAP. In this chapter, we continue moving ahead and cover a number of useful topics that you need to know to work with ABAP Objects.

We also cover the concepts of local and global classes along with demos and examples. We will move one more step forward. I will use the global as well as local classes to exemplify my point.

The following topics will be covered in this chapter:

- CASE TYPE OF used for determining the type of an object reference variable

- The NEW operator

- Defining types in classes

- Inline declaration

- Specifying constant values within classes

- Static constructor concept

- Method chaining and functional methods

- Event handling

© Rehan Zaidi 2019
R. Zaidi, *SAP ABAP Objects*, https://doi.org/10.1007/978-1-4842-4964-2_2

Finding the Type of an Object Reference Variable: Revisited

Depending on the requirements, it may be necessary to confirm if an object belongs to a particular class, i.e, for example, if an EMPLOYEE object is an instance of the ZCL_TEST_ EMPLOYEE class.

As mentioned in last chapter, since NetWeaver 7.50, we have a new expression called IS INSTANCE OF that can be used in conjunction with the IF statement to confirm if a particular object belongs to a particular class. The usage is very simple, just like any other expression within an IF statement.

Suppose we have the following code:

```
data employee type ref to ZCL_TEST_EMPLOYEE.
 create object employee
    EXPORTING
        number  = 10
        name = 'John Reed'
        country = 'England'.
```

Here, we defined a variable called EMPLOYEE that is a reference to the ZCL_TEST_ EMPLOYEE class. We then used the CREATE OBJECT statement to instantiate the given object with suitable attribute values for number, name, and country.

In this case, we use the IF statement with the IS INSTANCE OF addition on the given class, as shown here:

```
if employee is instance of ZCL_TEST_EMPLOYEE.
    NEW-LINE.
    write : 'This is an employee'.
 endif.
```

The output of this code is shown in Figure 2-1.

```
This is an employee
```

Figure 2-1. *Program output*

There is another way we can determine the type of the given employee.

This is done using the CASE.. ENDCASE control structure. A simple example of this in the context of our employee scenario is as follows:

```
CASE TYPE OF employee.
    WHEN TYPE zcl_test_employee.
        write : / 'This is an employee'.
    WHEN OTHERS.
ENDCASE.
```

Here, note that the TYPE OF addition has been used along with CASE, and the TYPE variant is written with the WHEN clause. This code also checks whether the employee object is an instance of the ZCL_TEST_EMPLOYEE class. The code output is the same as shown in Figure 2-1.

Using the New Operator to Create an Object

Starting with NetWeaver 7.4, ABAP allows creation of objects via the NEW operator. This operator provides an alternate to the CREATE OBJECT statement. There are a number of ways in which it may be used for objects' instantiation. The NEW operator may be used for creating instances of both local and global classes.

Before we look at the actual coding, let's go through the general syntax for the NEW operator. For object creation, the NEW operator may be used in the following two ways:

1. *Used in conjunction with the class name.* The construct for this is shown here:

   ```
   DATA MYOBJ TYPE REF TO MYCLASS.
           MYOBJ = NEW myclass(
                       param1 = val1
                       param2 = val2
                       paramN = valN).
   ```

   Using the inline declaration supported by ABAP 7.40, the same form may be written in one single statement:

```
DATA(MYOBJ) =      NEW myclass(
                        param1 = val1
                        param2 = val2
                           ...
                        paramN = valN).
```

In both of the previous cases, the NEW operator is used in conjunction with the class name. This will create an instance of the MYCLASS class and assign to the reference variable MYOBJ. In the latter case, there is an implicit declaration of MYOBJ based on the MYCLASS class (where the type of MYOBJ is derived from the content of the right side of the assignment). If the constructor of the class has mandatory importing parameters, the corresponding data must be passed to the instance constructor within the parentheses, as shown.

2. *Used with the # character.* Another form of the NEW operator is using it with the # character. The syntax is as follows:

```
DATA
    MYOBJ TYPE REF TO MYCLASS.
    MYOBJ =       NEW #( param1 = val1
                         param2 = val2
                            ...
                         paramN = valN).
```

We declare a variable called MYOBJ referred to the MYCLASS class. Since we already declared a reference variable based on the class in question, there is no need to specify the class again with the NEW operator. Instead of the class name, the # character can be used. Any non-optional parameters are provided in parentheses, as shown earlier.

To better understand how to use the two forms of the NEW operator, let's look at a few examples. In this example, we use the global football player class ZST6_FOOTBALL_PLAYER_CLASS that we defined earlier in the book.

Consider the following code block, which is a pre-ABAP 7.40 version:

```
DATA FOOTBALL_PLAYER TYPE REF TO ZST6_FOOTBALL_PLAYER_CLASS. CREATE OBJECT
FOOTBALL_PLAYER
"""""""" Without NEW Operator
```

```
    EXPORTING
      NAME    = 'Oliver Kahn'
      WEIGHT = '88'
      HEIGHT = '178'
      FOOTBALL_CLUB = 'Bayern Munich'.
FOOTBALL_PLAYER->DISPLAY_PLAYER_DETAILS( ).
```

We created an object of the global class using the CREATE OBJECT statement. The DISPLAY_PLAYER_DETAILS method was then called to print the details of the created football player. This block of code was earlier used to create a football player object.

We will now see two ways that we can instantiate the object of using the NEW operator (and not the CREATE OBJECT statement). The block of code shown in the previous listing may be replaced with the following:

```
DATA(FOOTBALL_PLAYER) =
 NEW ZST6_FOOTBALL_PLAYER_CLASS( NAME = 'Oliver Kahn'
                   WEIGHT = '88'
                   HEIGHT = '178'
                   FOOTBALL_CLUB = 'Bayern Munich' ).
FOOTBALL_PLAYER->DISPLAY_PLAYER_DETAILS( ).
```

We used the inline declaration of FOOTBALL_PLAYER along with the NEW operator in a single statement. This involves the implicit definition of FOOTBALL_PLAYER as a reference of class ZST6_FOOTBALL_PLAYER_CLASS. In this case, we did not have to declare a variable based on the class in a separate statement. An object for the given class is created and the reference variable FOOTBALL_PLAYER may then be used to display the player details.

Let's now look at another piece of code that uses the NEW operator in conjunction with the # character. The corresponding code is shown here:

```
DATA: FOOTBALL_PLAYER TYPE REF TO ZST6_FOOTBALL_PLAYER_CLASS.
FOOTBALL_PLAYER = NEW #( NAME = 'Oliver Kahn'
                     WEIGHT = '88'
                     HEIGHT = '178'
                     FOOTBALL_CLUB = 'Bayern Munich').
FOOTBALL_PLAYER->DISPLAY_PLAYER_DETAILS( ).
```

In this usage form, we declare a reference variable FOOTBALL_PLAYER for the class ZST6_FOOTBALL_PLAYER_CLASS. We use the NEW operator to create an object of the given class. Instead of specifying the name of the class, we use the # character. The reference to the newly created object is assigned to the FOOTBALL_PLAYER variable. The values for the various importing parameters are supplied as shown earlier. The complete class name is not required, as the system automatically detects it from the type of the variable to which the created object's reference is assigned (in our case, FOOTBALL_PLAYER).

The following block of code pertaining to our requirement will be unacceptable, as the class whose object is to be created is unknown:

```
DATA(FOOTBALL_PLAYER) =
                   NEW #( NAME = 'Oliver Kahn'
                          WEIGHT = '88'
                          HEIGHT = '178'
                          FOOTBALL_CLUB = 'Bayern Munich' ).
""   NOT ALLOWED
FOOTBALL_PLAYER->DISPLAY_PLAYER_DETAILS( ).
```

In the above code, the error appears as shown in Figure 2-2. An error results since the type (the class name) of the football player object cannot be determined.

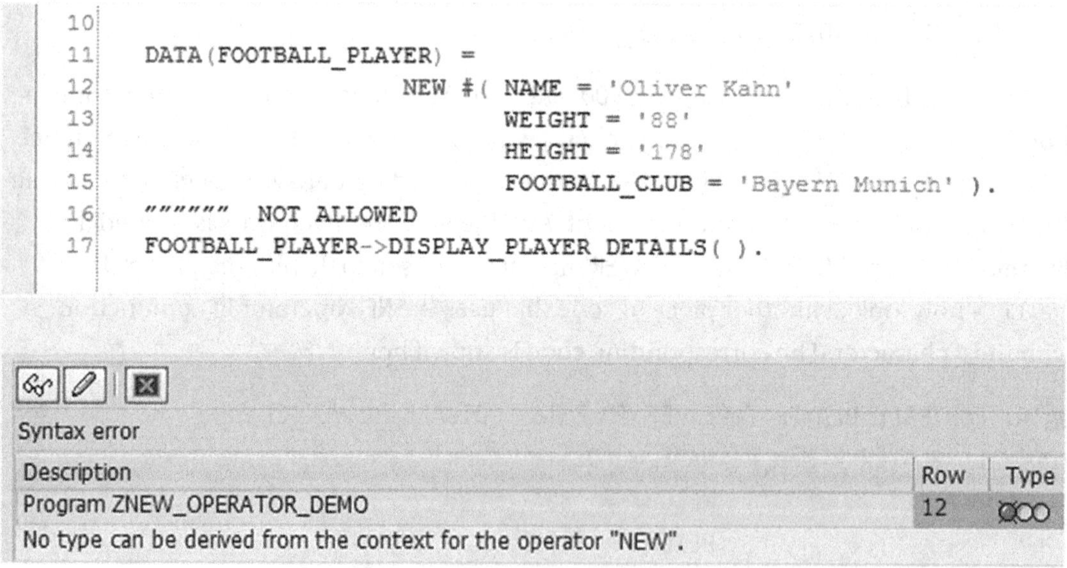

Figure 2-2. *Syntax error using the NEW operator*

Defining Our Own Types in Classes

In this section, we learn how to define our own types in local and global classes. You may define types within the class in the private or the public sections (as well as the protected section). We will first see how to define types in local classes.

A simple example of this is as follows:

```
class newclass definition.
   public section.
      types : myty_dec2 type p length 13 decimals 2.
   endclass.
......
```

Here we defined our own type based on the public section.

You may define your own variables within the class and outside using the `data` statement.

Based on a type defined within the public section, it is possible to define variables based on the define type. You may use the class name and the => symbol to address the define type. An example of this follows:

```
data INT type newclass=>myty_dec2.
```

As mentioned earlier, it is also possible to define a type in a global class. To define a type in an SE24 transaction, a few additional steps are required.

Go to the class in edit mode. Then, click on the Types tab. Enter the name of the type in the Type field. Enter Public as the visibility for this example. Then click the yellow arrow icon on the relevant row.

Class/Interface	ZST17_TOTAL_AVERAGE		Implemented / Active		

Properties	Interfaces	Friends	Attributes	Methods	Events	Types	Aliases

Type	Visibility	Typing	Associated...		Description
MYTY_DEC2	Public				
		Type			
		Type			
		Type			
		Type			
		Type			

Figure 2-3. *Defining types in SE24*

This will take you to the Class Builder code editor, where you may specify the complete specification (length and decimals). This is shown in Figure 2-4.

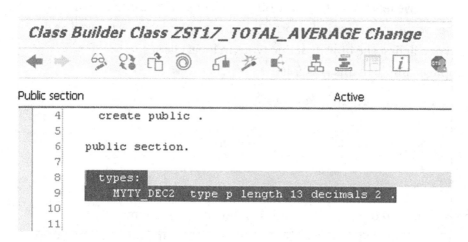

Figure 2-4. *Specifying type definition*

Save and activate the class.

Constants in Classes

Just like we have constants while making report programs, we can declare constants within local and global classes. Within the realm of classes, *constants* are special static attributes within a class. Constants may be public or private attributes and may not be changed within the class or outside the class.

For local classes, suppose we have a class called MYCLASS, as shown:

```
CLASS myclass DEFINITION.
  PUBLIC SECTION.
  CONSTANTS: myconstant TYPE string VALUE 'XYZ'.
ENDCLASS.

DATA myvalue TYPE string.

myvalue = myclass=>myconstant.
write myvalue.
```

Here we have the MYCLASS class, and within the public section, we defined a constant by the name MYCONSTANT and assigned it the value XYZ. Since this is a public attribute, it can be accessed outside the class using the => operator. The value is assigned to the string called myvalue. The contents of myvalue are printed.

Suppose you try to change the value of MYCONSTANT anywhere in the program? An error will occur at the time of the syntax check, as shown in Figure 2-5.

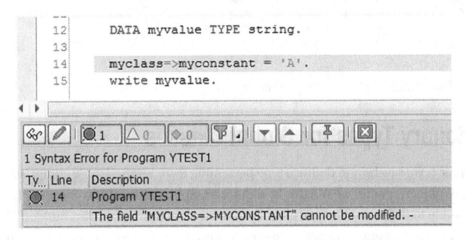

Figure 2-5. Syntax error

As mentioned, a constant can be defined in the private section of a class as well. Hence, the following class definition is also acceptable:

```
CLASS myclass DEFINITION.
    Private SECTION.
        CONSTANTS: myconstant TYPE string VALUE 'XYZ'.
ENDCLASS.
```

You may not be able to access myconstant outside the class, like all other private attributes.

It is also possible to define constants within global classes. Let's see how this is done using the Class Builder. Suppose we have a class called ZCL_TEST_EMPLOYEE (see Figure 2-6).

Here we defined a constant called SALUTATION_MR based on the type STRING, and assigned it the value 'MR'. For the Level, we specified CONSTANT, as shown in Figure 2-6.

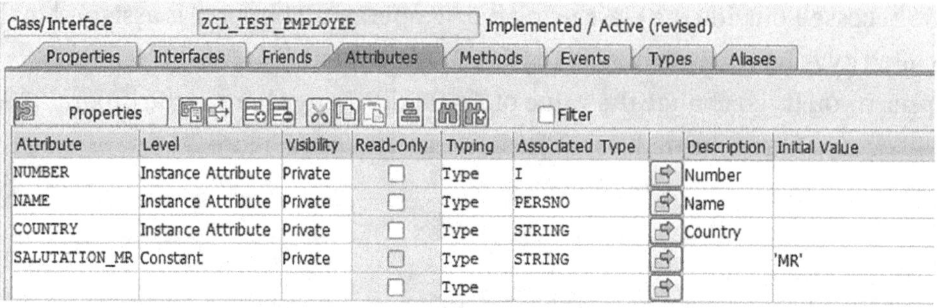

| Class/Interface | ZCL_TEST_EMPLOYEE | | | Implemented / Active (revised) | | | | |

| Properties | Interfaces | Friends | Attributes | Methods | Events | Types | Aliases |

Properties ▨ Filter

Attribute	Level	Visibility	Read-Only	Typing	Associated Type		Description	Initial Value
NUMBER	Instance Attribute	Private	☐	Type	I	⇨	Number	
NAME	Instance Attribute	Private	☐	Type	PERSNO	⇨	Name	
COUNTRY	Instance Attribute	Private	☐	Type	STRING	⇨	Country	
SALUTATION_MR	Constant	Private	☐	Type	STRING	⇨		'MR'
			☐	Type		⇨		

Figure 2-6. *The SALUTATION_MR constant*

Dictionary Types for Global Classes

In Chapter 1, we saw how to define a type pertaining to an internal table comprised of employee objects. Earlier we did this by defining a table type local to a program. It is also possible to define a table type globally in the transaction SE24 Class Builder. This may later be used in any program to create objects based on the underlying class. In this section, we see how this is done.

Suppose we have a class called ZCL_TEST_EMPLOYEE, defined in the Class Builder. To create a table type based on this class, follow these steps:

1.   Go to transaction SE11. This will display the screen shown in Figure 2-7.

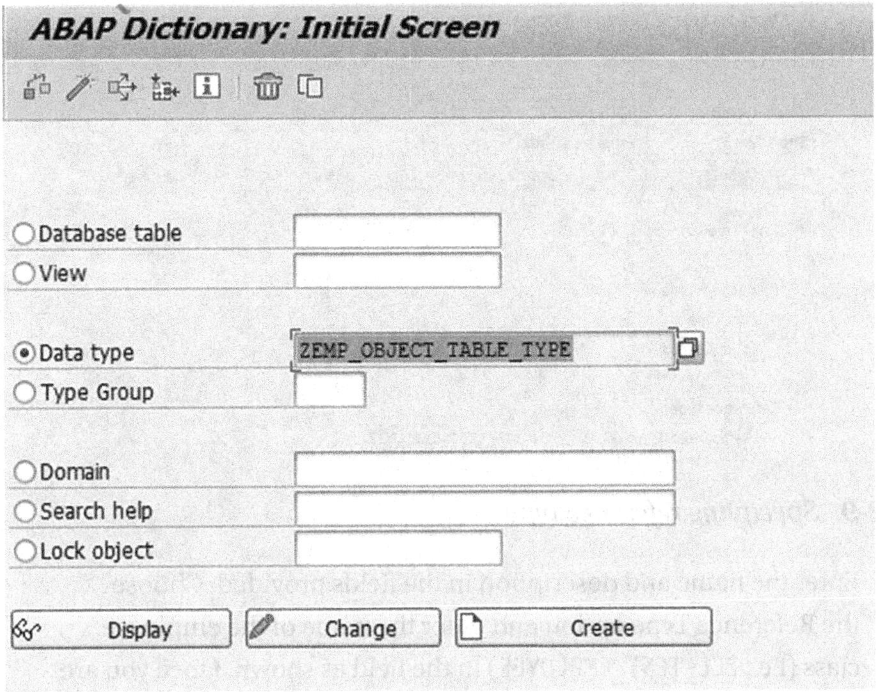

Figure 2-7. *Data type in SE11*

2. Enter the name of the table type that you want to create in the Data Type field and click the Create button. (As you will see, we called our type ZEMP_OBJECT_TABLE_TYPE.) This will display a small dialog box, as shown in Figure 2-8.

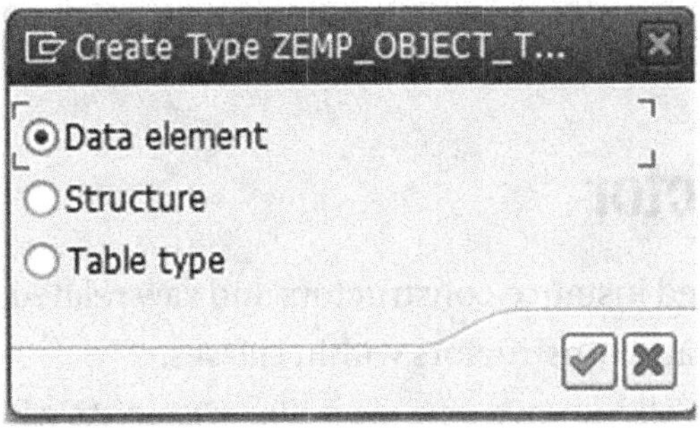

Figure 2-8. *Data type options*

3. Choose the Table Type option and press Enter. This will take you to the screen shown in Figure 2-9.

4. Choose the Reference type option.

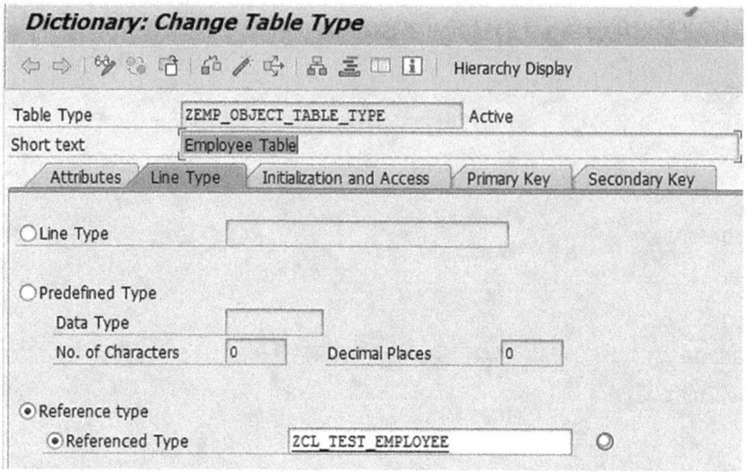

Figure 2-9. *Specifying reference type*

5. Enter the name and description in the fields provided. Choose
    the Reference Type option and enter the name of the employee
    class (i.e., ZCL_TEST_EMPLOYEE) in the field as shown. Once you are
    done, save and activate the type using the CTRL+F3 keys.

Now that we are done, we can use this type in any program. An example is shown here:

```
data EMPLOYEES type zemp_object_table_type.
```

This statement is the same as the following two statements:

```
Types emp type ref to ZCL_TEST_EMPLOYEE.
 data employees type STANDARD TABLE OF emp.
```

Static Constructor

In Chapter 1, we discussed instance constructors and saw related coding examples. It is
also possible to define static constructors within classes.

A *static constructor* is also known as a *class constructor*. As with the other static
methods, the static constructor is only able to address the static components residing
within the class in question.

We also have a static constructor in a class. This is called ONLY once for a class
(and internal session), prior to the first access made to the class.

The following statement shows the generic form of a static constructor declaration within a local class:

```
CLASS-METHODS class_constructor.
```

As you will see, we declared a static constructor by the name `class_constructor` of the class in question. This statement may only be written within the public section of the class (declaration). By default, every class has a built-in `class_constructor` method in the public section.

However, without the declaration, this constructor is blank.

In contrast to the instance constructor, the static constructor is executed *once* for each class within an internal session. This execution occurs before the first access to the class in question, such as an instance creation.

You can access any static component of the class using `=>`. It is also possible to call a static method within the static constructor.

Any failed attempt to dynamically address a nonexistent component of a class does not result in the static constructor being called.

Now that we have some knowledge of the working of static constructors, let's look at a fully working example:

```
CLASS my_class DEFINITION.
  PUBLIC SECTION.
    CLASS-METHODS class_constructor.
    CLASS-METHODS my_static_method.
ENDCLASS.

CLASS my_class IMPLEMENTATION.
  METHOD class_constructor.
    write : / 'Static Constructor Called'.
  ENDMETHOD.
 METHOD my_static_method.
    write : / 'Static Method Called'.
  ENDMETHOD.
ENDCLASS.

START-OF-SELECTION.
  my_class=>my_static_method( ).
```

Here we have a local class called MY_CLASS that has two static methods, namely CLASS_CONSTRUCTOR and MY_STATIC_METHOD. Within the two methods, there are specific messages outputted in order to show the sequence of method execution. We call the static method only using the component class selector =.>.

Calling the static method MY_STATIC_METHOD will result in the static constructor being executed prior to MY_STATIC_METHOD.

The output of the program is shown in Figure 2-10.

```
Static Constructor Called
Static Method Called
```

Figure 2-10.   *Program output*

Now let's look at the same requirement fulfilled using a global class. We assume for this example that a class already exists by the name ZCL_TEST_EMPLOYEE.

Follow the steps:

1.   Open the class in edit mode. Then click the Methods tab.

2.   Under the method list, enter the name CLASS_CONSTRUCTOR and press Enter. This will automatically populate Static Method into the Level field, as shown in Figure 2-11.

Class Builder: Change Class ZCL_TEST_EMPLOYEE

Class/Interface   ZCL_TEST_EMPLOYEE   Implemented / Active

Properties   Interfaces   Friends   Attributes   Methods   Events   Types   Aliases

Method	Level	Visibility	M...	Description
SHOW_DETAILS	Instance Method	Public		Show Employee details
GET_NAME_AND_COUNTRY	Instance Method	Public		Give Employee name and Country for Object
CONSTRUCTOR	Instance Method	Public	▦	Create object
CLASS_CONSTRUCTOR	Static Method	Public	▦	Class Constructor

Figure 2-11.   *Methods tab*

As you will see, the Level is set to Static Method and cannot be changed. In addition, the visibility column will be automatically populated with Public. It is worth noting that if any other visibility, such as Private, is entered in the column, upon pressing Enter, the Visibility will change back to Public.

Method Revisited

In Chapter 1, we saw local as well as global methods. In this section, we will go a few steps further with methods. We will see how to specify internal tables as method parameters, method chaining, and functional methods.

Specifying Internal Tables as Method Parameters

So far we have only seen integers and strings as types of method parameters. It is also possible to specify internal tables as exporting, importing, and returning parameters of class methods.

Let's now complicate things a bit. In this section, we see how we can specify an internal table as a parameter of the method of a class. In the football player example introduced in Chapter 1, we define a new method, called RETURN_LIST_OF_PLAYERS. Instead of writing the attributes of each player object on the screen, we will return the list of player objects in an internal table.

We will specify an internal table (of player objects) as a parameter to this method. Prior to this method, we specify a type called ty_player_tab based on the the ty_player type defined earlier.

```
class player DEFINITION DEFERRED.
 types : ty_player type ref to player.
 types : ty_player_tab type STANDARD TABLE OF ty_player.
```

We then define the static RETURN_LIST_OF_PLAYERS method. The signature of this method is shown in the Player class definition:

```
class player DEFINITION.
   public section.
    methods write_player_details.
    methods constructor importing name type string
                                  country type string
                                  club type string.
    class-methods display_list_of_players.
    class-methods return_list_of_players
        exporting players_tab
                type ty_player_tab.
```

```
  private section.
    data name type string.
    data country type string.
    data club type string.
    class-DATA: players_list type STANDARD TABLE OF ty_player.

 ENDCLASS.
```

As you will see, we have specified an exporting parameter called PLAYERS_TAB based on the TY_PLAYER_TAB type. It must be noted that the table type must be specified here. (This is a TYPE STANDARD TABLE type based on TY_PLAYER.)

Next, we write the code of the method within the Implementation section. Since we already have the internal table of objects stored in the PLAYERS_LIST static variable, we simply use an assignment operator to store the internal table contents in the exporting parameter, called PLAYERS_TAB.

```
 method return_list_of_players.
    players_tab[] = players_list[] .
 endmethod.
```

The internal table is then returned as an exporting parameter.

To call the method we will use the player class static method:

```
player=>return_list_of_players(          IMPORTING players_tab
                                         = data(players_tab) ) .
```

This method is called after instantiation of two player objects, as shown in our previous example, which shows the contents of our players_tab. We use inline declaration to return this in players_tab.

After execution of the program, the contents of the internal table will look like Figure 2-12.

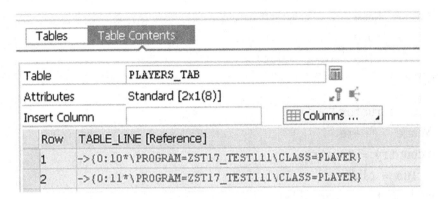

Figure 2-12. *Table contents*

The complete code of the football player exercise will now look like this:

```
class player DEFINITION DEFERRED.
 types : ty_player type ref to player.
 types : ty_player_tab type STANDARD TABLE OF ty_player.

 class player DEFINITION.
   public section.
    methods write_player_details.
    methods constructor importing name type string
                          country type string
                          club type string.
    class-methods display_list_of_players.
    class-methods return_list_of_players exporting players_tab type
    ty_player_tab.
    private section.
      data name type string.
      data country type string.
      data club type string.

class-DATA: players_list type STANDARD TABLE OF ty_player.

ENDCLASS.

class player IMPLEMENTATION .
  method write_player_details.
    skip.
```

```
  write :/ 'Name     :', me->name.
  write :/ 'Country :', me->country.
  write :/ 'Club     :', me->club.
endmethod.

method constructor.
  me->name =  name.
  me->country = country.
  me->club = club.
  append me to players_list.
ENDMETHOD.

method display_list_of_players.
  data : temp_player type ref to player.
  write :/ '------------PLAYERS LIST------------'.
  loop at players_list into temp_player.
    temp_player->write_player_details( ) .
  endloop.
  write :/ '----------------------------------'.
endmethod.

 method return_list_of_players.
  players_tab[] = players_list[] .
endmethod.

endclass.

start-OF-SELECTION.
data : player1 type ref to player.
data : player2 type ref to player.

CREATE OBJECT player1
  EXPORTING
    name    = 'John Mann'
    country = 'Germany'
    club    = 'Bayern Munich'.

CREATE OBJECT player2
  EXPORTING
```

```
    name    = 'Paul Goldberg'
    country = 'Britain'
    club    = 'Liverpool'.

  player=>return_list_of_players( IMPORTING
            players_tab  =   data(players_tab) ) .
  end-OF-selection.
```

Inline Declarations While Calling Methods

Since 740, ABAP supports inline declaration of variables. This holds true for method calls as well. We will see how to call methods and specify (as parameters) variables that were not declared earlier in the program.

Consider a situation where we have an employee class called ZCL_EMPLOYEE that has a method called GET_NAME_AND_COUNTRY that returns the name and country of the employee in question.

One of the ways to call this method is:

```
data name type string.
data country type string.

employee->get_name_and_country(
    IMPORTING
        name = name
        country = country ) .
```

This is the traditional method, where we first declare variables pertaining to the importing parameters of the method. The value of name and country is then returned in the declared variables.

There is another compact way of writing this using inline declaration. This is shown as:

```
employee->get_name_and_country(
    IMPORTING
        name = data(name)
        country = data(country) ) .
```

As you will see, we have not done any prior declaration of the two variables NAME and COUNTRY. Rather we used the feature of inline declaration while specifying the parameters of the method in question. The variable name to be declared inline must be in parentheses and must be preceded by data. The output of this piece of code and the one shown earlier are exactly the same.

Using inline declarations is not just restricted to exporting parameters of the method. They may also be used for RECEIVING parameters (we will discuss this in an upcoming section).

Functional Methods

So far, we have only seen methods that take as input a number of importing parameters and then export a number of parameters (exporting parameters). We also have a special type of method that returns a single result or returning value. Such methods are known as *functional methods*. These may be defined in local and global classes. It is also possible to have a functional method as a static method or an instance method within a class.

One such functional method is as follows:

```
class func_method_class DEFINITION.
    public section.
      class-methods calc_average IMPORTING
                          int1 type i
                          int2 type i
                 RETURNING value(average) type i.
 endclass.

 class func_method_class IMPLEMENTATION.
     method calc_average.
       average = ( int1 + int2 )  / 2.
     endmethod.
 endclass.
```

As you can see, the static method CALC_AVERAGE takes as input two integer values int1 and int2 and returns a single parameter called AVERAGE as the returning parameter. The example shows a local class, called func_method_class. As with other methods, the code of this is written in the IMPLEMENTATION of the class.

To call this method, we use the following formats:

```
func_method_class=>calc_average(
        exporting int1 = i1
                  int2 = i2
        RECEIVING average = av ).
```

As you will see, while calling the CALC_AVERAGE method, we use RECEIVING (corresponding to the RETURNING parameter AVERAGE). In addition, there is another way of calling the functional method using inline declaration:

```
func_method_class=>calc_average(
              exporting int1 = i1
                        int2 = i2
              RECEIVING average = data(av1) ).
```

A more meaningful and preferred format is shown in the following example:

```
data(i1) = 1.
data(i2) = 3.
data(av) =    func_method_class=>calc_average( int1 = i1  int2 = i2 ).
write : av.
```

Here we used the assignment operator to return the average result in the variable AV. When using a functional method, you do not have to specify the parameter names for the return value explicitly in the parameter list, as shown in the code.

We can also define a functional method for a global class. We will create a static method called CALC_AVERAGE having public visibility, as shown in Figure 2-13.

Class/Interface	ZST8_TEST1		Implemented / Active				
Properties	Interfaces	Friends	Attributes	Methods	Events	Types	Aliases

Method	Level	Visibility	Description
CALC_AVERAGE	Static Method	Public	Calculate the average of two numbers

Figure 2-13. *Global class with a functional method*

For the method, the next step involves specifying the parameters for the method. For the AVERAGE parameter, we need to select the Returning type. If you do not select the Pass Value checkbox for Average, the system automatically checks this indicator. The other two parameters are specified as Importing, as shown in Figure 2-14.

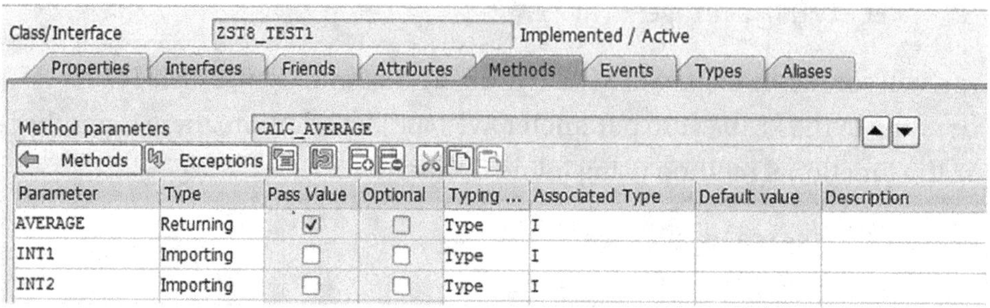

Figure 2-14. *Parameters of CALC_AVERAGE*

Next, we write the source code of the method, as shown in Figure 2-15.

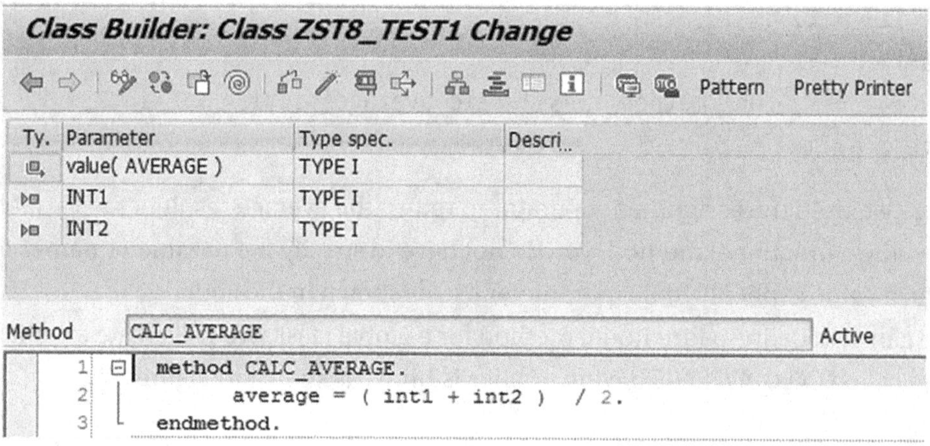

Figure 2-15. *Method source code*

When you are done, save and activate the class. The method created here may be called in programs the same way the local functional method was called.

A functional method can have only one returning parameter. You may not create two or more returning parameters. You must also ensure that the assignment operator is used with a method that has a returning parameter. If the method does not have a returning parameter, but you try to use it in an expression along with the assignment = operator, a syntax error occurs. Consider the example shown in Figure 2-16.

```
        data wa_p0006 type p0006.

            wa_p0006 = lr_container_data->PRIMARY_RECORD_REF( ).

            changed_record_data ?= lr_container_data->modify_primary_record(
```

Syntax error		
Description	Row	Type
Program ZST2_CHANGE_0006	55	◉○○
The method "PRIMARY_RECORD_REF" does not have a RETURNING parameter.		
You cannot call it in expressions.		

Figure 2-16. *Syntax error*

Here we have a method called PRIMARY_RECORD_REF that does not have a returning parameter. But we have used this improperly, which results in a syntax error.

When you try to create more than one returning parameter for a given method, a syntax error occurs, as shown in Figure 2-17.

1 Syntax Error for Program ZST17_TEST111		
Ty...	Line	Description
●	21	Program ZST17_TEST111
		".", "RAISING", "OPTIONAL", "DEFAULT ...", or "EXCEPTIONS ..." expected after "I".

Figure 2-17. *Syntax error*

This error occurs for global as well as local classes. Starting from NetWeaver 7.50, it is also possible to specify exporting parameters for functional methods.

Specifying Exporting and Returning Parameters for Functional Methods

The newer NetWeaver release provides an interesting feature of functional methods. In addition to a returning parameter, a functional method can also have an exporting parameter. However, note that functional methods support only one returning parameter and any number of other formal parameters, including importing and exporting. We can create local or global functional methods, which may be static or instance methods.

In the examples, we cover both scenarios of defining functional methods locally and globally that have both exporting and returning parameters. We use static method in these examples for better understanding.

This first example defines a functional method locally. We define a class with a static method to calculate the total sum and average of two given numbers. The sum will be returned as an exporting parameter, whereas the average will be a returning parameter. The code is shown:

```
class newclass definition.
  public section.
    types : myty_dec2 type p length 13 decimals 2.
    class-methods :  func_av_and_total importing
                          myint1 type i
                          myint2 type i
                        exporting
                          sum type i
                        returning
                          value(av) type myty_dec2.

  endclass.
```

As you see in the code, we defined a class locally within the program. The class name is newclass. A static method, func_av_and_total, is defined within the class, which calculates both the average and the sum of the two numbers supplied to the method.

This method has two import parameters (myint1 and myint2) of type Integer. The sum is the exporting parameter, whereas AV is the returning parameter of the type myty_dec2. (This is a user-defined type defined within the class.)

The class implementation is shown here:

```
class newclass implementation.
  method func_av_and_total.
    sum =  myint1 + myint2.
    av = sum / 2.
  endmethod.
endclass.
```

In the class implementation, we specified how the sum and the average are calculated. We add the two numbers to get sum and divide the total by 2 in order to get the average that is returned in parameter AV.

We can call this method in multiple ways. The example will show you how to use the assignment operator to read only the average value of the provided numbers.

```
data(av1) = newclass=>func_av_and_total(
                    exporting  myint1 = '2'
                               myint2 = '11'  ) .
```

In the example, a static method is called without creating a class instance. The variable AV is defined using an inline declaration. The method returns the average of the input parameters, which is captured in the variable AV. This may later be printed on the user screen.

In another example, we will show how you call the static method with exporting and importing parameters, along with the returning parameter.

```
data sum type i.
data(av1) = Newclass=>func_av_and_total(
exporting  myint1 = '2'
           myint2 = '11'
              importing sum =  sum ).

write : av1 ,  sum.
```

In this example, the func_av_and_total method is called with exporting integer parameters and an importing sum. The function will return the av value. Here, we have passed numbers 2 and 8 to MYINT1 and MYINT2, respectively. The average value is returned in the AV1 variable, whereas sum is assigned to the variable sum. The output is then printed on the screen, as shown in Figure 2-18.

```
6.50            13
```

Figure 2-18. *Program output*

Using Class Builder (transition SE24), we can define a similar method globally. An example of this is shown in Figure 2-19.

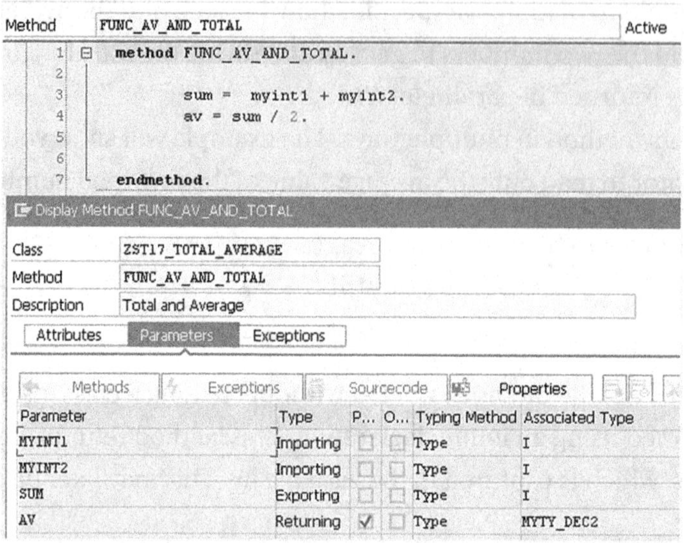

Method	FUNC_AV_AND_TOTAL		Active

```
1 ⊟    method FUNC_AV_AND_TOTAL.
2
3          sum = myint1 + myint2.
4          av = sum / 2.
5
6
7      endmethod.
```

☞ Display Method FUNC_AV_AND_TOTAL

Class	ZST17_TOTAL_AVERAGE
Method	FUNC_AV_AND_TOTAL
Description	Total and Average

Attributes	Parameters	Exceptions

← Methods	⚡ Exceptions	Sourcecode	Properties	

Parameter	Type	P...	O...	Typing Method	Associated Type
MYINT1	Importing	☐	☐	Type	I
MYINT2	Importing	☐	☐	Type	I
SUM	Exporting	☐	☐	Type	I
AV	Returning	☑	☐	Type	MYTY_DEC2

Figure 2-19. *Functional method in sE24*

In this class definition, SUM is defined as an exporting parameter and AV is defined as a returning parameter. The ty_dec2 type is defined using the Types tab.

The method may be tested using the standard test feature, as shown in Figure 2-20.

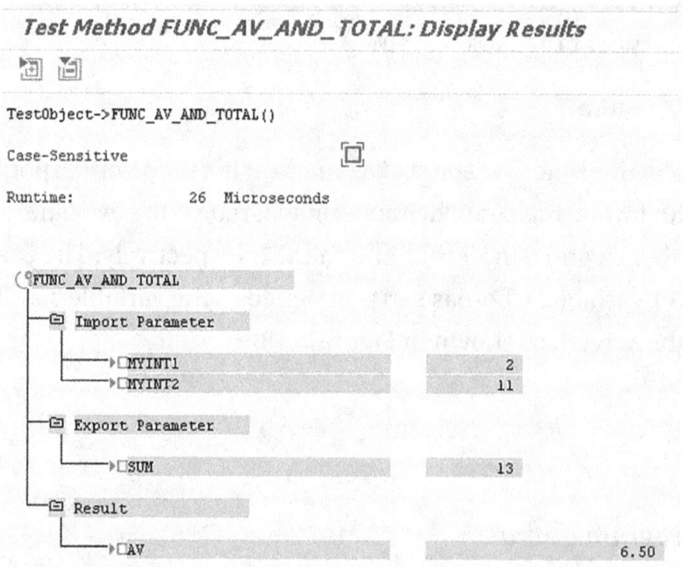

Test Method FUNC_AV_AND_TOTAL: Display Results

🗗 🗐

TestObject->FUNC_AV_AND_TOTAL()

Case-Sensitive   ☐

Runtime: 26 Microseconds

```
FUNC_AV_AND_TOTAL
  └─ Import Parameter
       ├─▸ ☐MYINT1                       2
       └─▸ ☐MYINT2                       11
  └─ Export Parameter
       └─▸ ☐SUM                          13
  └─ Result
       └─▸ ☐AV                          6.50
```

Figure 2-20. *Test feature*

Methods Calling Other Methods

A declared method can call other methods in the source code. For example, it is possible for a local class method to call a (public) method of another local class, or a static local method can call a static global or local method. At the time of calling, the control switches just like other modularization units, such as form subroutine and function modules, and returns to the calling method.

Method Chaining

A newer concept that has evolved is *method chaining*. This involves combining calls of functional methods (i.e., methods that have one returning value as output). The chaining of methods makes the code more compact and allows you to fulfill requirements without the need for additional reference variables. There are two types of chaining possible: chained method access and chained method call. (The primary emphasis of this section is on chained method access.) Let's take a look at what each of these means.

In chained method access, there could be two forms as follows:

```
obj_ref->inst_meth_a(..)->inst_meth_b(..)->inst_meth(..).
class=>static_meth_a(..)->inst_meth_b(..)->inst_meth(..).
```

The return value of one functional method is a reference to an object that is used to call the next method in the chain. The returning value of the last method is used as an operand.

In this case, the first use may be a class component selector (=>) or an object component selector (->). After that, all the methods are called using the component. Or, in other words, the first method may be a static or an instance method. Other than that, you must have all functional instance methods.

Chained attribute access, on the other hand, is similar to chained method calling. In this case, the instance attribute is used as an operand. The chained attribute access may be in the following forms:

```
obj_ref->inst_meth_a(..)->inst_meth_b(..)->inst_attr.
class=>static_meth_a(..)->inst_meth_b(..)->inst_attr.
```

The return value of the last method (INST_METH_B) must refer to the object that contains the INST_ATTR attribute. In this case, the return values of the previous functional methods are variables that refer to objects for the next method.

As an example of method chaining, consider the previous block of code that we used in our ALV example earlier, shown here:

```
data : functions type ref to cl_salv_functions.
functions = alv->get_functions( ).
functions->set_all( ).
```

Method chaining can be applied in this case. The three lines above can be replaced by a single line of code, as shown here:

```
alv->get_functions( )->set_all( ).
```

There is also no need to define the FUNCTIONS variable, and the coding is very compact.

Let's look at one more example of method chaining. Let's go back to our football example shown earlier involving the NEW operator:

```
DATA: FOOTBALL_PLAYER type ref to   ZST6_FOOTBALL_PLAYER_CLASS.
   FOOTBALL_PLAYER = NEW #( NAME = 'Oliver Kahn'
                            WEIGHT = '88'
                            HEIGHT = '178'
                            FOOTBALL_CLUB = 'Bayern Munich' ).
   FOOTBALL_PLAYER->DISPLAY_PLAYER_DETAILS( ).
```

We can combine the NEW operator shown earlier in the chapter with method chaining. The previous block of code can be written more compactly, as shown here:

```
NEW ZST6_FOOTBALL_PLAYER_CLASS(
        NAME = 'Oliver Kahn'
        WEIGHT = '88'
        HEIGHT = '178'
        FOOTBALL_CLUB =
    'Bayern Munich')->DISPLAY_PLAYER_DETAILS( ).
```

Event Handling in ABAP Objects

The topic of ABAP Objects is incomplete without one important component that may be included within a class definition—*events*.

Events are signals generated by a class or its object. They may be the result of changes in the state of an object, such as Employee Hired, Employee Changed, or Player Created.

Just like any other components of a class, there may be static or instance events. Static events are independent of any particular object of a class. Static events may be triggered from both static and instance methods, whereas instance events may be triggered from instance methods only.

At runtime, the handler method's code (the method that handles the event) is executed when the event is triggered (also known as event raised). Handling and generating events in your programs involves the following essential steps:

- Defining the method as an instance or static event within the respective class definition. The class containing the event may be a subclass of another class, or may have a number of subclasses derived from it. You may also define an event in an interface. (The event will then be part of the class(es) that implement(s) the interface.) To define the event as static, use this code:

  ```
  CLASS_EVENTS <event_name>.
  ```

  On the other hand, the following statement defines an instance event:

  ```
  EVENTS <event_name>.
  ```

- Raising the event at a suitable place using the `RAISE EVENT` statement.

  The parameters are specified after the `EXPORTING ADDITION`. For an instance event, an implicit parameter called `SENDER` is applicable. This parameter holds a reference to the object for which the event has been generated. For example, when the instance event called `PLAYER_CREATED` is raised, `SENDER` will contain the reference to the player object in question. For static events, the `SENDER` parameter is not there.

- Defining and implementing the event handler method. This may be defined in the same class or in a separate class. Within the handler class implementation, you write the method code to be executed upon event trigger. The parameters available to the method (i.e., the ones exported via the RAISE statement) may be used by the developer for fulfilling user requirements.

- Registering the method to react to events. The SET HANDLER statement is used for this purpose. If the event is static, the syntax may be of the form shown here:

  ```
  SET HANDLER <method_name>.
  ```

  In the case of an instance event, the SET HANDLER statement will contain the additions FOR ALL INSTANCES or FOR (referring to a specific object for whose event the event handler is to be executed). It is possible to specify all instances or a particular object instance whose raised event is to be caught and the handler method is executed.

  This is an important step that defines the link between the handler method and the event that is to be raised. If the registration is not performed, the handler method will not be executed even if the event gets triggered successfully with all essential information passed.

In the next section, we see these steps in detail as applied to our football player example.

A Working Example

In this section, we look at a full-fledged working example of event handling. For the sake of our example, we see how events may be defined and handled in local classes.

Triggering and Handling the PLAYER_CREATED Event

We add the event triggering functionality for our local football player class defined earlier. We create a separate event handler class for handling our PLAYER_CREATED event.

The following steps are required:

1. As mentioned, we need to define the event for our football player class. In our case, we name the event PLAYER_CREATED. This is defined as an instance event, as shown here:

```
events : player_created .
```

2. We make sure that the event is defined in the public section of the class. We then raise the event. This is done using the RAISE EVENT statement as shown here:

```
raise event player_created.
```

3. We put this in the constructor, as shown here:

```
method constructor.
        call method super->constructor
          exporting
            name = name
            weight = weight
            height = height.
        me->football_club = football_club.
        raise event player_created.
"" nothing exported
"" but created object passed
"" via implicit SENDER parameter
  endmethod .
```

4. We will not pass a parameter explicitly to the RAISE event. Next we create an event handler class with the name MYHANDLERCLASS. Within the class, there is a handler method called MYHANDLER defined as a static class method. Within the definition of the class for our handler method, we specify that it is for the PLAYER_ CREATED event of the football player class.

Note that the importing implicit parameter SENDER is also specified. The sender contains a reference to the object for which the event has been triggered.

The code for the handler class definition is shown here:

```
class myhandlerclass DEFINITION.
   public section.
     class-methods myhandler FOR EVENT player_created
     OF football_player importing sender.
   endclass.
```

Since we defined the event earlier as a public event, we are able to create a handler method in a separate class. Suppose the event was in the private section. In that case, an error would occur, as shown in Figure 2-21 .

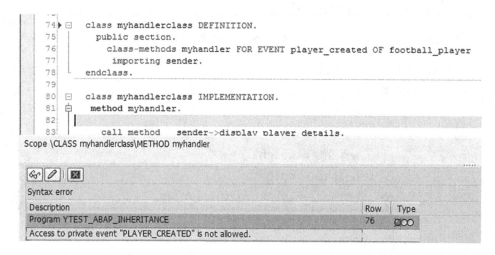

Figure 2-21. *Syntax error for a private event*

Next in the implementation section, we will write the code (for method MYHANDLER) to be executed when the PLAYER_CREATED event is triggered.

```
class myhandlerclass IMPLEMENTATION.
   method myhandler.
    write : 'Event Handler Executed'.
    call method sender->display_player_details.
   endmethod.
   endclass.
```

Within the method code, we will simply call the DISPLAY_PLAYER_DETAILS method of the football player class. This will display the various attributes of the newly created football player.

In this example, we have seen a football player class inherited from a player class. The inheritance concept will be explained in detail in the next chapter.

Next, we will register the handler method to react to the situation when the event occurs. We will use the SET HANDLER statement for this purpose, as shown here:

```
SET HANDLER myhandlerclass=>myhandler for all instances.
```

The name of the method along with class name is specified. Since the MYHANDLER is a static method, we use the class component selector (=>). We use the FOR ALL INSTANCES addition in order for the handler method to be executed for all instances of the FOOTBALL_PLAYER class.

When the program is executed, the CREATE OBJECT statement for the football player is executed. Whenever a new football player is created, a Player_Created event is triggered. This is an instance event raised via a RAISE EVENT statement in the constructor of the FOOTBALL_PLAYER class. Since we have registered the MYHANDLER method for the PLAYER_CREATED event of all instances of the football player class, the handler method gets executed. The method receives SENDER as an importing parameter, which is the reference to the football player object for which the event is raised. Within the handler method, we call the DISPLAY_PLAYER_DETAILS method of the FOOTBALL_PLAYER class to display the details of the football player object that is created.

The output of the program is shown in Figure 2-22.

```
Event Handler Executed
Player Name:  Oliver Kahn
Height    :  188
Weight    :  95.00
Club Name  :  Bayern Munich
```

Figure 2-22. *Program output*

The complete code listing is shown here:

```
class player DEFINITION.
    public section.
      methods constructor importing  name type string
                        weight type p  height type i.
      methods display_player_details.
```

```
          PROTECTED SECTION.
              data : name type string.
              data : height type i.
              data : weight type p decimals 2.
     endclass.
class player IMPLEMENTATION.
        method constructor .
            me->name = name.
            me->height = height.
            me->weight = weight.
        ENDMETHOD.

  method display_player_details.
        write :/  'Player Name:   ',15 me->name ,
              /  'Height     :      ',15   me->height LEFT-JUSTIFIED ,
              /  'Weight      :',15 me->weight LEFT-JUSTIFIED.
  ENDMETHOD.

endclass.

class football_player DEFINITION INHERITING
        FROM player.
     public section.
       methods constructor importing
                              name type string
                              weight type p
                              height type i
                              football_club type string.
        methods display_player_details REDEFINITION.

        events : player_created  .

   private section.
        data : football_club type string.
endclass.

class football_player IMPLEMENTATION.
        method constructor.
```

```
      call method super->constructor
          exporting
            name = name
            weight = weight
            height = height.
      me->football_club = football_club.
      raise event player_created.
    endmethod .

    method display_player_details.
    call method super->display_player_details.
    write:/ 'Club Name  :          ',15 me->football_club.
    endmethod .

  endclass.

class myhandlerclass DEFINITION.
  public section.
    class-methods myhandler FOR EVENT player_created
    OF football_player importing sender.
endclass.

class myhandlerclass IMPLEMENTATION.
 method myhandler.
   write : 'Event Handler Executed'.
   call method sender->display_player_details.
 endmethod.
endclass.

 START-OF-SELECTION.

 data : myfootball_player type ref to football_player.
 set HANDLER myhandlerclass=>myhandler for all instances.
   create object myfootball_player
            exporting name =  'Oliver Kahn'
                      weight = '95'
                      height =  '188'
                      football_club = 'Bayern Munich'.
```

Summary

In this chapter, we covered a number of useful topics that you need to know in order to work with ABAP Objects. We discussed the CASE TYPE OF construct used for determining the type of an object reference variable followed by a discussed of the "new" NEW operator.

We also saw how to apply inline declaration in ABAP Objects, constant declaration, method chaining, and functional methods. Finally, we saw a fully working demo of event handling.

CHAPTER 3

More on Object-Oriented ABAP

After the basic introduction to ABAP provided in Chapters 1 and 2, this chapter dives deeper into the topic. It starts by showing how inheritance applies to ABAP Objects. Then, the chapter covers the concept of casting—upcasting and downcasting—and how we can achieve polymorphism using casting.

Inheritance: Super and Subclasses

ABAP lets you derive (inherit) a new class from a given class. This is called *inheritance* and the inherited class is referred to as a subclass of the main class in question, which is known as the *superclass*. Within ABAP, you may have any number of classes derived from a given base class. For example, if we have class B inherited from class A, then class A is the direct superclass of class B. It is also possible to derive another class, class C, from class B. Then, both A and B are superclasses of C, but B is the direct superclass of C, as shown in Figure 3-1.

© Rehan Zaidi 2019
R. Zaidi, *SAP ABAP Objects*, https://doi.org/10.1007/978-1-4842-4964-2_3

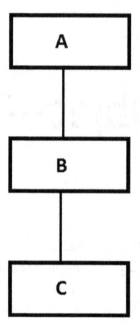

Figure 3-1. *Inheritance tree*

The diagram shown in Figure 3-1 is referred to as the inheritance hierarchy or tree. These trees may contain multiple levels of class inheritance. (For simplicity's sake, only two levels are shown along with single inheritance only.)

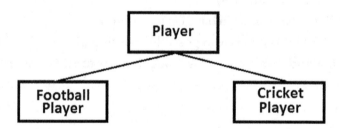

Figure 3-2. *Inheritance tree of players*

Within ABAP, you may have multiple direct subclasses for a given superclass. Conversely, you may have only one direct superclass of a given class (subclass). This is called a single inheritance.

You may view a superclass as having the common (general) characteristics of its subclasses. The level of specialization in the tree increases as we move down through each level. Likewise, as you move up the hierarchy (i.e., toward the root node), the classes tend to be more general.

For example, we may have a class called PLAYER that is the superclass of Football_player and Cricket_player. The PLAYER class has properties of both football and cricket players. However, the Cricket_player will have specific characteristics to that of a cricketer, which are not possessed by a football player, and vice versa.

Note   The predefined empty class called OBJECT is the root node of all inheritance trees.

There is a general class called OBJECT from which all inheritance trees originate. This class has no attributes or methods. The PLAYER class is actually a subclass of the OBJECT class. For simplicity's sake, it is not shown in Figure 3-2.

Up until this point, we have looked at two types of class components—private and public. With the advent of inheritance, another type comes into play, *protected*. Of primary importance is the "protected" section within a superclass. The protected section contains components that are accessible from within the subclasses of the given superclass.

Within the superclass, there may be protected, private, and public components. The components of the superclass become part of the derived subclass(es). (Although the private components are included in the subclass, only the private and public components within are visible in the subclass.) Because of this, all public and protected components of classes within a given inheritance hierarchy must have unique names. For private components, you must make sure that they are uniquely named within a class.

An inherited class contains the components that are defined in ALL its superclasses (i.e., the direct superclass and the above).

Let's illustrate this concept with an example.

Suppose we have the following inheritance tree, where two classes—B and C—are derived from a common superclass A. We can have a private attribute INT1 in classes A, B, and C. However, we cannot have a protected attribute INT1 in the superclass A and at the same time a public attribute INT1 defined in the subclass B.

The syntax for defining a subclass locally within a program is via the addition INHERITING FROM, shown as follows:

```
CLASS <MYSUBCLASS> DEFINITION INHERITING FROM <MYSUPERCLASS>.
...
ENDCLASS.
```

For example, in the following code excerpt, we have a player class called
Football_player that is inherited from the generic class PLAYER.

```
class football_player DEFINITION INHERITING
     FROM player.

endclass.
```

Suppose within the PLAYER class, we have an instance constructor and a method
called DISPLAY_PLAYER_DETAILS. We also have protected attributes called NAME, WEIGHT,
and HEIGHT. The attributes are protected so that they may be addressed by the subclasses
inherited from the PLAYER class. See the code block as follows.

```
class player DEFINITION.
    public section.
      methods constructor importing
                            name type string
                            weight type p
                            height type i.

       methods display_player_details.
    protected section.
      data : name type string.
      data : height type i.
      data : weight type p decimals 2.
endclass.
```

We can then have a subclass called FOOTBALL_PLAYER that's inherited from the given
PLAYER class. Another attribute, called FOOTBALL_CLUB, has been defined that is specific to
FOOTBALL_PLAYER. This class has its own instance constructor, which has four importing
parameters (Football_Club is included in addition to the three parameters contained
in the player's constructor). The DISPLAY_PLAYER_DETAILS method is redefined in the
FOOTBALL_PLAYER class. It contains no parameters, as in the player class:

```
class football_player DEFINITION INHERITING
     FROM player.
    public section.
      methods constructor importing
                            name type string
```

```
            weight type p
            height type i
            football_club type string.
    methods display_player_details REDEFINITION.

  private section.
    data : football_club type string.
endclass.
```

We will take a closer look at the instance constructors for subclasses and the redefinition of superclass methods in detail in upcoming sections.

While naming attributes within subclasses, a few restrictions apply. Let's look at an example. Suppose you try to define a private attribute with the name HEIGHT within the FOOTBALL_PLAYER class, as shown:

```
class  football_player DEFINITION INHERITING
      FROM player. "BADCODE
.......
    private section.
      data  height type i.   """ NOT ALLOWED
endclass.
```

In this case, a syntax error occurs (see Figure 3-3).

Syntax error
Description
Program YTEST_ABAP_INHERITANCE
"HEIGHT" has already been declared

Figure 3-3. *Syntax error*

This is because the HEIGHT attribute is already declared in the superclass PLAYER as a protected attribute. The protected and public attribute of the superclass becomes part of the derived subclass. If the superclass contained HEIGHT in its private section instead, this code would not have given an error.

Redefining Methods

As mentioned, an important aspect we need to see within the ABAP Objects is the redefinition of inherited methods defined in the subclasses.

An instance method inherited from a superclass may be redefined in the subclasses. This allows you to add more specific functionality to the redefined method in the subclass (or subclasses).

During redefinition, you may not change the visibility section of the method. For example, it is not possible to have a private method redefined as a public method in a subclass. The signature of the instance method also *cannot* be changed during the redefinition. For example, it is not possible to add a new parameter to the method in the definition or change the type of a given parameter.

It is also important to note that static methods cannot be redefined in subclasses. Only instance methods can be redefined.

Within a local subclass, we may redefine a given instance method using the REDEFINITION keyword. Let's take a look at an example of this.

```
class football_player DEFINITION INHERITING
    FROM player.
  public section.
    methods display_player_details REDEFINITION.

    ........
endclass.
```

It is possible to call the superclass' method DISPLAY_PLAYER_DETAILS within the redefined method using SUPER->DISPLAY-PLAYER_DETAILS.

Instance Constructors

As discussed, every class has an instance constructor. Within the inheritance tree, the various instance constructors (of a class, its superclasses, and subclasses) are independent of each other. You may *not* redefine an instance constructor of a class in its subclasses.

The instance constructor is called automatically upon instantiation (creation) of the object (via the CREATE OBJECT statement). Within the constructor of the subclass, the immediate superclass constructor may be called. You may call the constructor of a superclass from a subclass using the following statement:

```
CALL METHOD SUPER->CONSTRUCTOR .......
```

This statement must not be used in the class that's a direct subclass of the OBJECT class.

After the SUPER->CONSTRUCTOR call, the code for assigning values to the attributes specific to the subclass is written, as shown in the following example.

```
class football_player IMPLEMENTATION.
    method constructor.
      call method super->constructor
        exporting
          name = name
          weight = weight
          height = height.

      me->football_club = football_club.
    endmethod .
endclass.
```

When you instantiate a class that has an instance constructor with a set of parameters (interface), appropriate values must be then supplied using the EXPORTING addition within the CREATE OBJECT statement:

```
create object myfootball_player
        exporting name =   'Oliver Kahn'
                  weight = '95'
                  height =   '188'
                football_club = 'Bayern Munich'.
```

Likewise, when you call a superclass constructor from a subclass, appropriate values must be supplied for the various parameters (mandatory, non optional). A class that is instantiated at the bottom of the inheritance tree may need to pass parameters to the class constructor that is close to the root.

> **Note**   If a given SUPERCLASS has an instance constructor that contains the call of a method via the self-reference variable me, then the method as defined in the SUPERCLASS is called and not the ones redefined in any of the subclasses.

Working Example

In this section, we look at how these concepts can be applied to solve a simple requirement.

We create a superclass player and its subclass Football_player. A suitable Football_player object is created and its attributes are displayed onscreen.

We first define a PLAYER class having three attributes in the protected section, including NAME, HEIGHT, and WEIGHT. Two methods are defined within the public section—the instance constructor and the DISPLAY_PLAYER_DETAILS method. Appropriate parameters are specified for the CONSTRUCTOR for creating instances belonging to the PLAYER class. The DISPLAY_PLAYER_DETAILS method has no parameters. The definition of the class looks like this:

```
class player DEFINITION.
    public section.
      methods constructor importing
                            name type string
                            weight type p
                            height type i.

      methods display_player_details.
    protected section.
      data : name type string.
      data : height type i.
      data : weight type p decimals 2.
endclass.
```

Within the implementation section of the PLAYER class, we write the code for constructor, by initializing the attributes NAME, HEIGHT, and WEIGHT. Within the DISPLAY_PLAYER_DETAILS method, we include the WRITE statement to display the attribute values on the user screen.

```
class player IMPLEMENTATION.
     method constructor .
        me->name = name.
        me->height = height.
        me->weight = weight.
     ENDMETHOD.

 method display_player_details.
   write :/  'Player Name:    ',15 me->name ,
          /  'Height     :    ',15  me->height
                LEFT-JUSTIFIED ,
                 /  'Weight      :',15 me->weight
                    LEFT-JUSTIFIED.
            ENDMETHOD.
            endclass.
```

Next, we define the FOOTBALL_PLAYER class. The constructor of the class takes as an importing parameter the player's name, weight, and height, as well as the name of the football club. The private section contains the FOOTBALL_CLUB attribute—this is specific to the football player class.

A redefined method for displaying the player's detail is also DISPLAY_PLAYERS_ DETAILS defined.

```
class football_player DEFINITION INHERITING
     FROM player.
   public section.
     methods constructor importing
                         name type string
                         weight type p
                         height type i
                         football_club type string.
     methods display_player_details REDEFINITION.
   private section.
     data : football_club type string.
endclass.
```

Within the implementation of the class, we have the code written for the subclass constructor and DISPLAY_PLAYER_DETAILS.

```
class football_player IMPLEMENTATION.
    method constructor.
      call method super->constructor
        exporting
          name = name
          weight = weight
          height = height.

    me->football_club = football_club.
  endmethod .

method display_player_details.
    call method super->display_player_details.
    write:/ 'Club Name   :        ',15
                  me->football_club.
  endmethod .
  endclass.
```

The full code of the example is shown here:

```
class player DEFINITION.
  public section.
    methods constructor importing
                          name type string
                          weight type p
                          height type i.

    methods display_player_details.
  protected section.
    data : name type string.
    data : height type i.
    data : weight type p decimals 2.
endclass.
```

```abap
class player IMPLEMENTATION.
      method constructor .
         me->name = name.
         me->height = height.
         me->weight = weight.
      ENDMETHOD.

 method display_player_details.
    write :/  'Player Name:    ',15 me->name ,
          /  'Height      :    ',15  me->height
             LEFT-JUSTIFIED ,
         /  'Weight      :',15 me->weight
             LEFT-JUSTIFIED.
 ENDMETHOD.

endclass.

class football_player DEFINITION INHERITING
      FROM player.
    public section.
      methods constructor importing
                          name type string
                          weight type p
                          height type i
                          football_club type string.
      methods display_player_details REDEFINITION.

    private section.
      data : football_club type string.
endclass.

class football_player IMPLEMENTATION.
      method constructor.
        call method super->constructor
          exporting
            name = name
            weight = weight
            height = height.
```

```
        me->football_club = football_club.
    endmethod .

    method display_player_details.
     call method super->display_player_details.
     write:/ 'Club Name  :          ',15
       me->football_club.
    endmethod .

  endclass.

  START-OF-SELECTION.

  data : myfootball_player type ref to
         football_player.

  create object myfootball_player
         exporting name =  'Oliver Kahn'
                   weight = '95'
                   height =  '188'
                football_club = 'Bayern Munich'.

 call method


myfootball_player->display_player_details.
```

We have defined a reference variable typed with the FOOTBALL_PLAYER class. We then created the football player object using the CREATE OBJECT statement. Appropriate values are supplied for instantiation of the football player object. The values exported from the program to the CREATE OBJECT statement are imported into the constructor. First, the constructor of the FOOTBALL_PLAYER class is executed, within which the constructor of the superclass PLAYER is called. The code of the super->constructor assigns values to the NAME, HEIGHT, and WEIGHT attributes, whereas the last line of the subclass' constructor assigns a supplied value to the FOOTBALL_CLUB attribute.

Once the football player object is created, we called the DISPLAY_PLAYER_DETAILS method using the reference variable FOOTBALL_PLAYER. The method contains a call to the

SUPER->DISPLAY_PLAYER_DETAILS method, which displays the three attribute values—player name, height, and weight. The football club name is printed via the WRITE statement within the redefined DISPLAY_PLAYER_DETAILS method of the football player class.

The output of the program is shown in Figure 3-4.

```
Player Name:  Oliver Kahn
Height    :   188
Weight    :   95,00
Club Name :   Bayern Munich
```

Figure 3-4. *Program output*

Casting and Polymorphism

Related to the concept of inheritance is *casting*. Within the arena of inheritance and ABAP Objects, *upcasting* and *downcasting* are both possible. Let's take a closer look at these concepts.

Using upcasting, a reference variable typed with reference to a subclass may be assigned to a variable typed via reference to its direct superclass (or any of its superclasses).

```
superclass_type = subclass_type.   "Upcasting
```

This statement is permissible because a subclass contains all components of all its superclasses. Moreover, the interfaces of methods of a superclass cannot be changed in subclasses. The reference variable SUPERCLASS_TYPE may then be used to address the components visible to the given superclass. In this case, no specific functionality added to the subclasses may be addressed. For example, any new attribute added to the subclasses, or any new method added to the subclasses, may not be accessed using the variable SUPERCLASS_TYPE. (We will look at a working example of upcasting and its role in implementing polymorphism in the latter part of this section.)

On the other hand, downcasting involves assignment of a reference variable (based on a reference of a superclass) to a reference variable typed via reference to a subclass:

```
subclass_type ?= superclass_type.   "Downcasting
```

In this case, the downcasting operator ?= must be used. If we use the equals (=) sign instead, a syntax error will occur at the time of program check.

> **Note**   In upcasting, we assign a reference variable to a more general reference variable type; i.e we go up the inheritance hierarchy. On the other hand, in the case of downcasting, the target is a more specific type (i.e., we move downward within the inheritance tree).

Downcasting is particularly useful when we need to access components. For example, when we have a method that is defined in the more specific subclass, but we have a reference to superclass and not to the subclass itself. Let's now consider the following example (pertaining to ALV classes) in order to understand downcasting and how to use it.

```
DATA: ALV TYPE REF TO CL_SALV_TABLE.
DATA: MYCOLUMNS TYPE REF TO CL_SALV_COLUMNS_TABLE.
DATA: ONE_COLUMN TYPE REF TO CL_SALV_COLUMN_TABLE.
....
....
 MYCOLUMNS = ALV->GET_COLUMNS( ).
 ONE_COLUMN ?= MYCOLUMNS->GET_COLUMN( 'COLNAME' ).
```

The GET_COLUMN method returns an instance of the CL_SALV_COLUMN class, but we need to call the methods of the CL_ALV_COLUMN_TABLE class. For example, the SET_KEY method used for setting a column as a key field is available in the CL_SALV_COLUMN_TABLE class and not in CL_SALV_COLUMN. (The CL_SALV_COLUMN class is a superclass (not direct) of the CL_SALV_COLUMN_TABLE class.)

In this case, downcasting is useful. The returned reference is assigned to the ONE_COLUMN variable, based on CL_SALV_COLUMN_TABLE. Once the downcasting is successful, we can call the methods that are provided via the CL_SALV_COLUMN_TABLE class using the reference variable ONE_COLUMN. To catch any exceptions that occur during casting, we can use the exception class CX_SY_MOVE_CAST_ERROR.

As an example, let's add another class called Cricket_player to our PLAYER and FOOTBALL_PLAYER example. Two objects are created, one for Football_player and the other for the Cricket_player class. Their details are printed using a single reference variable, based on superclass PLAYER.

If you redefine a given instance method in multiple subclasses, it is possible to access the various method implementation via one reference variable, based on the superclass type. Addressing the different implementations using a single reference variable is called *polymorphism*. Upcasting may be used to implement polymorphism.

We declare another class, CRICKET_PLAYER, that is also inherited from the class PLAYER. We add a new attribute called COUNTY_NAME with type STRING. The constructor of this class is also added with COUNTY_NAME as an importing parameter. As with the FOOTBALL_PLAYER class previously shown, the DISPLAY_PLAYER_DETAILS method is redefined in the class. The definition of this class is shown here:

```
class cricket_player definition inheriting
      from player.
  public section.
    methods constructor importing
                        name type string
                        weight type p
                        height type i
                        county_name type string.
    methods display_player_details redefinition.

  private section.
    data : county_name type string.
endclass.
```

Next, within the constructor in the CRICKET_PLAYER implementation, we call SUPER->CONSTRUCTOR and assign the importing parameter. COUNTY_NAME to the private attribute COUNTY_NAME defined in the class.

In the redefined method DISPLAY_PLAYER_DETAILS, we add a WRITE statement that displays the county for which the cricketer plays, that is the COUNTY_NAME.

```
class cricket_player implementation.
  method constructor.
    call method super->constructor
      exporting
        name   = name
        weight = weight
        height = height.
```

```
    me->county_name = county_name.
  endmethod .

  method display_player_details.
    call method super->display_player_details.
    write:/ 'County Name  :          ',
    15 me->county_name.
  endmethod .

endclass.
```

We then create two objects belonging to the FOOTBALL_PLAYER and CRICKET_PLAYER classes respectively, using CREATE OBJECT statements.

```
data : myfootball_player type ref to football_player.
  create object myfootball_player
    exporting
      name          = 'Oliver Kahn'
      weight        = '95'
      height        = '188'
      football_club = 'Bayern Munich'.

data : mycricket_player type ref to cricket_player.
  create object mycricket_player
    exporting
      name        = 'James Reed'
      weight      = '98'
      height      = '178'
      county_name = 'Surrey'.
```

We now declare a reference variable based on the PLAYER class (the superclass of the FOOTBALL_PLAYER and CRICKET_PLAYER classes defined earlier). We then use upcasting to assign the created object MYFOOTBALL_PLAYER to the PLAYER variable. The method of DISPLAY_PLAYER_DETAILS is then called using the reference variable PLAYER. This is repeated for the CRICKET_PLAYER class. The code for this follows:

```
data : player type ref to player.

player = myfootball_player.
player->display_player_details( ).

player = mycricket_player.
player->display_player_details( ).
```

The output of the program is shown in Figure 3-5.

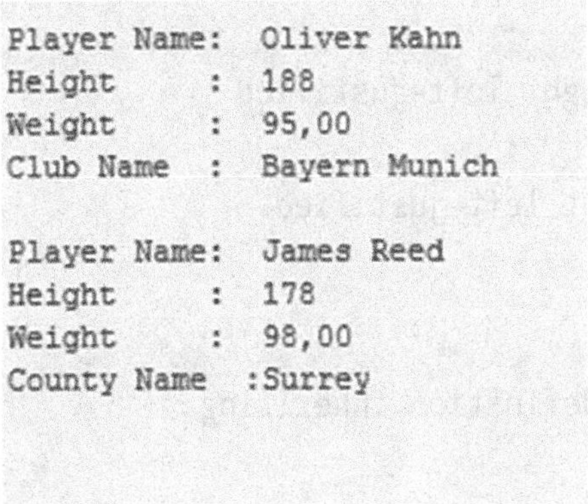

```
Player Name:  Oliver Kahn
Height     :  188
Weight     :  95,00
Club Name  :  Bayern Munich

Player Name:  James Reed
Height     :  178
Weight     :  98,00
County Name  :Surrey
```

Figure 3-5. *Program output*

The complete listing for the program exhibiting polymorphism is as follows:

```
class player definition.
  public section.
    methods constructor importing
                        name type string
                        weight type p
                        height type i.
    methods display_player_details.

  protected section.
    data : name type string.
    data : height type i.
```

```
    data : weight type p decimals 2.

endclass.

class player implementation.
  method constructor .
    me->name = name.
    me->height = height.
    me->weight = weight.
  endmethod.

  method display_player_details.
    write :/  'Player Name:    ',15 me->name ,
           / 'Height     :     ',
           15   me->height left-justified ,
           / 'Weight      :',
           15 me->weight left-justified.
  endmethod.
endclass.

class football_player definition inheriting
      from player.
  public section.
    methods constructor importing
                          name type string
                          weight type p
                          height type i
                          football_club type string.
    methods display_player_details redefinition.
  private section.
    data : football_club type string.
endclass.

class football_player implementation.
  method constructor.
    call method super->constructor
      exporting
        name    = name
```

```
        weight = weight
        height = height.
    me->football_club = football_club.
  endmethod .

  method display_player_details.
    call method super->display_player_details.
    write:/ 'Club Name  :         ',
    15 me->football_club.
    skip.
  endmethod .

endclass.

class cricket_player definition inheriting
      from player.
  public section.
    methods constructor importing
                          name type string
                          weight type p
                          height type i
                          county_name type string.

    methods display_player_details redefinition.

  private section.
    data : county_name type string.
endclass.

class cricket_player implementation.
  method constructor.
    call method super->constructor
      exporting
        name   = name
        weight = weight
        height = height.
```

```
    me->county_name = county_name.
  endmethod .

  method display_player_details.
    call method super->display_player_details.
    write:/ 'County Name   :        ',
    15 me->county_name.
  endmethod .

endclass.

start-of-selection.

data : myfootball_player type ref to football_player.
  create object myfootball_player
    exporting
      name          = 'Oliver Kahn'
      weight        = '95'
      height        = '188'
      football_club = 'Bayern Munich'.

data : mycricket_player type ref to cricket_player.
  create object mycricket_player
    exporting
      name          = 'James Reed'
      weight        = '98'
      height        = '178'
      county_name = 'Surrey'.

  data : player type ref to player.

  player = myfootball_player. "UPCASTING
  player->display_player_details( ).

  player = mycricket_player.
  player->display_player_details( ).
```

Global Subclasses and Redefinition of Methods

We have discussed how to define and implement subclasses locally within a program. In this section, we learn how to define global classes that are derived from other global classes (superclasses). Let's take a look at how to do this.

We will define a class ZST6_FOOTBALL_PLAYER_CLASS (a football player class) that is derived from the superclass ZST6_PLAYER_CLASS. For the sake of this example, we assume that the superclass ZST6_PLAYER_CLASS (the PLAYER class) already exists.

The global PLAYER class is similar to the one used as the superclass in the previous example of our locally defined class. One important point to keep in mind is that the final checkbox on the Properties tab must not be selected (see Figure 3-6). This is because we will have to define the FOOTBALL_PLAYER subclass based on the PLAYER class.

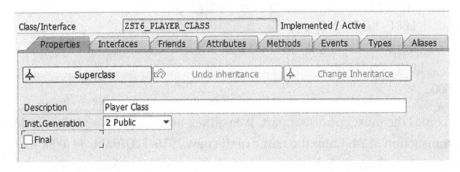

Figure 3-6. *Player class*

Three attributes (NAME, WEIGHT, and STRING) with protected visibility are defined for the PLAYER class, as shown in Figure 3-7.

Attribute	Level	Visibility	R...	Typing	Associated Type		Description
NAME	Instance ...	Protected	☐	Type	STRING	⇨	Name
WEIGHT	Instance ...	Protected	☐	Type	I	⇨	Weight
HEIGHT	Instance ...	Protected	☐	Type	I	⇨	Height

Figure 3-7. *Attributes of the player class*

An instance constructor and a `DISPLAY_PLAYER_DETAILS` method are also defined. The code of the constructor of the PLAYER class is shown here.

```
method CONSTRUCTOR.
      me->name = name.
      me->height = height.
      me->weight = weight.
endmethod.
```

The `DISPLAY_PLAYER_DETAILS` method will remain the same as shown earlier in the local class example:

```
method DISPLAY_PLAYER_DETAILS.
     write :/  'Player Name:    ',15 me->name ,
       / 'Height     :    ',15  me->height
          LEFT-JUSTIFIED ,
       / 'Weight      :',15 me->weight
          LEFT-JUSTIFIED.
ENDMETHOD.
```

Now comes the most important part. We will see how the inherited class is defined.

Call transaction SE24. Enter the name of the new ZST6_FOOTBALL_PLAYER_CLASS in the field provided. Then click the Create button. Choose the option class from the small popup box that appears and then click the Continue button. This will display the dialog box shown in Figure 3-8.

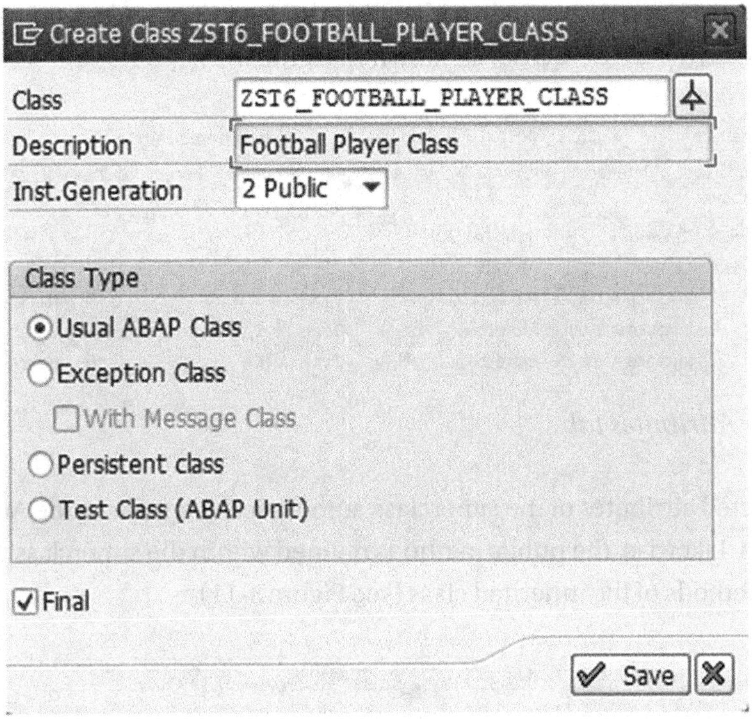

Figure 3-8. Creating the football player class

Enter the description in the field provided. Then click the Save button. This will take you to the screen shown in Figure 3-9.

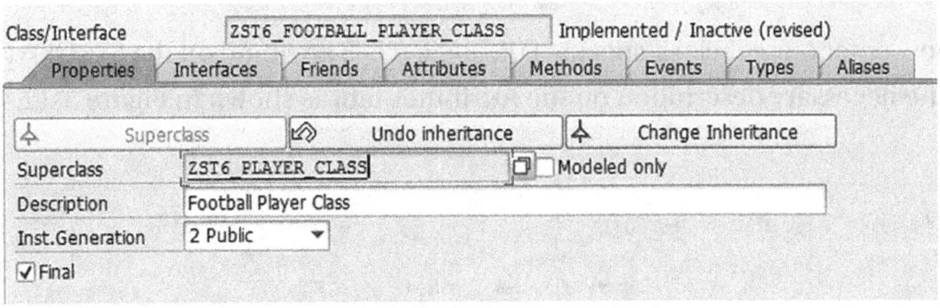

Figure 3-9. Properties of the football player class

On the Properties tab, click the [🔱   Superclass   ] button. This will make the superclass field visible and ready for input. Enter the name of the superclass in the field provided (in our case, ZST6_PLAYER_CLASS). Then press Enter to save your entries.

By saving your class, you automatically fill in the Attributes and Methods tabs from the superclass ZST6_PLAYER_CLASS, as shown in Figure 3-10.

Class/Interface	ZST6_FOOTBALL_PLAYER_CLASS			Implemented / Active			
Properties	Interfaces	Friends	Attributes	Methods	Events	Types	Aliases

Attribute	Level	Visibility	Read-Only	Typing	Associated Type		Description
NAME	Instance Attribute	Protected	☐	Type	STRING	⇨	Name
WEIGHT	Instance Attribute	Protected	☐	Type	I	⇨	Weight
HEIGHT	Instance Attribute	Protected	☐	Type	I	⇨	Height

Figure 3-10. Attributes tab

The protected attributes of the superclass automatically appear in the Attributes tab of the subclass. Likewise, the public methods defined within the superclass are made available as methods of the inherited class (see Figure 3-11).

Class/Interface	ZST6_FOOTBALL_PLAYER_CLASS			Implemented / Active			
Properties	Interfaces	Friends	Attributes	Methods	Events	Types	Aliases

Method	Level	Visibility	Method type	Description
CONSTRUCTOR	Instance Method	Public		Constructor
DISPLAY_PLAYER_DETAILS	Instance Method	Public		Display Player Details

Figure 3-11. Methods tab

We now enter our subclass-specific FOOTBALL_CLUB attribute on the STRING type and include the necessary description on the Attributes tab, as shown in Figure 3-12.

Attribute	Level	Visibility	R...	Typing	Associated Type		Description
NAME	Instance ...	Protected	☐	Type	STRING	⇨	Name
WEIGHT	Instance ...	Protected	☐	Type	I	⇨	Weight
HEIGHT	Instance ...	Protected	☐	Type	I	⇨	Height
FOOTBALL_CLUB	Instance ...	Private	☐	Type	STRING	⇨	Football club

Figure 3-12. Football club attribute

We now have a total of four attributes in the subclass (NAME, WEIGHT, HEIGHT, and FOOTBALL_CLUB).

Next, we need to define the instance constructor of our subclass FOOTBALL_PLAYER. Click the Constructor button ☐ Constructor . This will display the dialog box shown in Figure 3-13.

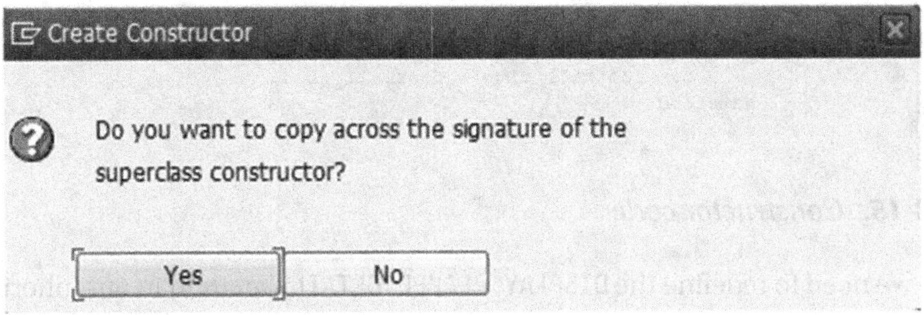

Figure 3-13. *Creating a constructor*

Click the Yes button, as we need the parameters of the superclass' constructor for the instance constructor of our inherited class. On the parameters list, the NAME, WEIGHT, and HEIGHT parameters will be added. Then, we will add the fourth parameter in the list of importing parameters of our instance constructor, as shown in Figure 3-14.

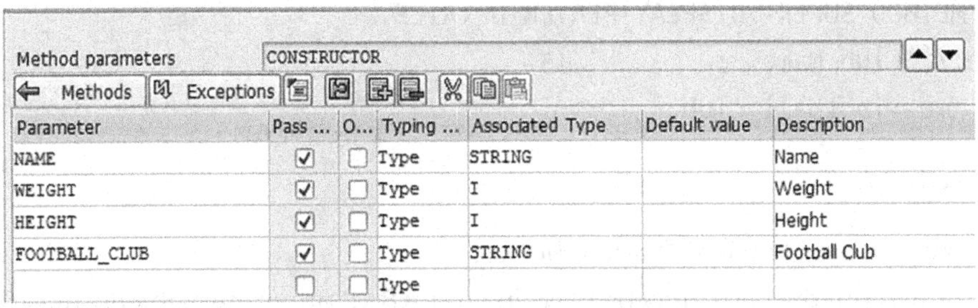

Figure 3-14. *Parameters of subclass instance constructor*

Within the code of the constructor, the superclass constructor is called, as well as a statement included to assign the value imported via FOOTBALL_CLUB to the corresponding attribute of the class. The code is shown in Figure 3-15.

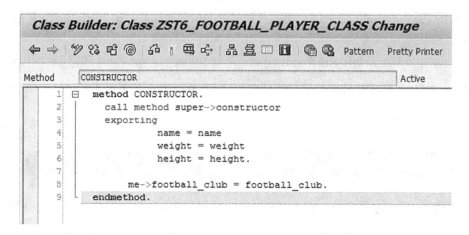

Figure 3-15. *Constructor code*

Next, we need to redefine the DISPLAY_PLAYER_DETAILS method in our inherited class. We need to make the method "specific" to the football player class in order for it to print the name of the football club that the player is associated with.

To redefine a method, while on the Methods tab, select the DISPLAY_PLAYER_DETAILS method and click the 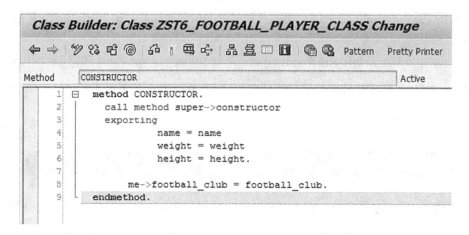 button.

You will then be taken to the code editor. Add the following code to the redefined method:

```
method DISPLAY_PLAYER_DETAILS.
  CALL METHOD SUPER->DISPLAY_PLAYER_DETAILS.
  write:/ 'Club Name  :        ',15
       me->football_club.

endmethod.
```

Once you are done, activate your subclass.

After activation, the class may be used in your ABAP programs. Objects may be instantiated based on the newly created subclass ZST6_FOOTBALL_PLAYER_CLASS. The code for doing so is shown here:

```
data : myfootball_player type ref
         to ZST6_FOOTBALL_PLAYER_CLASS.
  create object myfootball_player
         exporting name =  'Oliver Kahn'
                   weight = '95'
```

```
              height =  '188'
              football_club = 'Bayern Munich'.

call method myfootball_player->display_player_details.
```

This will create an object for the football player and print its details, as shown earlier.

Interfaces

In ABAP Objects, interfaces are also of importance. Interfaces may be simply defined as a set of components (events, attributes, and methods) that may be reused (implemented) in classes, thus may be used to extend the scope of classes. Interfaces cannot have instances (unlike classes), but are only used to implement classes.

Interfaces only have a public section and have no implementation part. The implementation (of the interface's methods) is done in the various classes that implement the interface.

You may have one class implement more than one interface. Also one interface may be used in multiple classes. For example, we may have an interface called INT_PLAYER that's used in the FOOTBALL_PLAYER and CRICKET_PLAYER classes. The interfaces may only be used in the public section of the class that implements them.

They may *not* be used in the private or protected sections. An interface may be composed of one or more interfaces—these are called *composite interfaces*. We use the following syntax to create an interface locally within a program:

```
INTERFACE int_name.
......
ENDINTERFACE.
```

For example, say we have an INTERFACE with the same DISPLAY comprised of a DISPLAY_PLAYER_DETAILS method, as shown here:

```
INTERFACE display.
  METHODS display_player_details.
ENDINTERFACE.
```

The particular interface may then be used in a class using the INTERFACES keyword within the public section of the class definition (as mentioned earlier).

Suppose we use this interface to extend the PLAYER class. The following code shows how this is done:

```
class player DEFINITION.
   public section.
     methods constructor importing
                            name type string
                            weight type p
                            height type i.

     INTERFACES display.   ""INTERFACE used
   private section.
     data : name type string.
     data : height type i.
     data : weight type p decimals 2.

endclass.
```

Within the implementation of the PLAYER class, we have the code of the DISPLAY_PLAYER_DETAILS method, as shown here:

```
method display~display_player_details.
   write :/  'Player Name:   ',15 me->name ,
         /  'Height     :   ',15  me->height
            LEFT-JUSTIFIED ,
         /  'Weight      :',15 me->weight
            LEFT-JUSTIFIED.
 ENDMETHOD.
```

You may note how the name of the method is indicated, i.e., the name of the interface followed by the method name, separated by a tilde (~). The tilde is also known as the Interface component selector.

Suppose we have a class called myclass that has implemented an interface called myinterface, and the variable classref points to an object in the myclass class. Then, we can have an assignment:

```
   intref = classref.
```

After this, the interface reference in intref will point to the object as the class reference in classref.

To call the relevant interface methods from a program, there are two possible approaches:

- We declare two reference variables, one for the PLAYER class and the other for the display interface. The MY_PLAYER object is then created. We assign the MY_PLAYER object reference to the MY_DISPLAY interface reference. The relevant method can then be called to display the player's details on the user screen.

```
data : my_display type ref to display.
data : my_player type ref to player.
create object my_player
        exporting name =  'Oliver Kahn'
                  weight = '95'
                  height =  '188'.
my_display = my_player.
my_display->display_player_details( ).
```

- Alternatively, we declare only one variable, called MY_DISPLAY, based on the PLAYER class. An object is created via the CREATE OBJECT statement. We then use the MY_PLAYER reference and the interface component selector (~) to call the DISPLAY_PLAYER_DETAILS method.

```
data : my_display type ref to player.
create object my_player
        exporting name =  'Oliver Kahn'
                  weight = '95'
                  height =  '188'.

my_player->display~display_player_details( ).
```

The result of this code is the same (i.e., the player details are displayed on the user screen) as shown in Figure 3-16.

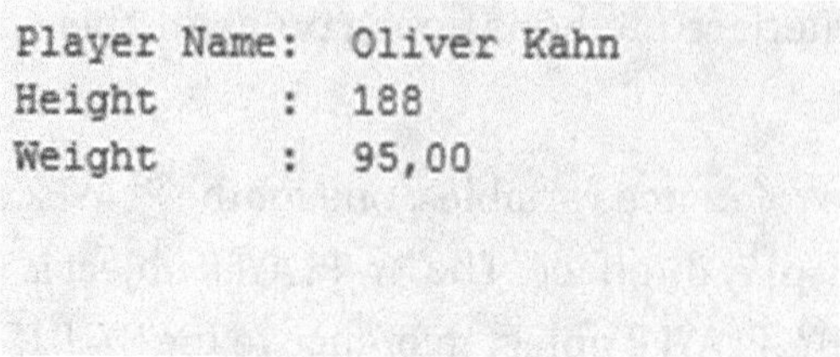

```
Player Name:  Oliver Kahn
Height     :  188
Weight     :  95,00
```

Figure 3-16. Program output

The complete listing of the program is shown here (the first approach is shown):

```
INTERFACE display.
  METHODS display_player_details.
ENDINTERFACE.

class player DEFINITION.
    public section.
      methods constructor importing
                            name type string
                            weight type p
                            height type i.

      INTERFACES display.
    private section.
      data : name type string.
      data : height type i.
      data : weight type p decimals 2.

endclass.

class player IMPLEMENTATION.
      method constructor .
         me->name = name.
         me->height = height.
         me->weight = weight.
      ENDMETHOD.

 method display~display_player_details.
    write :/ 'Player Name:    ',15 me->name ,
         / 'Height     :    ',15  me->height
```

```
          LEFT-JUSTIFIED ,
    /  'Weight      :',15 me->weight
          LEFT-JUSTIFIED.
  ENDMETHOD.

endclass.

  START-OF-SELECTION.

  data : my_display type ref to display.
  data : my_player type ref to player.
  create object my_player
        exporting name =  'Oliver Kahn'
                  weight = '95'
                  height =  '188'.

  my_display = my_player.
  my_display->display_player_details( ).
my_player->display~display_player_details( ).
```

Creating Global Interfaces

To define global interfaces using the Class Builder, follow these steps.

1. Call transaction SE24. Enter the name of the interface in the field provided (in our case, Z_INTERFACE_PLAYER) and click the Create button. The dialog box shown in Figure 3-17 appears.

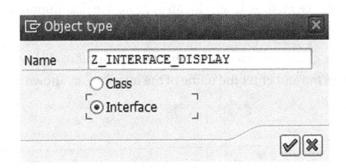

Figure 3-17. *Choosing the interface object type*

2. In this case, select the Interface checkbox and click the Continue button. The popup box appears, as shown in Figure 3-18.

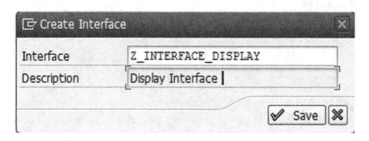

Figure 3-18. *The Create Interface dialog box*

3. Enter the description of the interface in the field provided and click the Save button. This will take you to the screen shown in Figure 3-19.

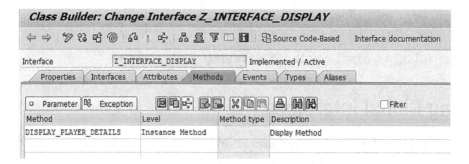

Figure 3-19. *Adding methods to the interface*

4. On the Methods tab, add the DISPLAY_PLAYER_DETAILS method as an Instance Method level with an appropriate description. Save and activate your interface.

5. To use the global interface in a global class definition, click on the Interfaces tab and enter the name of the interface, as shown in Figure 3-20.

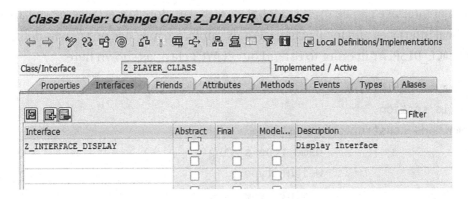

Figure 3-20.   *Using an interface in a global class*

6.   Once you save your class, the Methods tab will be populated with the Interface method (Z_INTERFACE_DISPLAY~DISPLAY_PLAYER_ DETAILS). See Figure 3-21.

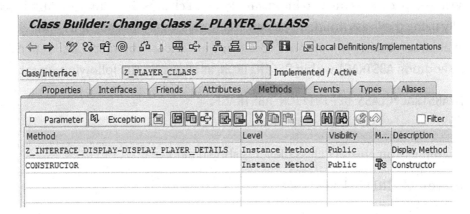

Figure 3-21.   *Interface method added*

7.   You can double-click on the method name. This will take you to the editor to add the method code. Then, you can activate the class in question.

A global interface can be used in global classes and global interfaces as well as within local interfaces and local classes. For example, we may use our newly-defined Z_INTERFACE_DISPLAY in order to extend our PLAYER class, as shown here:

```
class player DEFINITION.
    public section.
      methods constructor importing
                          name type string
                          weight type p
                          height type i.

      INTERFACES Z_INTERFACE_DISPLAY. "global
              " interface Z_INTERFACE_DISPLAY.
```

Abstract and Final Classes

In this section, we discuss the two important types of classes that can be defined locally or globally using the Class Builder. You can create classes as *abstract* or as *final*.

With abstract classes, you may not create any instances. Abstract classes are defined using the addition ABSTRACT within DEFINITION, as shown in the following syntax.

```
CLASS MYABSTRACTCLASS DEFINITION ABSTRACT.
ENDCLASS.
```

An example of an abstract class player is shown below:

```
class player DEFINITION abstract.
    public section.
      methods constructor importing
                          name type string
                          weight type p
                          height type i.
      methods display_player_details.

      PROTECTED SECTION.
      data : name type string.
      data : height type i.
      data : weight type p decimals 2.

endclass.
```

If you try to create an instance of an abstract class, a syntax error results, as shown in Figure 3-22.

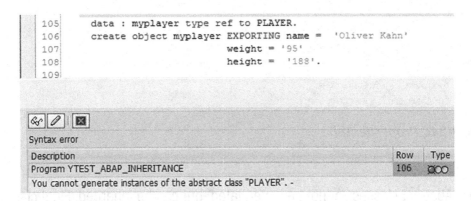

Figure 3-22. *Syntax error on abstract class instantiation*

With global classes, you can define an abstract class by choosing abstract as the instance generation field on the Create Class dialog, as shown in Figure 3-23.

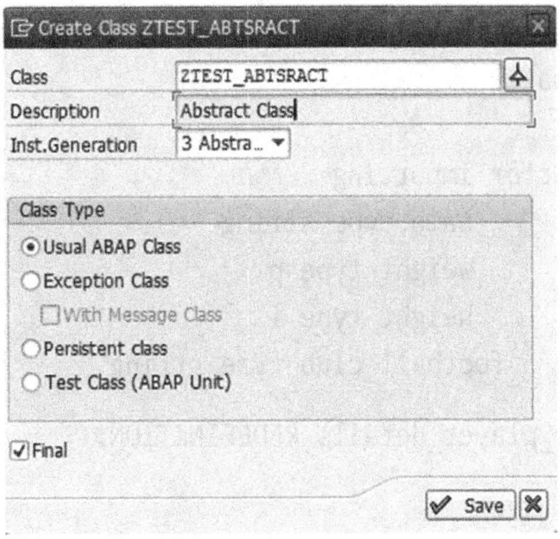

Figure 3-23. *The Create Class dialog*

The same field may be edited from the Properties tab, as shown in Figure 3-24.

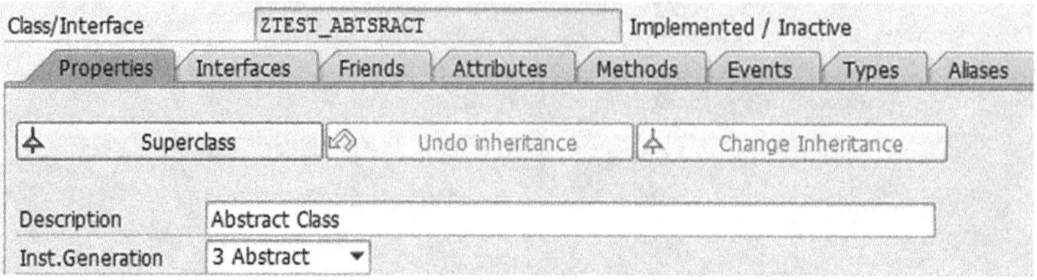

Figure 3-24. *Properties tab*

Note   Abstract classes cannot be instantiated, but can be inherited. Final classes cannot be inherited, but can be instantiated.

Final classes are classes that may not be inherited, i.e. they cannot have subclasses. They may be defined locally in a program or globally using the Class Builder. A final class is specified locally via the addition FINAL, as shown here:

```
class football_player DEFINITION INHERITING
      FROM player final.
   public section.
      methods constructor importing
                           name type string
                           weight type p
                           height type i
                        football_club type string.

      methods display_player_details REDEFINITION.

   private section.
      data : football_club type string.
endclass.
```

With global classes, you need to check the Final checkbox on the Properties tab, as shown in Figure 3-25.

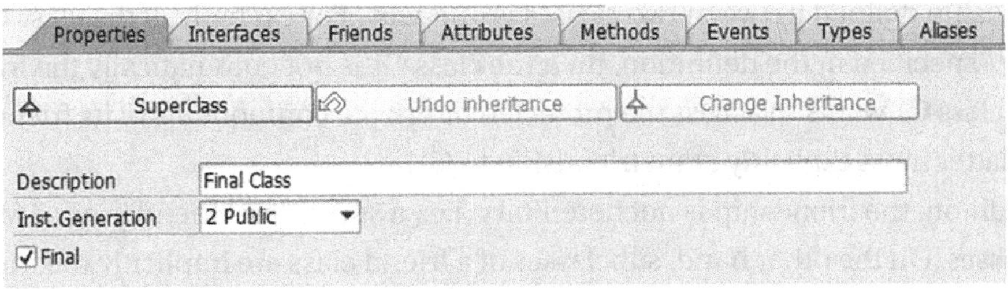

Figure 3-25. *Final checkbox on the Properties tab*

If you try to derive a class from a FINAL class, a syntax error occurs, as shown as in Figure 3-26.

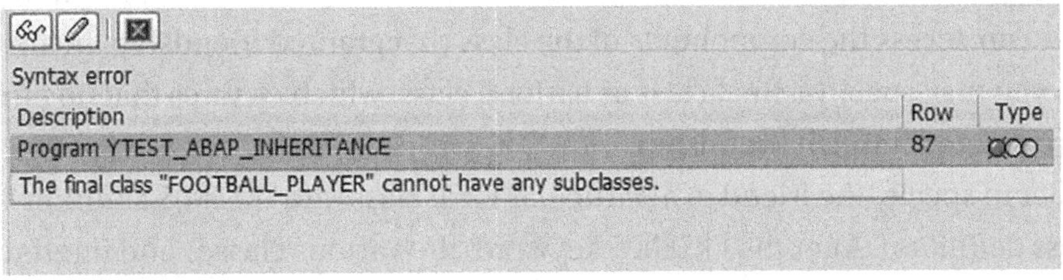

Figure 3-26. *Error on final class*

Friendships

Another important concept within ABAP Objects is the concept of *friend classes*. From outside the class, you can only access the public components of the class in question. The protected components are only visible to the subclasses of the given class.

In some very special cases, it may be required to grant another class access to a class' private components. This is done by designating the class as a friend (class) to the one whose private components are to be accessed. In this way, only friends may have access to these invisible components. This does not grant access to any other classes.

A class A may be specified as a friend to a given class. In addition, you may specify an interface I as a friend. In this way, all classes that implement the friend interface are friends of the given class and may access its private, public, and protected components.

Note   Friends are given access to all components of the class that offers the friendship, irrespective of the visibility section.

Friendship defined between two classes is one-way. For example, if the class C1 has a friend F1 specified in the definition, then the class C1 is not automatically the friend of F1. If the class C1 wants to access the protected or private components of its friend F1, then the latter must explicitly grant friendship to C1.

In addition, the friendship is not hereditary, i.e., a superclass' friend is not a friend of its subclasses. On the other hand, subclasses of a friend class are implicitly the friends of the given class that granted the friendship. For example, consider the following scenario.

Suppose we have a class C1 that has a friend F1 that has subclasses F2 and F3. Once class C1 has granted friendship to F1, F2 and F3 automatically become friends of C1 and can access private (and protected) components of C1.

You must therefore be very cautious when granting friendship to a class. A high-position friend class within an inheritance hierarchy means that a number of subclasses can access the components of the class that granted friendship. In an ideal situation, you may specify a final class as a friend class, which ensures that no other classes are granted implicit friendship.

In order to specify the friend of a particular local class, the FRIENDS addition is used in the class definition. After the FRIENDS keyword, the various classes and interfaces (to which the friendship is granted) are listed. Friendship can be granted to all classes or interfaces of the same program.

In addition to accessing the components of a class, friend classes can also create instances of the given class that granted friendship, irrespective of whether private instantiation has been specified in the class definition.

To specify a particular global class as a friend of another class, you must enter the name of the former on the Friends tab, as shown in Figure 3-27.

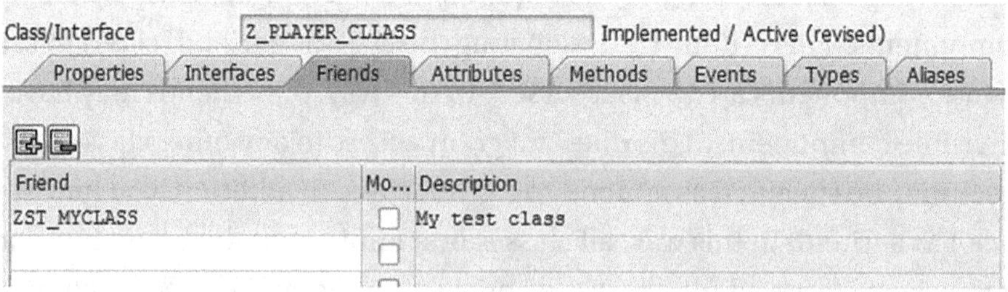

Figure 3-27. *Friends tab*

Let's now look at how a friendship can be created between classes. (We will look at an example of a local friend class shortly.) Consider the following piece of code:

```
class friend1 definition.
  public section.
    methods display.
endclass.

class myclass definition create private friends friend1.
  private section.
    data private_int type i value 200.
endclass.

class friend1 implementation.
  method display.
    data myobject type ref to myclass.
    create object myobject.
    write : myobject->private_int.
  endmethod.
endclass.

start-of-selection.
  data friend1 type ref to friend1.
  create object friend1.
  friend1->display( ).
```

We created a class called FRIEND1 with a display method in its definition. Another class, called MYCLASS, has a private instantiation defined with FRIEND1 specified as its friend. This class has a private attribute PRIVATE_INT with an initial value of 200. Within the DISPLAY method of the FRIEND1 class, an object called MYCLASS is created using a CREATE OBJECT statement and the value of the private attribute PRIVATE_INT is then printed. Finally, we define a reference to the FRIEND1 class and create a corresponding object. The DISPLAY method is then called. The DISPLAY method creates an object of MYCLASS and displays its private attribute value 200 on the user screen. If the FRIEND addition is not specified, the following syntax error occurs when trying to create an instance of MYCLASS within the DISPLAY method of FRIEND1. See Figure 3-28.

Syntax error		
Description	Row	Type
Program YTEST_FRIEND	24	000
You cannot create an instance of the class "MYCLASS" outside the class.		

Figure 3-28. *Error related to private instantiation*

Summary

In this chapter, we learned about inheritance and redefining of methods. We then covered instance constructors and interfaces. A section on casting and polymorphism was also included. We also discussed abstract and final classes. Finally, we discussed the friendship concept within classes, along with looking at fully working coding examples.

CHAPTER 4

Class Builder

Global classes are defined in the Class Builder, which has the transaction code SE24. Global classes and interfaces can be accessed by all ABAP programs in the R/3 system.

In this chapter, we first see how we can use the Object Navigator as an alternative transaction for creating global classes. We then move on to the Class Builder, where we will spend some time exploring its various tabs, particularly the Methods tab. We take a brief look at the Class Browser, and then return to the Class Builder, where we learn to test instance methods and view some examples.

Finally, we see a number of examples using the transaction SE24 that will be tested using the transaction itself rather than having to create a program for them.

Transaction SE80

One easy way to create a new global class is by using the Object Navigator, which has the transaction code SE80. The navigator is split into two areas: the navigation area and the tool area. A screenshot of the Object Navigator is shown in Figure 4-1.

© Rehan Zaidi 2019
R. Zaidi, *SAP ABAP Objects*, https://doi.org/10.1007/978-1-4842-4964-2_4

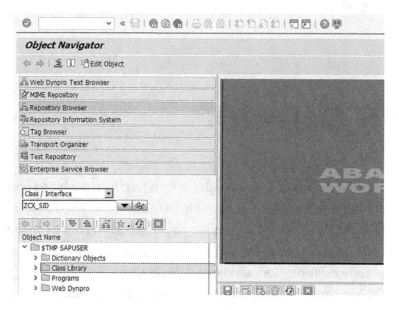

Figure 4-1. *The Object Navigator*

The left side of the window is the navigation area, and right side is the tool area. It also makes it easy for us to use the navigation area in order to navigate through the various components of the global class.

Follow these steps to create a global class using SE80:

1. To create a new global class, use the context menu in the navigation area.

2. First select the package node or select the Class Library node within the package and right-click it. From the context menu that appears, choose the Create option. A dialog box will open.

3. Input the class name and description, select the Usual ABAP Class option, and uncheck the Final checkbox, as shown in Figure 4-2. Click the Save button.

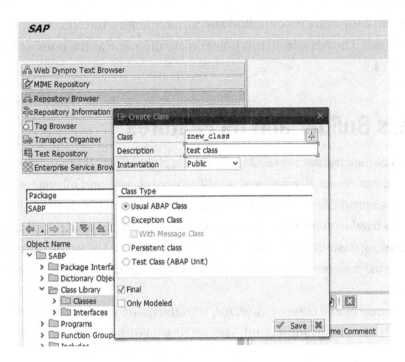

Figure 4-2. *Create Class dialog box*

The global class will then appear in the Class Builder (in the right pane), which you can find in the tool area of the Object Navigator. It will display various tabs like Interface, Attributes, Methods, etc., as you can see in Figure 4-3.

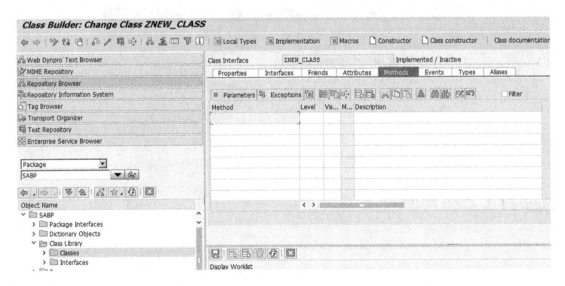

Figure 4-3. *Creating a class*

Here, we can define any new method and its parameters, the class attributes, and other components. The steps from this point on are the same as the ones when using the transaction SE24.

The Class Builder and Its Features

As mentioned earlier, transaction SE24 is the main global Class Builder. With this transaction, we can create, display, and modify global classes and interfaces. Together, these form the *Central Class Library,* which is accessible throughout the SAP system. Class Builder is used to define or create new custom global classes. It may be used to modify the existing custom SAP ABAP classes and interfaces. Using the Class Builder, it is also possible to implement inheritance of classes and the redefining of the inherited methods.

To create a new global class or interface, start the name with Y or Z (the convention followed for all custom developments). This will distinguish it from a standard class or interface.

We may use the transaction SE24 to display the standard SAP classes. Now, let's look at one of the standard ABAP classes. Let's take the example of CL_ABAP_REGEX. We start with the initial screen of the Class Builder. The Class Builder (SE24) initial screen is shown in Figure 4-4.

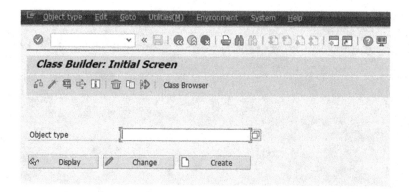

Figure 4-4. *Class Builder*

Enter the name of the CL_ABAP_REGEX class in the Object Type field (see Figure 4-5) and click Display.

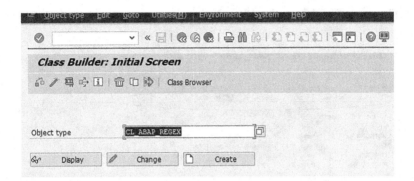

Figure 4-5. *Class Builder with a standard SAP class*

The screen—with the Properties, Interfaces, Friends, Attributes, Methods, Events, Types, and Aliases tabs—appears. See Figure 4-6.

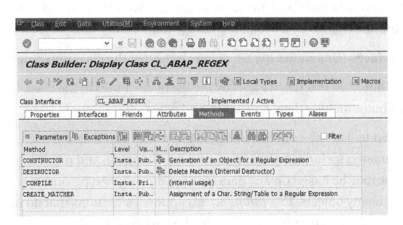

Figure 4-6. *Display mode*

These methods can be called from any ABAP program.

Class Builder Tabs

A global class includes several components, all of which have a visibility—public, private or protected. The various tabs on the Class Builder are shown in Figure 4-7.

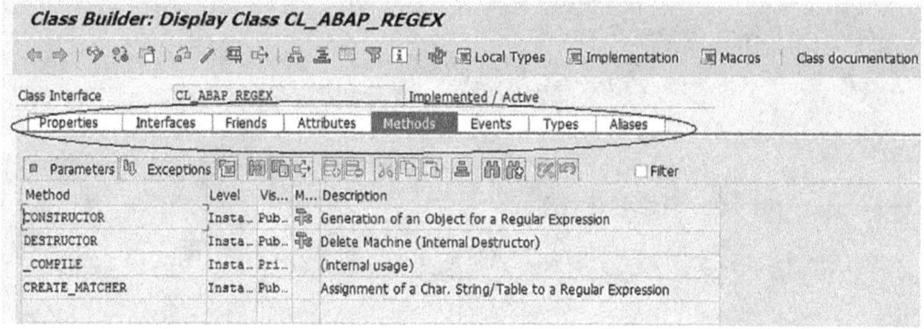

Figure 4-7. *Global class methods*

The tabs on the Class Builder transaction SE24 are as follows:

- **Properties**. This tab includes the properties, such as a short description of the class, the name of the user who created it, the date of the last change by a user, the package name, etc.

- **Interfaces**. This shows the list of interfaces that the class implements.

- **Attributes**. In this tab, we specify the list of attributes of the class. Attributes include data, constants, and types.

- **Methods**. The tab has two subtabs: Parameters and Exceptions. *Parameters* include importing, exporting, changing, and returning. These may be based on any data types or dictionary types, or may refer to any objects. *Exceptions* are exceptional situations that do not allow a method to proceed normally during execution. These may be raised within the code and may be used to avoid the method from resulting in a runtime error (and short dump).

- **Events**. On this tab, we can define several events for the class. A corresponding method can be triggered when an event occurs.

- **Types.** On this tab, we define or declare any user-defined types, which we can then use in method parameters. To declare a user-defined type, go to the Types tab and input the type name, its visibility, an associate type, and a description, then click Save. See Figure 4-8.

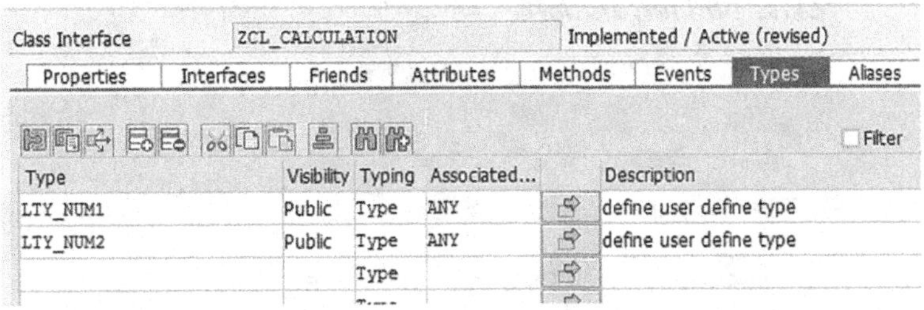

Class Interface	ZCL_CALCULATION				Implemented / Active (revised)			
Properties	Interfaces	Friends	Attributes	Methods	Events	Types	Aliases

Type	Visibility	Typing	Associated...		Description
LTY_NUM1	Public	Type	ANY	⇨	define user define type
LTY_NUM2	Public	Type	ANY	⇨	define user define type
		Type		⇨	

Figure 4-8. Types tab

When you click on the direct type entry icon (the yellow arrow), it will take you to the ABAP editor where the type is declared. You can now use this user-defined type in the method parameters.

```
TYPES lty_num1 TYPE any.
TYPES lty_num2 TYPE any.
```

- **Aliases.** On this tab, we can declare any aliases. These are only used in conjunction with interfaces and may be used to form short names to components existing in an interface that is implemented by a given class.

Useful Functions of the Class Builder

In this section, we discuss the various functions within the Class Builder.

Where-Used Lists

This is one of the functions used in the Class Builder as well as in the methods of a class. As its name suggests, the where-used list shows every place (in a program, class or enhancement) where a class or method is used.

To create a where-used list for a class (e.g., CL_SALV_TABLE), go to Utilities ➔ Where-Used List (CTRL+Shift+F3), as shown in Figure 4-9.

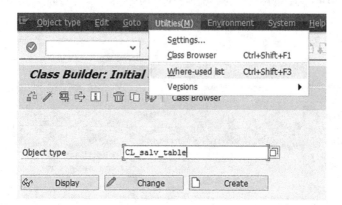

Figure 4-9. *Creating a where-used list*

A dialog box will appear with the class/interface name CL_SALV_TABLE, as shown in Figure 4-10. Select the top three options to see which program or classes/interfaces use them, then click to continue.

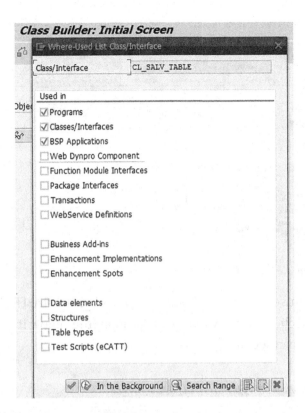

Figure 4-10. *Where-Used List dialog box*

A dialog box appears with a message, as shown in Figure 4-11. Click Yes.

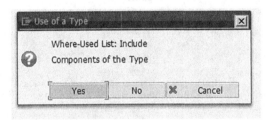

Figure 4-11. *Confirm your where-used list*

The output will display a hit list showing each place the CL_SALV_TABLE class is used or defined in the program. In this case, there are around 149 programs using this class. From this hit list, you can select the location of the object's exact usage.

In this way, the where-used list function makes it easy for us to search for any object in programs. See Figure 4-12.

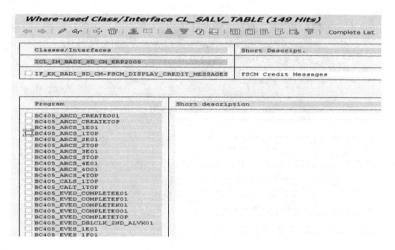

Figure 4-12. *Hit list*

To create a where-used list for methods, go to the CL_SALV_TABLE class, go to the
DISPLAY method, and click on the where-used list icon (the yellow icon with a tree
structure), which you can see in Figure 4-13.

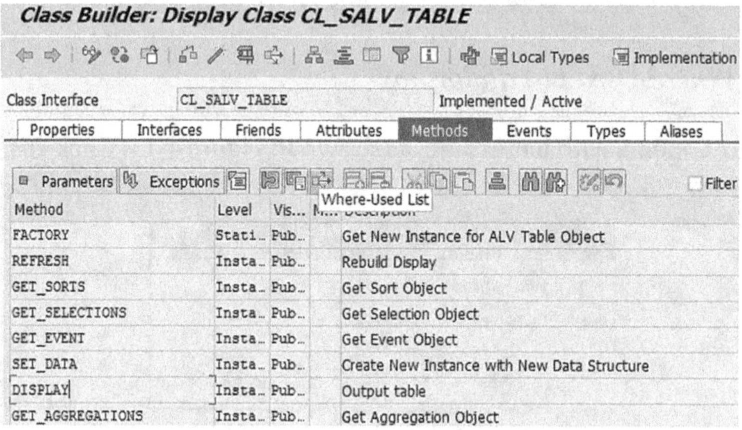

Figure 4-13. *Where-used list icon*

A dialog box will appear with the class/interface and method name with the selected
option program, classes, and BSP application, as shown in Figure 4-14.

Figure 4-14. *Where-Used List dialog box*

Click Continue. A hit list will then appear. In this example, you can see that the
`Display` method is used in 96 programs, as shown in Figure 4-15.

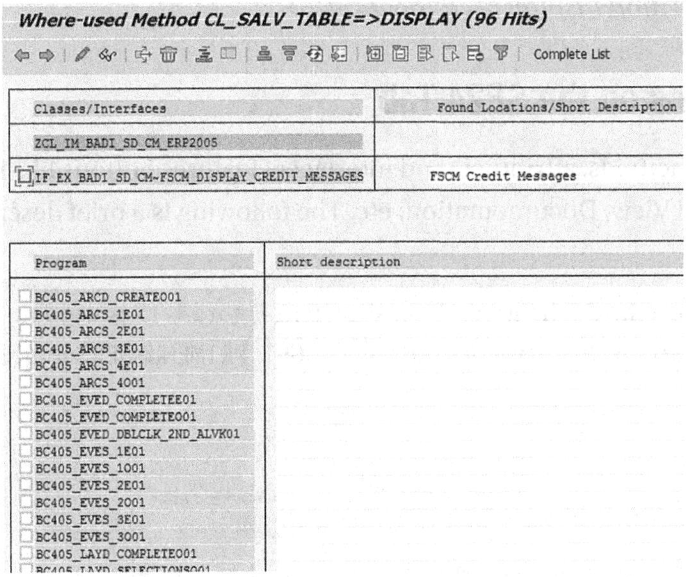

Figure 4-15. *Hit list*

To check where the method is used, double-click on an object name. This will take you to the exact location where it is used, as shown in Figure 4-16.

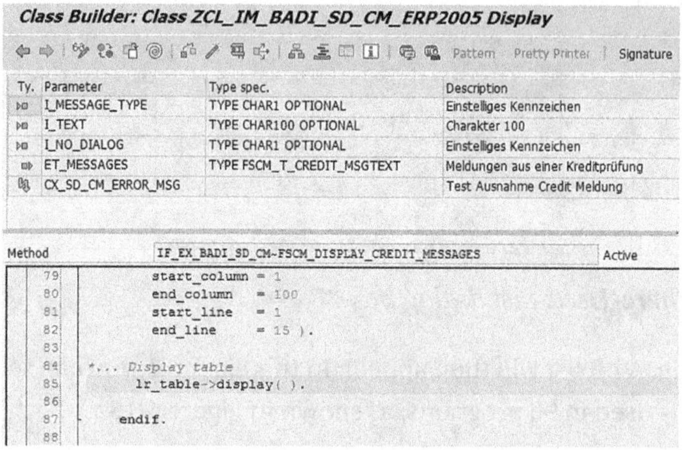

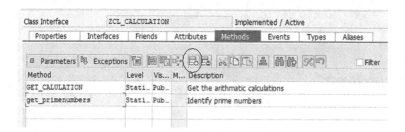

Figure 4-16. Method display used location

Useful Buttons on the SE24 Tab

Every SE24 tab (methods, attributes, and interfaces) features buttons like Insert, Delete, Copy, Sort, Detail View, Documentation, etc. The following is a brief description of some of these buttons.

- **Insert method.** The green icon shown in Figure 4-17 is used to add methods. Here, we are adding the GET_PRIMENUMBERS method to a class.

Figure 4-17. Add Method icon

- **Delete method.** The red icon shown in Figure 4-18 is used to delete a method. Here, we are deleting the GET_PRIMENUMBERS method from the column.

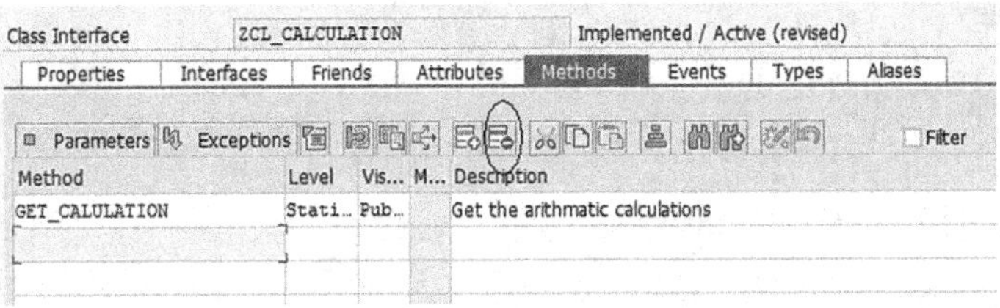

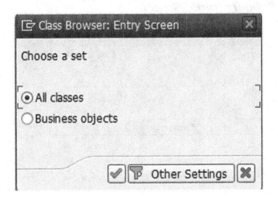

Figure 4-18. *Delete Method icon*

Class Browser

This is used to display all the global classes and interfaces or business objects in the class library. The transaction code is CLABAP. We can do this via the Class Builder, or we can use the transaction CLABAP directly.

You'll find a screen with the options All Classes and Business Objects, as shown in Figure 4-19.

Figure 4-19. *SAP easy access screen*

Choose the All Classes option. You'll get a screen showing all the standard SAP global classes and interfaces, as you can see in Figure 4-20.

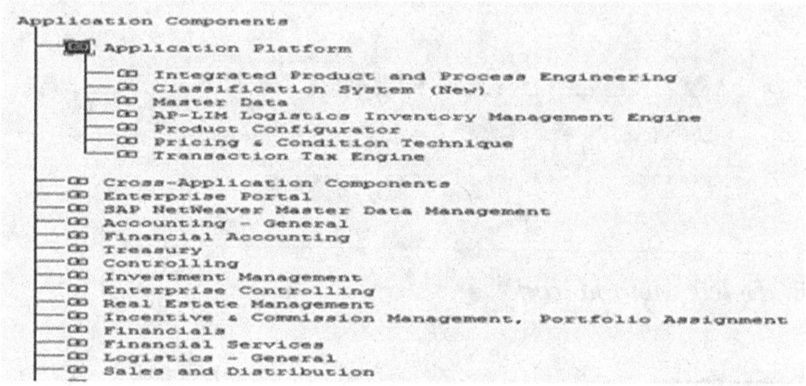

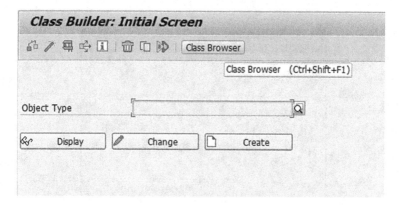

Figure 4-20. *All classes screen*

The other way to access the class browser is through the Class Builder (SE24). Go to SE24, click on Utilities, and select Class Browser. A similar dialog box of options will appear, as shown in Figure 4-21, and you can search through the classes and interfaces.

Figure 4-21. *Class Browser screen*

Testing Classes in SE24

The Class Builder allows you to test your class and its methods without creating a test program. The test function within the class lets you specify test data and check the behavior of both static and instance methods. These may contain table parameters or not.

In this section, we look at a number of examples that will be tested via SE24.

Testing a Static Method

Let's look at the steps needed to test a static method. To serve as the example, we will create a class called ZMY_PERCENTAGE to calculate the percentage of the two inputted numbers.

Go to SE24 and input the class name ZMY_PERCENTAGE. Click on the Create option, as shown in Figure 4-22.

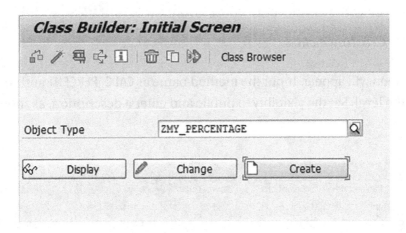

Figure 4-22. *Inputting a class name*

Choose the Class option from the dialog box that appears and then press Enter.

The dialog box shown in Figure 4-23 will appear. Input the description, select the Usual ABAP Class option, uncheck the Final checkbox, and click the Save button.

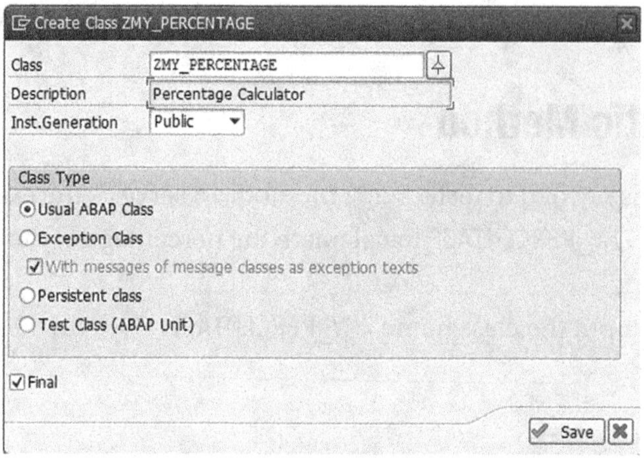

Figure 4-23. *Creating a class*

A new screen will appear. Input the method name as CALC_PERCENT and select Static Method for the level. Set the visibility to public and enter a description, as shown in Figure 4-24.

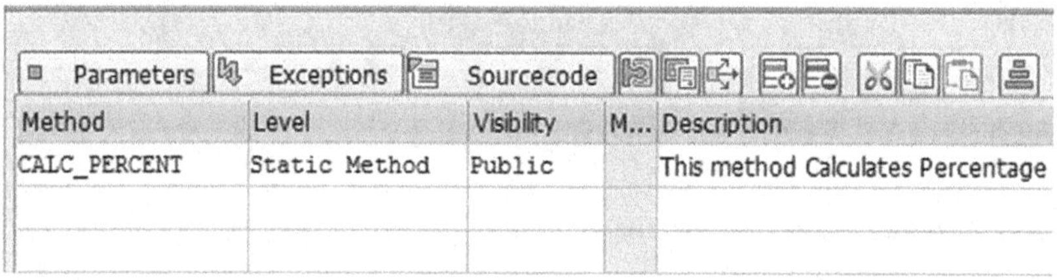

Figure 4-24. *Setting the class description*

Now, go to Method and select the Parameters tab. Input MYNUMBER1 and MYNUMBER2 as the importing parameters of type INTEGER and input CALC_PERCENT as an exporting parameter of type INTEGER. This is shown in Figure 4-25. Click Save.

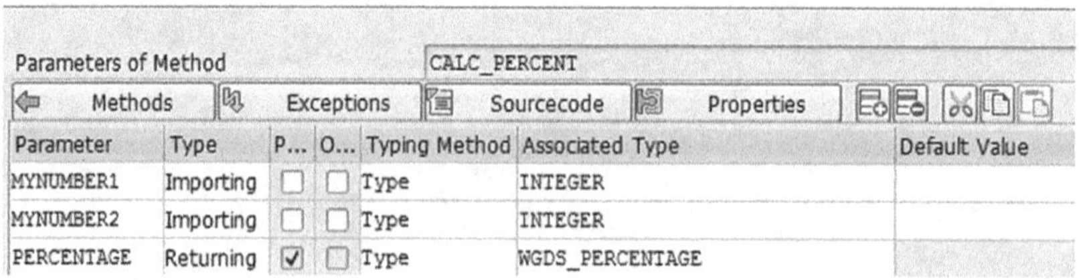

Figure 4-25. *Method parameters*

Go back to Method to implement source code for CALC_PERCENT. Select the method by clicking on it. You'll get the screen shown in Figure 4-26.

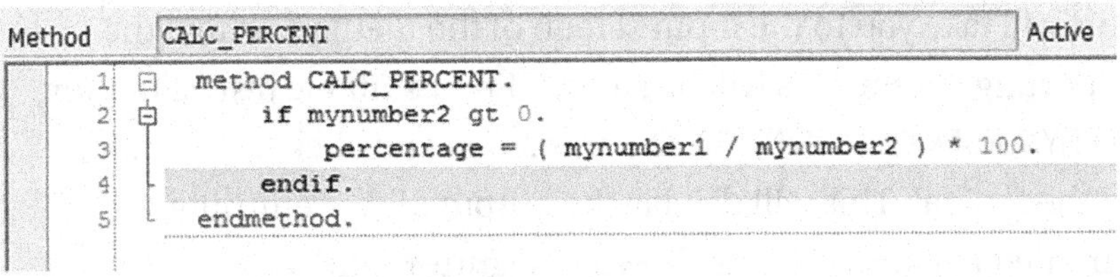

```
Method    CALC_PERCENT                                                    Active
      1  □     method CALC_PERCENT.
      2  □         if mynumber2 gt 0.
      3                 percentage = ( mynumber1 / mynumber2 ) * 100.
      4             endif.
      5         endmethod.
```

Figure 4-26. *Source code screen*

Here, we have written the logic of the program to calculate percentage. Now, check the syntax for errors using the check option (or CTRL+F2), save (CTRL+S) every element of the class, and activate the class (CTRL+F3).

To test the static method CALC_PERCENT of the ZMY_PERCENTAGE class, follow these steps:

1. Click the 🔲 button. This will take you to the screen shown in Figure 4-27.

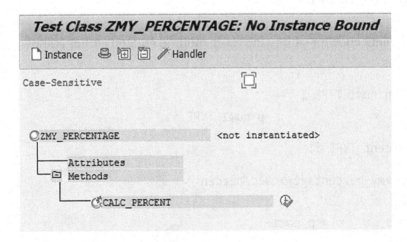

Figure 4-27. *Testing ZMY_PERCENTAGE*

2. We do not need to create an instance of the object since we have to test a static method (in our case, CALC_PERCENT). Simply click the ⊕ next to the method.

3. This will take you to the input screen of the method, where the importing parameters will be shown. Enter suitable test values for the MYNUMBER1 and MYNUMBER2 parameters and click the ⊕ button on the toolbar. This will display the output of the returning parameter PERCENTAGE, as shown in Figure 4-28.

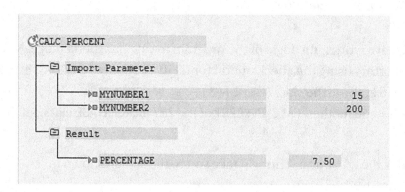

Figure 4-28. *Percentage output*

The equivalent code for calling the static method created earlier is shown in the code, as follows.

```
PARAMETERS: p_num1 TYPE i ,

                    p_num2 TYPE i.

DATA cal_percent TYPE i.

CALL METHOD zmy_percentage=>calc_percent
  EXPORTING
    mynumber1        = p_num1
    mynumber2        = p_num2
  IMPORTING
    cal_percent = cal_percent.

WRITE: 'Percentage =', cal_percent.
```

In this code, we are again calculating percentage through an ABAP program. We've declared the P_NUM1 and P_NUM2 parameters of type string, so that we can take the input values from the selection screen. The result is stored in CAL_PERCENT, which is of the integer type.

We have now called the CALC_PERCENT method from a ZMY_PERCENTAGE class, which calculates the percentage. The importing parameters of the MYNUMBER1 and MYNUMBER2 methods are exported with P_NUM1, P_NUM2, and CAL_PERCENT stored as the result.

Testing Instance Methods

Now let's look at a simple example of testing pertaining to instance methods.

We will create the class to calculate the cubic value of a number. In this code, we will use the constructor method to calculate the cubic value of the inputted number (importing parameter of the constructor) and set the cubic value as an attribute of the class. We will then use the Class Builder to instantiate an object of the class and calculate the cubic value. Let's see how this is done.

Go to the SE24 Class Builder, input the object type name ZCL_MY_CUBE_CALCULATOR, and click on Create, as shown in Figure 4-29.

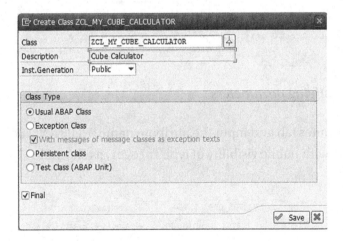

Figure 4-29. *Creating a cube class*

Go to the Methods tab and input the method name CONSTRUCTOR, then press Enter. A constructor symbol is created, showing you that this is a constructor method, as you can see in Figure 4-30. For the constructor, choose a visibility of Public.

☐ Parameters ⬚ Exceptions ⬚ Sourcecode				
Method	Level	Visibility	M...	Description
CONSTRUCTOR	Instance Method	Public	⬚	Constructor

Figure 4-30. *Constructor method*

Go to the CONSTRUCTOR method you've just created and click on the Specifying parameters. Input the parameter name MYNUMVALUE, type integer, as shown in Figure 4-31.

Class Builder: Change Class ZCL_MY_CUBE_CALCULATOR

⬚ Local Definitions/Implementations   ⬚ Local Test Classes

Class/Interface	ZCL_MY_CUBE_CALCULATOR	Implemented / Inactive (revised)

Properties	Interfaces	Friends	Attributes	Methods	Events	Types	Aliases

Parameters of Method	CONSTRUCTOR	▲ ▼

⬚ Methods ⬚ Exceptions ⬚ Sourcecode ⬚ Properties

Parameter	Pass Value	Optional	Typing Method	Associated Type	Default Value	Description
MYNUMVALUE	☐	☐	Type	INTEGER		Whole Number with +/- Sign (-2.147.483.648 ..
	☐	☐	Type			

Figure 4-31. *Specifying parameters*

Select the Attributes tab and input the attribute name MYCUBICVALUE. Set it as an instance attribute with public visibility of type integer, as shown in Figure 4-32.

Class/Interface	ZCL_MY_CUBE_CALCULATOR	Implemented / Active

Properties	Interfaces	Friends	Attributes	Methods	Events	Types	Aliases

⬚ Properties   ☐ Filter

Attribute	Level	Visibility	R...	Typing	Associated Type
MYCUBICVALUE	Instance Attribute	Public	☐	Type	INTEGER
			☐	Type	

Figure 4-32. *Attributes tab*

Go back to the method constructor and double-click on it. Write the logic of the code to calculate the cube of the input number, as shown in Figure 4-33.

```
1  ⊟    method CONSTRUCTOR.
2 ▸ |        mycubicvalue  =   mynumvalue * mynumvalue * mynumvalue.
3    L   endmethod.
```

Figure 4-33. *Calculation code*

Save the class and activate all the elements of the class.

Once the class is activated, we can execute the constructor method using the Test feature of the Class Builder.

From the Class Builder, click the ⊞ button or use the F8 key. The Create Instance screen appears, as shown in Figure 4-34.

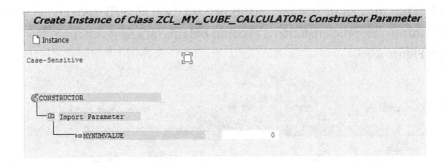

Figure 4-34. *Create Instance screen*

Here, you will be provided space to enter value(s) for the importing parameter(s) of the constructor. In our case, there is only one parameter—MYNUMVALUE.

We will enter a value of 10 in the input field and click the ☐ Instance button on the toolbar. This will create an instance of the class and will assign a value equal to the inputted number's cube value of the MYCUBICVALUE attribute, as shown in Figure 4-35.

121

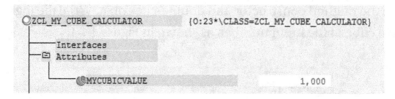

Figure 4-35. *Cubic value calculated*

In short, you'll get the cube of the number stored in the given attribute, without the need to develop a test program with relevant coding.

E

We will now see another example—a bank account demo—where will test instance methods (other than the constructor) using the functions of the Class Builder. As an example, we will use a bank account for bank customers. The class we will use is ZCL_MY_ACCOUNT_DEMO.

This class has the private instance attribute called BALANCE, based on the type BETRG. We will use this to store the customer's account balance at any given time. This attribute is shown in Figure 4-36.

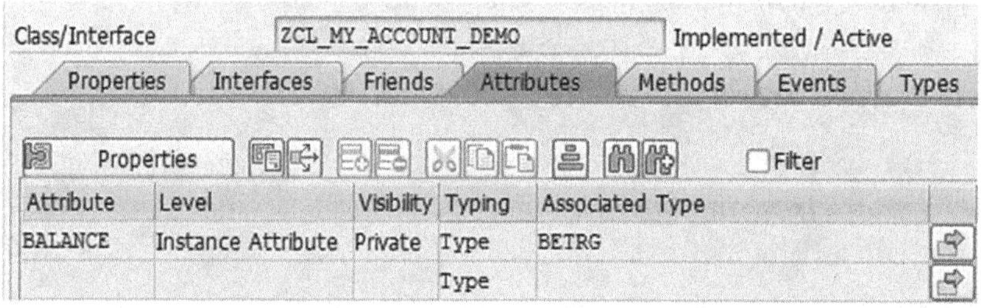

Class/Interface	ZCL_MY_ACCOUNT_DEMO			Implemented / Active	

Properties	Interfaces	Friends	Attributes	Methods	Events	Types

Attribute	Level	Visibility	Typing	Associated Type	
BALANCE	Instance Attribute	Private	Type	BETRG	
			Type		

Figure 4-36. *Account attributes*

The class also has three methods, all of which have public visibility, as shown in Figure 4-37. The methods are DEPOSIT_MONEY, WITHDRAW_MONEY, and SET_ACCOUNT_BALANCE.

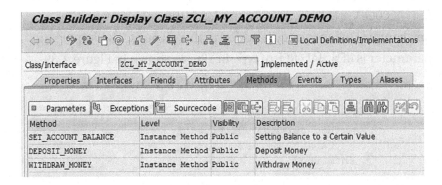

Figure 4-37. *Class methods*

The methods are defined as follows:

- DEPOSIT_MONEY. This method adds a deposit to the current balance and returns the new one. The importing parameter is AMOUNT_DEPOSITED of type BETRG, and the returning parameter is NEW_BALANCE of type BETRG, as shown in Figure 4-38.

| Method | DEPOSIT_MONEY | | | | | | Active |

```
1 ⊟  method deposit_money.
2       balance = balance +  amount_deposited.
3
4       new_balance  = balance.
5 ⌐  endmethod.
```

Display Method DEPOSIT_MONEY

Class	ZCL_MY_ACCOUNT_DEMO
Method	DEPOSIT_MONEY
Description	Deposit Money

Attributes / Parameters / Exceptions

| | Methods | | Exceptions | | Sourcecode | | Properties | | |

Parameter	Type	Pass Value	Optional	Typing Method	Associated Type
AMOUNT_DEPOSITED	Importing	☐	☐	Type	BETRG
NEW_BALANCE	Exporting	☐	☐	Type	BETRG

Figure 4-38. *Method deposit balance*

- SET_ACCOUNT_BALANCE. This method sets the balance with the
  new amount when money is added to the account. The importing
  parameter is NEW_BALANCE of type BETRG, as shown in Figure 4-39.

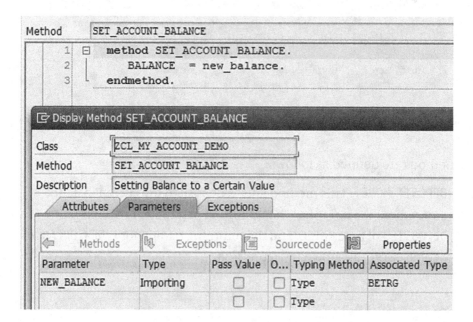

Figure 4-39. *NEW_BALANCE method*

- WITHDRAW_MONEY. When an amount is withdrawn from the balance,
  this method returns the new amount. The importing parameter is
  AMOUNT_WITHDRAWN of type BETRG, and the exporting parameter is
  NEW_BALANCE of type BETRG, as shown in Figure 4-40.

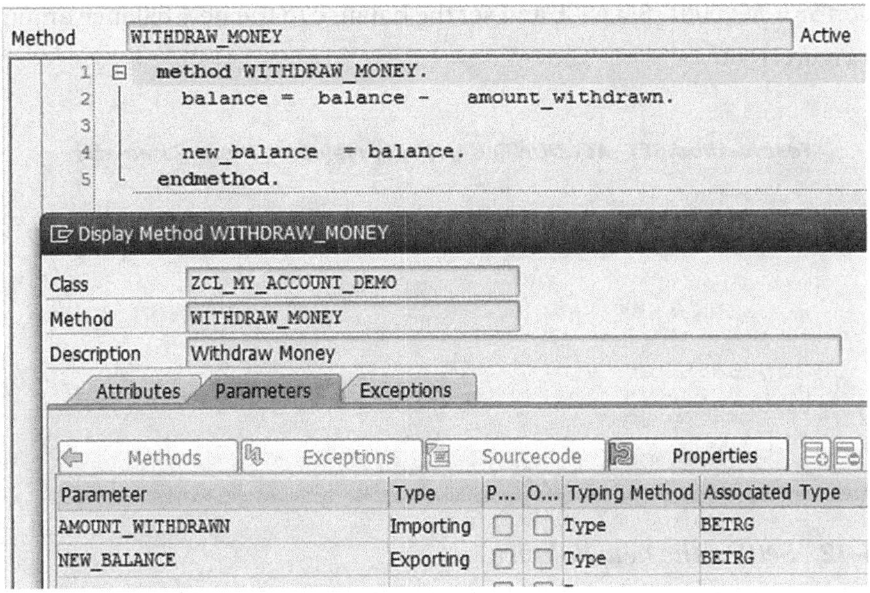

```
Method      WITHDRAW_MONEY                                              Active
   1  ⊟    method WITHDRAW_MONEY.
   2          balance = balance -   amount_withdrawn.
   3
   4          new_balance  = balance.
   5  └     endmethod.
```

```
 ☞ Display Method WITHDRAW_MONEY

Class          ZCL_MY_ACCOUNT_DEMO
Method         WITHDRAW_MONEY
Description    Withdraw Money
      Attributes   Parameters   Exceptions

  ⇦    Methods    ⓦ   Exceptions   ▤  Sourcecode  ▣  Properties   ⊟⊟
 Parameter                      Type       P... O... Typing Method Associated Type
 AMOUNT_WITHDRAWN               Importing  ☐   ☐   Type           BETRG
 NEW_BALANCE                    Exporting  ☐   ☐   Type           BETRG
```

Figure 4-40. *Debit amount method*

To test the object, activate all the elements of the global class and click on the Test button. The screen shown in Figure 4-41 appears.

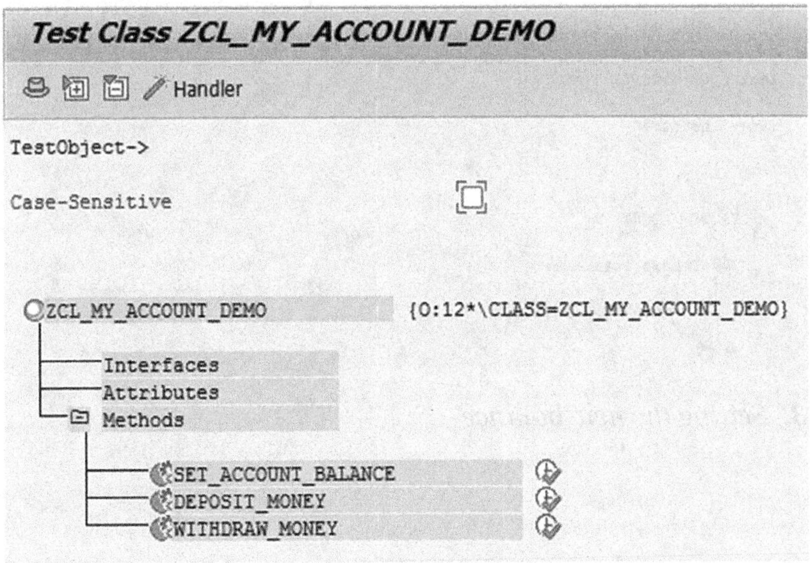

Test Class ZCL_MY_ACCOUNT_DEMO

```
 ⊟ 回 回 ∅ Handler

TestObject->

Case-Sensitive                        ▢


○ZCL_MY_ACCOUNT_DEMO              {0:12*\CLASS=ZCL_MY_ACCOUNT_DEMO}
  │
  ├── Interfaces
  ├── Attributes
  └─⊟ Methods
       │
       ├── ⚙SET_ACCOUNT_BALANCE        ⊕
       ├── ⚙DEPOSIT_MONEY              ⊕
       └── ⚙WITHDRAW_MONEY             ⊕
```

Figure 4-41. *Testing the object*

Click on SET_ACCOUNT_BALANCE and set the balance to the new balance amount, as shown in Figure 4-42.

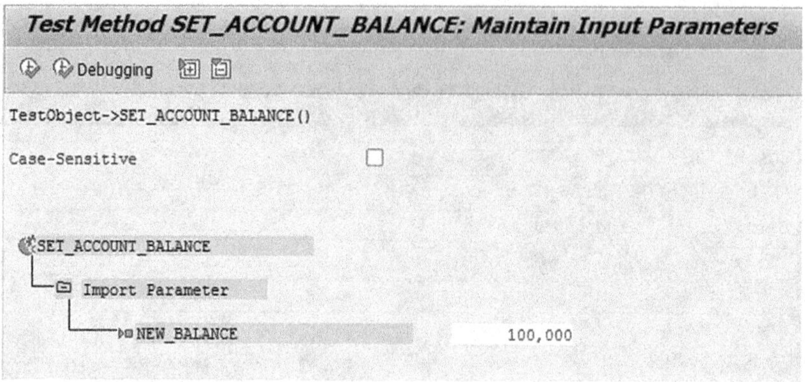

Figure 4-42. *Setting the new balance*

Click Execute. The account balance is now set, and you will return to the previous screen.

Go to DEPOSIT_MONEY and enter the deposit amount as 200, as shown in Figure 4-43.

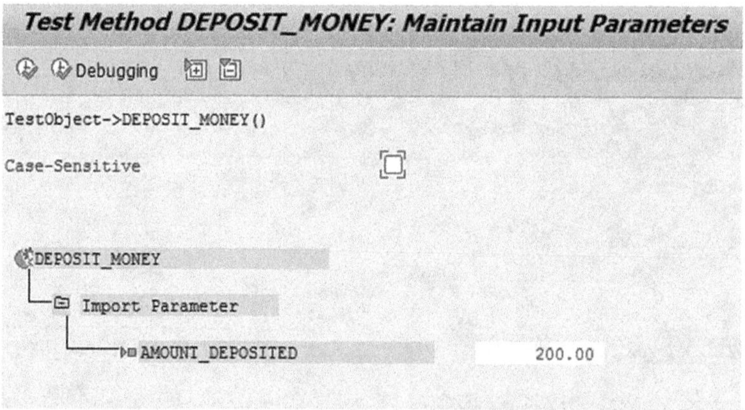

Figure 4-43. *Setting the new balance*

Click the Execute button. The output of this method is shown in Figure 4-44. As you can see in Figure 4-44, the new balance in the account is 100,200.

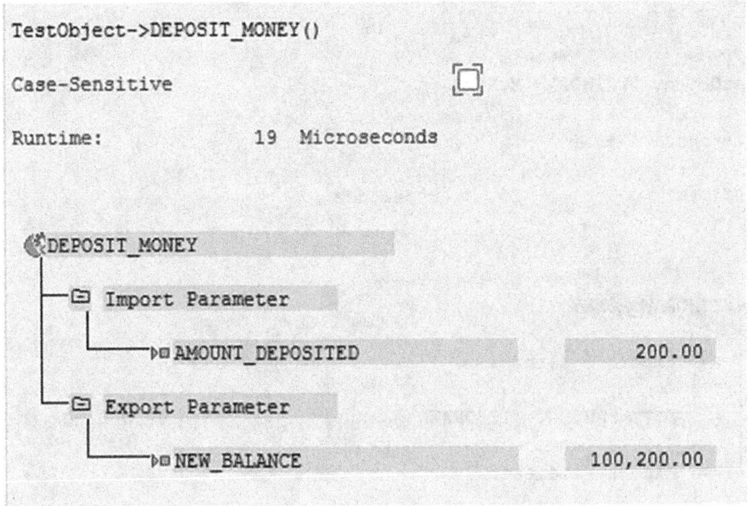

```
TestObject->DEPOSIT_MONEY()

Case-Sensitive                                  [ ]

Runtime:              19  Microseconds


  DEPOSIT_MONEY

    ├─ 🗀 Import Parameter

    │        ▶ AMOUNT_DEPOSITED                    200.00

    └─ 🗀 Export Parameter

             ▶ NEW_BALANCE                     100,200.00
```

Figure 4-44. *Setting the new balance*

Let's withdraw 99,000 from the current balance. We can see this step in Figure 4-45.

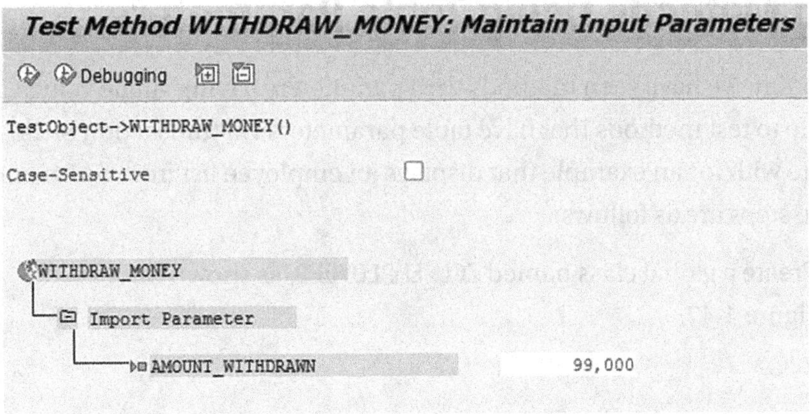

```
Test Method WITHDRAW_MONEY: Maintain Input Parameters

🕀 🕀 Debugging   🗇 🗇

TestObject->WITHDRAW_MONEY()

Case-Sensitive                                  [ ]


  WITHDRAW_MONEY

    └─ 🗀 Import Parameter

             ▶ AMOUNT_WITHDRAWN                   99,000
```

Figure 4-45. *Setting the new balance*

As you can see in Figure 4-46, the balance remaining in the account is 1,200.

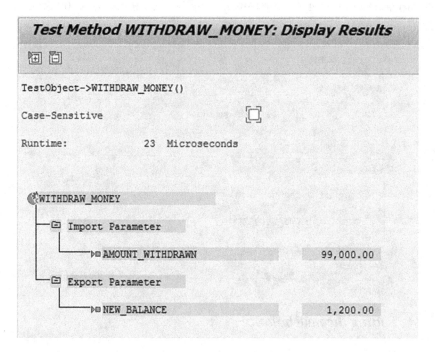

Figure 4-46. Setting the new balance

Testing Methods Using Table Parameters

Up to this point, we have seen methods with parameters having single values. It is also possible to test methods that have table parameters via transaction SE24. We will demonstrate with for an example that displays an employee list from SAP standard table PA0002. The steps are as follows:

1. Create a global class named ZCL_EMPLOYEES, as shown in Figure 4-47.

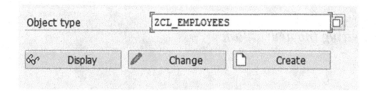

Figure 4-47. Global class ZCL_EMPLOYEES

2. Declare the instance attributes with visibility set to public in the Attributes tab. P_BEGDA and P_ENDDA are used to select the employee start date and end date. WA_PA0002 is a work area, and IT_PA0002 is a table. You can see this step in Figure 4-48.

Class Interface	ZCL_EMPLOYEES			Implemented / Active			
Properties	Interfaces	Friends	Attributes	Methods	Events	Types	Aliases

Attribute	Level	Vis...	Re...	Typing	Associated Type		Description	Initial value
P_BEGDA	Instanc.	Public		Type	BEGDA	⇨	Start Date	
P_ENDDA	Instanc.	Public		Type	ENDDA	⇨	End Date	
WA_PA0002	Instanc.	Public		Type	PA0002	⇨	HR Master Record: Infoty.	
IT_PA0002	Instanc.	Public		Type	ZPA0002_TT	⇨	Table type	
				Type		⇨		

Figure 4-48. *Declaring instance attributes*

3. In the Methods tab, declare the instance methods as GET_EMPLOYEES and DISPLAY_EMP, with public visibility. The GET_EMPLOYEES method will list the entries in an internal table, and DISPLAY_EMP will display the employee details. You can see this step in Figure 4-49.

Class Interface	ZCL_EMPLOYEES			Implemented / Active			
Properties	Interfaces	Friends	Attributes	Methods	Events	Types	Aliases

Method	Level	Vis...	M...	Description
GET_EMPLOYEES	Insta...	Pub...		Employees details
DISPLAY_EMP	Insta...	Pub...		Display employee details

Figure 4-49. *Methods tab*

4. To write the logic for the code, double-click on the GET_EMPLOYEES method. This will take you inside the method. Here, we select all the data from table PA0002 and insert it into table IT_PA0002. You can see this step in Figure 4-50.

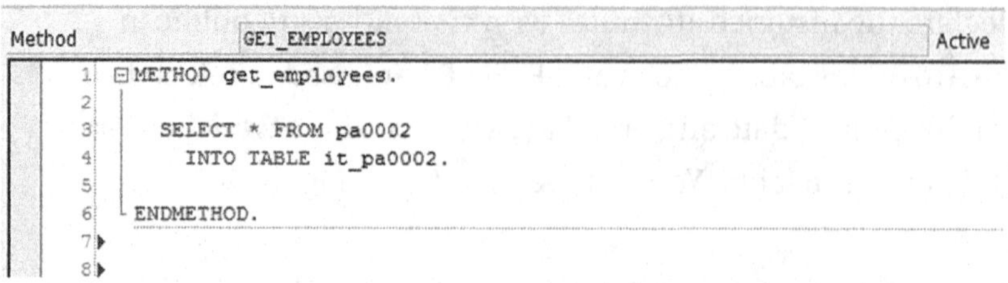

Method	GET_EMPLOYEES	Active

```
1  ⊟ METHOD get_employees.
2
3       SELECT * FROM pa0002
4          INTO TABLE it_pa0002.
5
6  └ ENDMETHOD.
7 ▶
8 ▶
```

Figure 4-50. *Writing the code*

5. In the DISPLAY_EMP method, use the LOOP AT statement to display all the records, as shown in Figure 4-51.

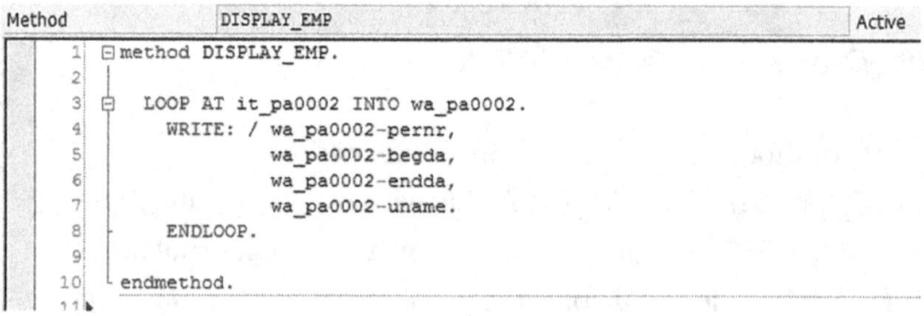

Method	DISPLAY_EMP	Active

```
 1  ⊟ method DISPLAY_EMP.
 2
 3  ⊟    LOOP AT it_pa0002 INTO wa_pa0002.
 4          WRITE: / wa_pa0002-pernr,
 5                   wa_pa0002-begda,
 6                   wa_pa0002-endda,
 7                   wa_pa0002-uname.
 8          ENDLOOP.
 9
10  └ endmethod.
11 ▶
```

Figure 4-51. *Using the LOOP AT statement*

6. Activate all the elements of the global class and test the class.

7. On the screen, you need to input the employee start date and end date, as you can see in Figure 4-52.

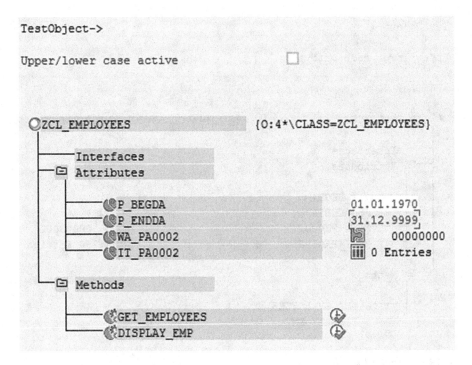

Figure 4-52. *Selection screen*

8. When you click the Execute button from the GET_EMPLOYEES method, it will give you a number of entries in the internal table IT_PA0002, as shown in Figure 4-53.

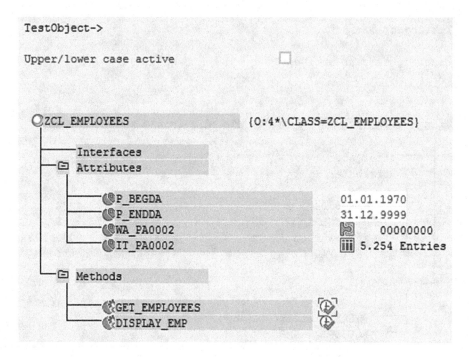

Figure 4-53. *Internal table*

9. When you execute the DISPLAY_EMP method, it will display all the records, as shown in Figure 4-54.

```
TestObject->DISPLAY_EMP()

Upper/lower case active                    [□]


00000000 09.09.1967 31.12.9999
00000010 22.05.1967 31.12.9999 WEISSANJA
00000069 01.01.1956 31.12.9999 HOLDERM
00000070 01.01.1921 31.12.9999 HOLDERM
00000071 09.09.1967 31.12.9999 HOLDERM
00000072 08.09.1965 31.12.9999 HOLDERM
00000073 09.09.1956 31.12.9999 HOLDERM
00001000 05.09.1960 04.10.2006 WECKESSER
00001000 05.10.2006 31.12.9999 HRADMIN
00001001 05.06.1960 31.12.9999 LIMPERT
00001002 05.09.1960 31.12.9999 WAECHTERH
00001003 09.06.1970 31.12.9999 LIMPERT
00001004 01.01.1994 31.12.9999 LIMPERT
00001005 31.05.1970 31.12.9999 LIMPERT
00001006 29.04.1960 31.12.9999 BONIN
00001007 07.12.1955 31.12.9999 LIMPERT
00001008 12.03.1955 31.12.9999 LIMPERT
00001009 16.11.1938 31.12.9999 LIMPERT
00001010 12.03.1944 31.12.9999 LIMPERT
00001011 01.01.1970 31.12.9999 MIERZWA
00001012 01.01.1970 31.12.9999 WOLTERA
00001013 01.01.1970 31.12.9999 WOLTERA
00001014 01.01.1960 31.12.9999 CURA
00001015 13.11.1952 31.12.9999 WEISSANJA
00001016 26.10.1954 31.12.9999 LIMPERT
00001017 16.10.1960 31.12.9999 LIMPERT
00001018 13.06.1940 31.12.9999 MIERZWA
00001019 19.09.1950 31.12.9999 LIMPERT
```

Figure 4-54. *Record display*

Equivalent code to call this method from a program is shown here:

```
REPORT  ZCL_EMPLOYEES.

PARAMETERS: p_begda TYPE begda,
            p_endda TYPE endda.

DATA: obj_emp TYPE REF TO ZCL_EMPLOYEES.

CREATE OBJECT obj_emp.

CALL METHOD obj_emp->get_employees.

CALL METHOD obj_emp->display_emp.
```

The output of this code is shown in Figure 4-55.

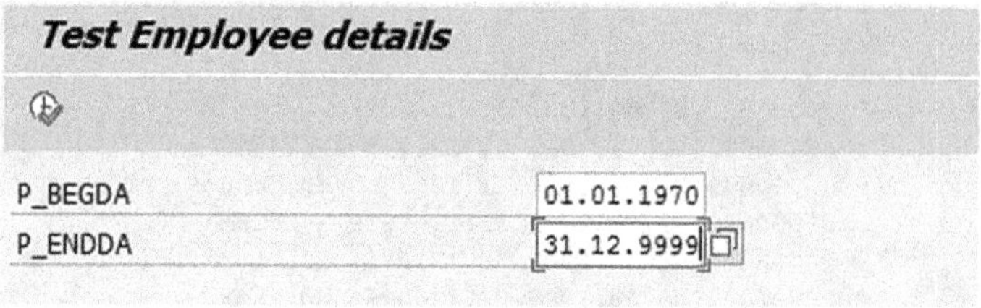

Figure 4-55. *Output*

Here, we want to fetch all the employee records from table PA0002. We have declared the parameters P_BEGDA and P_ENDDA. Data OBJ_EMP refers to class ZCL_EMPLOYEES. Now, we create an object called OBJ_EMP, which has instance attributes, and we call the GET_EMPLOYEES and DISPLAY_EMP methods to get the required output, which is shown in Figure 4-56.

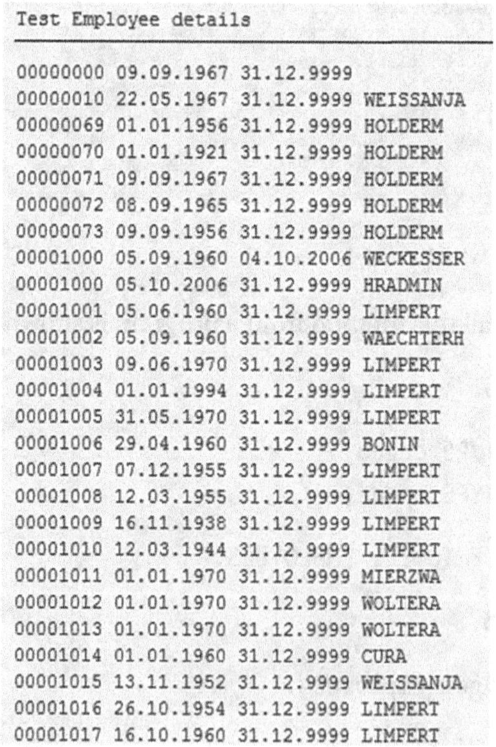

Figure 4-56. *Output*

Summary

In this chapter, we saw how we can use the Object Navigator to create global classes. We then explored the various tabs of the Class Builder, particularly the Methods tab. We discussed the Class Browser, and other useful options of the transaction SE24. Finally, we saw a number of examples using the transaction SE24 that could be tested using the transaction itself rather than having to create a program for them.

CHAPTER 5

Exceptions, Shared, and Persistent Objects

In this chapter, we cover some special topics and techniques that will help you create better programs and respond to users' requirements.

We start with a brief introduction of exception and exception handling as applied to ABAP Objects. We then see how we can create persistent objects in object-oriented ABAP. Finally, we learn about the theory and working code for shared objects.

These are some of the topics that this chapter will address:

- Exception handling and exception classes

- Singleton classes

- Persistent objects

- Shared memory objects

Exception Handling and Exception Classes

An important concept related to ABAP Objects is the exception class. You can create your own exception class. In this section, we learn how to create our own exception class and use it in an ABAP program.

During program execution, certain erroneous situations may arise and interrupt normal processing. In such situations, exceptions are raised. These may either be generated by the ABAP runtime environment or triggered explicitly through coding. If a suitable handler is not found for the exception, a runtime error occurs. Typical examples include arithmetic overflow, memory consumption problems, or a syntax error in a SQL statement.

© Rehan Zaidi 2019
R. Zaidi, *SAP ABAP Objects*, https://doi.org/10.1007/978-1-4842-4964-2_5

Developers must use their understanding to judge situations that may allow the program to halt specific to their program. For example, in our player class scenario, if we try to create a football player who weighs 0 (zero) kg, the object must not be created and an exception must be raised.

Within ABAP Objects, it is best practice to use class-based exceptions. Exception classes are special classes that allow you to handle exceptional (erroneous) situations. They may be defined globally in the Class Builder or defined locally within a program. In addition to the standard exception classes, you can also create your own exception classes and use them in your programs. It is possible to define text related to the exceptions, which may be short or more descriptive and long. These descriptors provide more details about the error that has occurred. It is possible to create text based on an OTR (Object Text Repository), or you may base your exception text on messages residing in the message classes.

An exception class has to be a subclass of one of the standard classes CX_STATIC_ CHECK, CX_DYNAMIC_CHECK, or CX_NO_CHECK, which are all derived from the CX_ROOT class.

For exceptions derived from CX_STATIC_CHECK, the exception must either be handled via TRY and CATCH statements or passed along via declaration in a method's interface using the RAISING clause. The handling of such exceptions is checked by the compiler. If an exception is not handled locally within a method and not declared in the method's interface, a syntax warning is generated.

The CX_DYNAMIC_CHECK category refers to exceptions that are not checked by the complier during syntax check. They "may" be declared in the methods interface via the RAISING clause. If these exceptions are not handled within a method or propagated to the caller via RAISING, a runtime error occurs during program execution.

For the CX_STATIC_CHECK and CX_DYNAMIC_CHECK categories, if the exceptions are declared in a method's interface using a RAISING clause, the exception passes the method interface at runtime, if the exception is not handled within the method itself.

The exception classes that are subclasses of CX_NO_CHECK can be handled within a method, or otherwise are automatically forwarded. They must not be declared in the interface of methods, and they do not result in any syntax check warnings. If such exceptions are not handled within a call hierarchy, they are assigned to the top-most call level. If they are not handled there, a runtime error occurs. A typical example of this category is a situation involving resource bottlenecks.

RAISE and TRY .. ENDTRY Statements

The RAISE EXCEPTION statement is used to raise an exception. This statement may be used in the method of a class. The syntax of the RAISE statement is as follows:

```
raise exception type zcx_player_exception.
```

After RAISE EXCEPTION, we specify the exception class using the TYPE keyword (in the example, it is ZCX_PLAYER_EXCEPTION). If the exception is not caught in the program, a runtime error occurs.

A RAISE statement may also have exporting parameters. For example, you may pass HEIGHT as a parameter to the RAISE statement.

```
raise exception type zcx_player_exception
exporting height = height .
```

The TRY...ENDTRY block is used for exception handling in our program, as follows:

```
TRY.
...
  CATCH zcx_player_exception INTO
  EXCEPTION_OBJECT.
...
  ENDTRY.
```

Within the block, we first write the set of statements (for example, creation of a player object) that may trigger an exception. The exception class is specified using the CATCH statement. The CATCH block is an exception handler. When the exception specified within the TRY block occurs, the code after CATCH statement is executed. (If all goes well, and no exception is raised, this code is not executed.) When the exception is raised, an exception object gets generated at runtime (based on the exception class specified). The reference to the exception object is stored in the reference variable MY_EXCEPTION_OBJ.

Suppose we have an exception raised within a program and the exception is not caught in the program at runtime. In this case, a short dump will occur stating that the exception was raised but not caught in the program.

Resumable Exceptions

The code syntax shown in this section is for non-resumable exceptions. It is also possible to raise resumable exceptions. In this case, the coding may slightly vary.

Creating an Exception Class

In this section, we learn how to define a global exception class.

We will create an exception class called ZCX_MY_EXCEPTION that will be used for our PLAYER class that we defined earlier.

To define an exception class, call transaction SE24. The screen shown in Figure 5-1 appears.

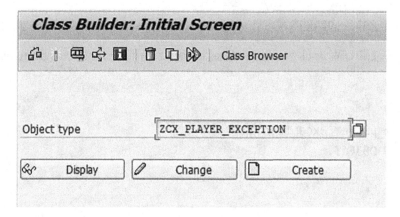

Figure 5-1. *Entering the exception class name*

Enter the name of the class in the field provided. The name of the exception class should begin with ZCX or YCX. If this naming connection is not followed, an error is displayed, as shown in Figure 5-2.

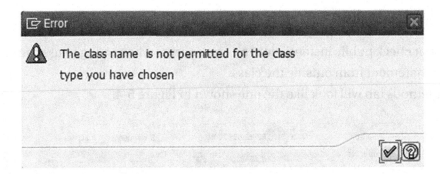

Figure 5-2. *Error due to improper naming*

Once the correct name is entered and you click the Create button, the dialog box shown in Figure 5-3 will be displayed.

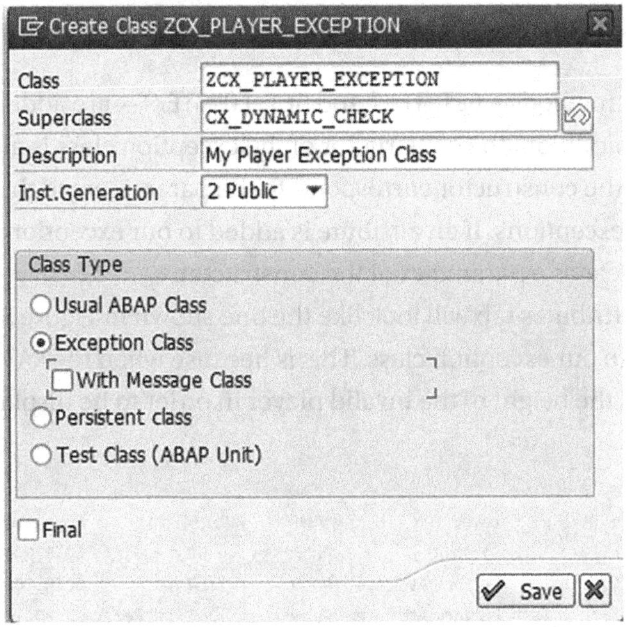

Figure 5-3. *Create an exception class*

Make sure that the CX_DYNAMIC_CHECK class is entered in the Superclass field. Enter a suitable description in the Description field. For the Inst. Generation, choose Public from the listbox. In addition, make sure that the Exception class radio button is switched on and that the With Message Class checkbox is not selected. Once you are done with the settings, click the Save button to proceed.

Public Instantiation

If you do not check public instantiation, an error occurs when trying to use the exception in a RAISE statement from outside the class.

The Methods tab will look like the one shown in Figure 5-4.

Method	Level	Visibility	Description
IF_MESSAGE~GET_TEXT	Instance..	Public	Returns message short text
IF_MESSAGE~GET_LONGTEXT	Instance..	Public	Returns message long text
GET_SOURCE_POSITION	Instance..	Public	Returns Position in Source Text
CONSTRUCTOR	Instance..	Public	CONSTRUCTOR

Figure 5-4. *Methods of an exception class*

Two important methods—GET_TEXT and GET_LONGTEXT—are added to our exception class. In addition, the constructor of the exception class is also generated. The parameters of the constructor correspond to the parameters of the RAISE statement used to trigger the exceptions. If an attribute is added to our exception class, the attribute parameter will appear as a parameter of the constructor.

Likewise, the Attributes tab will look like the one shown in Figure 5-5. We will add a HEIGHT attribute to our exception class. This is because when the RAISE statement is called, we will pass the height of the invalid player in order to be displayed with the long exception text.

Attribute	Level	Visibility	R...	Typing	Associated Type
CX_ROOT	Constant	Public	☐	Type	SOTR_CONC
TEXTID	Instance Attribute	Public	☑	Type	SOTR_CONC
PREVIOUS	Instance Attribute	Public	☑	Type Ref ..	CX_ROOT
KERNEL_ERRID	Instance Attribute	Public	☑	Type	S380ERRID
IS_RESUMABLE	Instance Attribute	Public	☑	Type	ABAP_BOOL
HEIGHT	Instance Attribute	Public	☐	Type	I

Figure 5-5. *Adding HEIGHT to the exception class attributes*

This adds the HEIGHT attribute as a parameter to the constructor of the exception class, as shown in Figure 5-6.

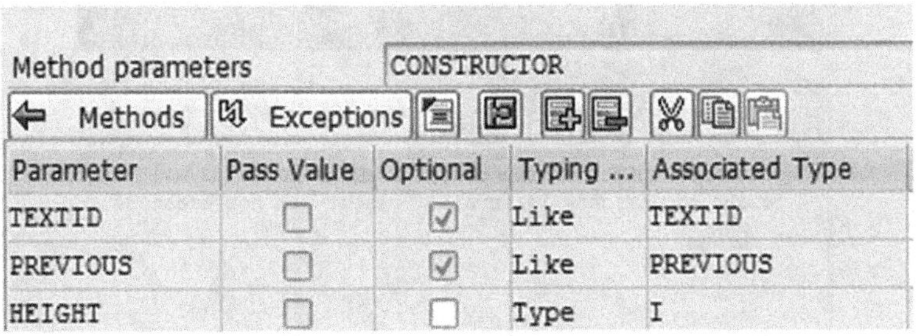

Method parameters		CONSTRUCTOR		
← Methods Exceptions				
Parameter	Pass Value	Optional	Typing ...	Associated Type
TEXTID	☐	☑	Like	TEXTID
PREVIOUS	☐	☑	Like	PREVIOUS
HEIGHT	☐	☐	Type	I

Figure 5-6. HEIGHT parameter

If no text is defined for your exception class, when an exception occurs in a program and is caught via a CATCH statement in a TRY.. ENDTRY block, you will see the text An Exception occurred of the CX_ROOT class.

Next, we will define the short and the long text for the exception ID. This text is stored in the OTR of the system (as we unchecked the With Message Class checkbox while creating the class). To define the text, click on the Texts tab. Then, for the ZCX_ PLAYER_EXCEPTION class, enter the text Player Height Invalid, as shown in Figure 5-7.

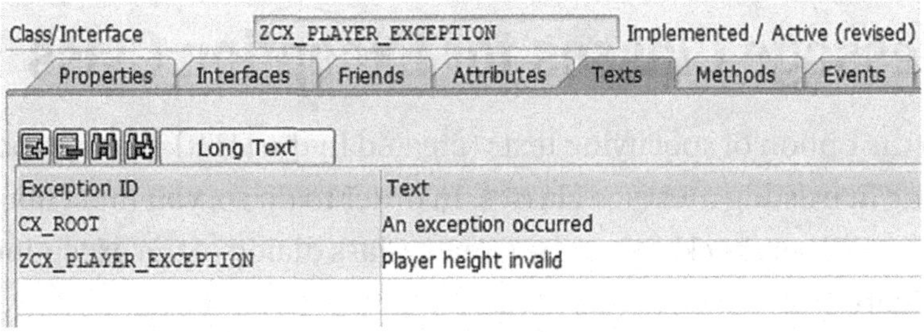

Class/Interface	ZCX_PLAYER_EXCEPTION	Implemented / Active (revised)

Properties	Interfaces	Friends	Attributes	Texts	Methods	Events

 Long Text

Exception ID	Text
CX_ROOT	An exception occurred
ZCX_PLAYER_EXCEPTION	Player height invalid

Figure 5-7. Defining exception text

Next, we will define the long text for the exception. Place the cursor on the name of the class (in our case, ZCX_MY_EXCEPTION) and then click the long text button. The long text editor will appear, as shown in Figure 5-8.

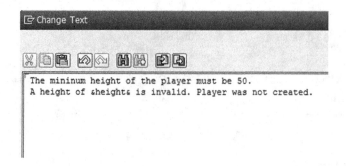

Figure 5-8. *Entering long text for an exception*

Enter the text as shown in Figure 5-8. Since we will also be displaying the HEIGHT attribute in the long text, we have included it in ampersands. This will serve as the placeholder of the height passed as a parameter of the RAISE statement. At runtime if an exception raised, the height along with the other text shown is generated as long text (we will see the output in the latter part of this chapter).

Once you have completed all the steps, save and activate your exception class.

Using Message Classes for Exception Class Text

In addition to the option of specifying texts (created in the OTR), it is also possible to use the text residing in existing message classes. In order to do so, you must make sure that the With Message Class checkbox on the Create Class dialog of the exception class is on, as shown in Figure 5-9.

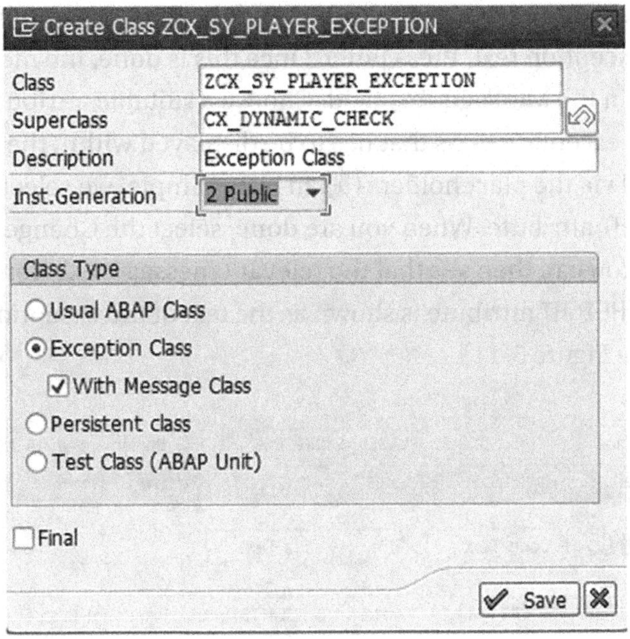

Figure 5-9. *Choosing the With Message Class option*

Once this is done, the following steps are required:

1. Click the Texts tab while you are in Change mode for the exception
    class using transaction SE24. Then, click the [✏ Message Text]
    button. The dialog appears, as shown in Figure 5-10.

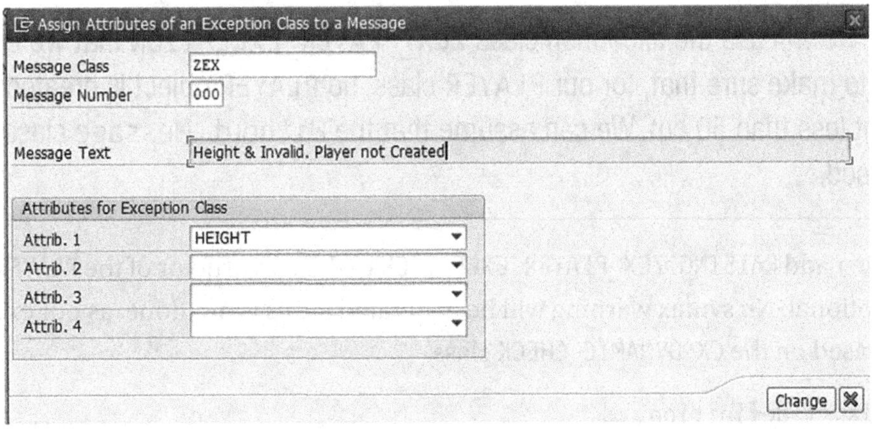

Figure 5-10. *Assign attributes to a message*

2. Enter the name of the message class and the message number
for the exception text. Press Enter. Once this is done, the message
appears in the Message Text field. Choose a suitable attribute
from the exception class that has to be displayed within the text
specified via the placeholders (&). In our example, we selected
the HEIGHT attribute. When you are done, select the Change
button. You can then see that the relevant message text along
with the HEIGHT attribute is shown as the text of the exception
class (see Figure 5-11).

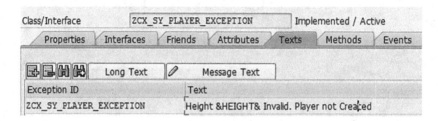

Figure 5-11. *The Texts tab*

A Working Example

In this section, we learn how the exception class that we defined can be used for
exception handling in ABAP programs.

Note   We will use the exception class ZCX_PLAYER_EXCEPTION that we created
earlier to make sure that, for our PLAYER class, no PLAYER object is created with
a height less than 50 cm. We can assume that the Without Message class has
been used.

We first add RAISING ZCX_PLAYER_EXCEPTION to the constructor of the PLAYER class.
This is optional. No syntax warning will be generated if this is not done, as our exception
class is based on the CX_DYNAMIC_CHECK class.

```
class player definition.
  public section.
    methods constructor  importing
             name    type string
```

```
          weight type p
          height type i
    raising zcx_player_exception.
  methods display_player_details.

  protected section.
    data : name type string.
    data : height type i.
    data : weight type p decimals 2.

endclass.
```

We will make a small change to the constructor of the PLAYER class. We will use the raise exception ZCX_PLAYER_EXCEPTION via a RAISE statement if the height of the player to be created is less than 50. The height is also supplied as a parameter in the RAISE statement. The code in this case is as follows:

```
class player implementation.
  method constructor .
    if height lt 50.
      raise exception
      type zcx_player_exception
      exporting height = height .
    endif.

    me->name = name.
    me->height = height.
    me->weight = weight.

  endmethod.
......
endclass.
```

Next, we will use the CREATE OBJECT statement to attempt to create a player 1 cm tall. The block of code is enclosed within a TRY.. ENDTRY block.

The CREATE OBJECT statement results in the constructor being called that raises the ZCX_PLAYER_EXCEPTION exception. The height supplied as the parameter (in our case, 1 cm) is also an exporting parameter of the RAISE statement (see the constructor code in the PLAYER class implementation).

```
try .
    create object my_player
      exporting
        name   = 'Wrong Player'
        weight = '80'
        height = '1'.  "" Height is wrong

catch zcx_player_exception into exception_obj.
  short_text =  exception_obj->get_text( ).
  long_text = exception_obj->get_longtext( ).
  write / : short_text , long_text.
endtry.
```

The PLAYER object is not created. Rather, the exception object is generated at runtime, whose reference is stored in the EXCEPTION_OBJ variable. The GET_TEXT and GET_LONGTEXT methods are called to return the short and long text of the exception, respectively. SHORT_TEXT and LONG_TEXT are then outputted to the user screen. (If the exception is not caught in the program, a short dump occurs.)

The output of the program is shown in Figure 5-12.

```
Player height invalid
The mininum height of the player must be 50. A height of 1 is invalid. Player was not created.
```

Figure 5-12. *Program output*

The complete code listing is shown as follows:

```
class player definition.
  public section.
    methods constructor  importing
                 name    type string
                 weight type p
                 height type i
      raising zcx_player_exception.
    methods display_player_details.

  protected section.
    data : name type string.
```

```
    data : height type i.
    data : weight type p decimals 2.

endclass.

class player implementation.
  method constructor .
    if height lt 50.
      raise exception
      type zcx_player_exception
      exporting height = height .
    endif.

    me->name = name.
    me->height = height.
    me->weight = weight.
  endmethod.

  method display_player_details.
    write :/  'Player Name:    ',
           15 me->name ,
            / 'Height      :    ',
           15 me->height left-justified ,
            / 'Weight      :',
           15 me->weight left-justified.
  endmethod.
endclass.

start-of-selection.

  data :  my_player type ref to player,
          exception_obj type ref to
          zcx_player_exception,
          short_text type string,
          long_text type string.
  try .
      create object my_player
        exporting
```

```
          name    = 'Wrong Player'
          weight = '80'
          height = '1'.  "" Height is wrong

  catch zcx_player_exception into exception_obj.
    short_text =  exception_obj->get_text( ).
    long_text = exception_obj->get_longtext( ).
    write / : short_text , long_text.
  endtry.
```

Singleton Classes

A *singleton* is simply defined as a class that has a maximum of one instance created by the user of an internal session. Any attempt to create a second instance must not be allowed and results in an error saying, for example, that "an object already exists". It is possible to create a singleton class locally or globally in the Class Builder.

In this section, we learn how to create a singleton design pattern class using a static method and static attributes. For simplicity's sake, we will create a class locally in a program.

We will start with the definition of a class (we will name it BEST_PLAYER based on the PLAYER class we used earlier). In the definition, the addition CREATE PRIVATE is added. This will ensure that instances of the given class may be created only inside the class. Any attempt to instantiate from outside the class or instantiate from subclasses is disallowed when the CREATE PRIVATE addition is used.

In addition to the CREATE PRIVATE addition, we will use a static attribute OBJECT, which is a reference variable based on the BEST_PLAYER class. (The single instance of the class is referred to by the OBJECT variable.) We also have a static method called CREATE_OBJECT that takes the importing parameters NAME, WEIGHT, and HEIGHT and returns R_OBJECT a reference to the BEST_PLAYER class. The definition of the class is as follows:

```
class best_player definition create private.
  public section.
    class-methods create_object
      importing name            type string
                weight          type p
                height          type i
```

```
returning value(r_object) type ref to
                            best_player.

methods constructor   importing
                          name    type string
                          weight type p
                          height type i.

methods display_player_details.

  private section.

  class-data object type ref to best_player.

  data : name type string.
  data : height type i.
  data : weight type p decimals 2.
endclass.
```

Next, we write the implementation of the class. In the implementation, we write the code of the CREATE_OBJECT method, in which we first check whether the static attribute OBJECT is already bound (i.e., instantiated) or not. If it is already bound, no new object is created and a message saying "Best Player Already exists, no new object created" is displayed.

If the OBJECT attribute is not bound yet, we create the object via the CREATE OBJECT statement (exporting the necessary parameters NAME, HEIGHT, and WEIGHT). The reference of the created object is assigned to the returning parameter R_OBJECT.

```
class best_player implementation.
  method create_object.
    if object is not bound.
      create object object
        exporting
          name   = name
          height = height
          weight = weight.

    else.
      write :/ 'Best Player Already exists',
               'no new object created'.
```

```
    endif.
    r_object = object.
  endmethod.
......

......
```

To create an object of the BEST_PLAYER class and display its details, we call the static method CREATE_OBJECT. Since this method returns the reference to the BEST_PLAYER class, the DISPLAY_PLAYER_DETAILS method may be chained in the same statement to write the details of the player on the screen. The code is as follows:

```
best_player=>create_object(
name = 'Player'  weight = '80'
height = '100' )->display_player_details( ).
```

Since it is the first time that the CREATE_OBJECT method is called, the BEST_PLAYER object is successfully created and the relevant details are displayed on the user screen as shown.

If the block of code is executed again, no new object is created. A message appears, and the details of the same player object are displayed.

The complete code for the singleton class BEST_PLAYER is as follows.

```
class best_player definition create private.
  public section.
   class-methods create_object
     importing name               type string
               weight             type p
               height             type i
     returning value(r_object) type ref to
                               best_player.

   methods constructor   importing
                         name    type string
                         weight type p
                         height type i.

   methods display_player_details.

  private section.
```

```
    class-data object type ref to best_player.

    data : name type string.
    data : height type i.
    data : weight type p decimals 2.
endclass.

class best_player implementation.
  method create_object.
    if object is not bound.
      create object object
        exporting
          name   = name
          height = height
          weight = weight.

    else.
      write :/ 'Best Player Already exists',
               'no new object created'.
    endif.
    r_object = object.
  endmethod.

  method constructor .
    me->name = name.
    me->height = height.
    me->weight = weight.

  endmethod.

  method display_player_details.
    write :/  'Player Name:   ',
          15 me->name ,
          /  'Height     :     ',
          15 me->height left-justified ,
          /  'Weight     :',
          15 me->weight left-justified.
  endmethod.
```

```
endclass.

start-of-selection.

  best_player=>create_object(
  name = 'Player'  weight = '80'
  height = '100' )->display_player_details( ).

  skip.

  best_player=>create_object(
  name = 'Player'  weight = '80'
  height = '100' )->display_player_details( ).
```

Persistent Objects

By default, objects in ABAP are transient in nature, i.e., they are alive in memory until the execution time of the program. However, it is also possible to store the attributes of an object in the database. The persistence service for ABAP Objects lets you achieve this. These objects are called *persistent objects* and the class on which they are based is known as a *persistence class*. In this section, we learn how to define a persistent class.

Persistent classes are defined globally in the Class Builder transaction SE24. Before creating a persistent class, we need to define a database table that is used to store the attributes of the object in question. The fields of the table must correspond to the attributes of the class whose objects are to be stored in the database.

Note   There are three options for storing persistent objects, including using business keys, GUIDs, and using a combination of GUID and business keys. For simplicity's sake, we will build an object using the business key option.

Let's use the PLAYER class example that we defined earlier and define a similar table in the database. In addition to the NAME, WEIGHT, and HEIGHT attributes, we will add PLAYERID as the key field, as shown in Figure 5-13.

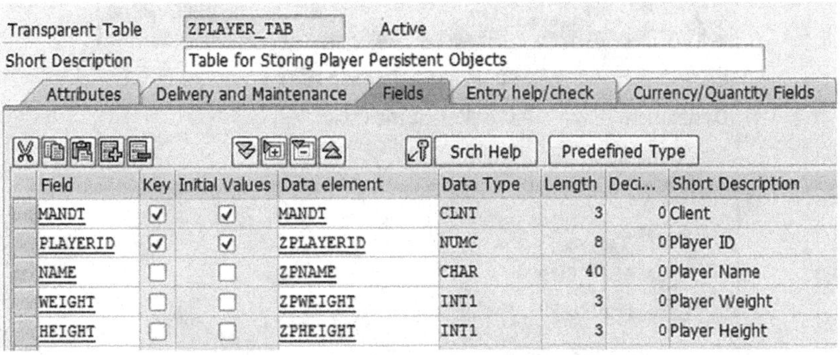

Field	Key	Initial Values	Data element	Data Type	Length	Deci...	Short Description
MANDT	✓	✓	MANDT	CLNT	3	0	Client
PLAYERID	✓	✓	ZPLAYERID	NUMC	8	0	Player ID
NAME	☐	☐	ZPNAME	CHAR	40	0	Player Name
WEIGHT	☐	☐	ZPWEIGHT	INT1	3	0	Player Weight
HEIGHT	☐	☐	ZPHEIGHT	INT1	3	0	Player Height

Transparent Table ZPLAYER_TAB Active
Short Description Table for Storing Player Persistent Objects

Attributes   Delivery and Maintenance   Fields   Entry help/check   Currency/Quantity Fields

Srch Help   Predefined Type

Figure 5-13. *Database table for storing persistent objects*

Prior to defining this table, we created data elements and domains pertaining to the player ID, weight, height, and name.

We will now create a persistence class. Call the transaction SE24. The screen shown in Figure 5-14 appears.

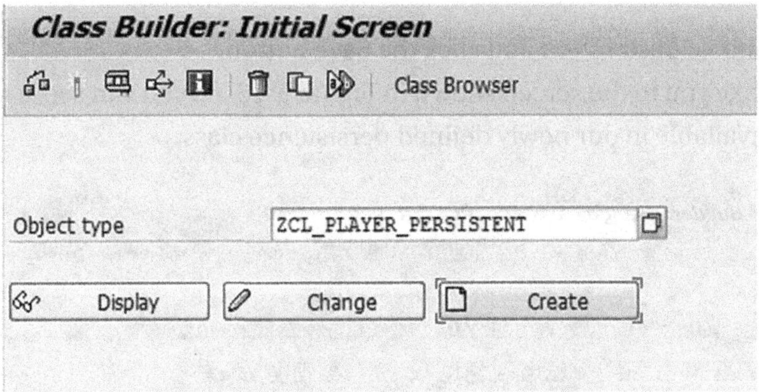

Class Builder: Initial Screen

Class Browser

Object type   ZCL_PLAYER_PERSISTENT

Display   Change   Create

Figure 5-14. *Class Builder*

Enter a suitable name in the field provided (in our case, ZCL_PLAYER_PERSISTENT) and click the Create button. The Create Class dialog box appears. Choose the Persistent Class option, as shown in Figure 5-15.

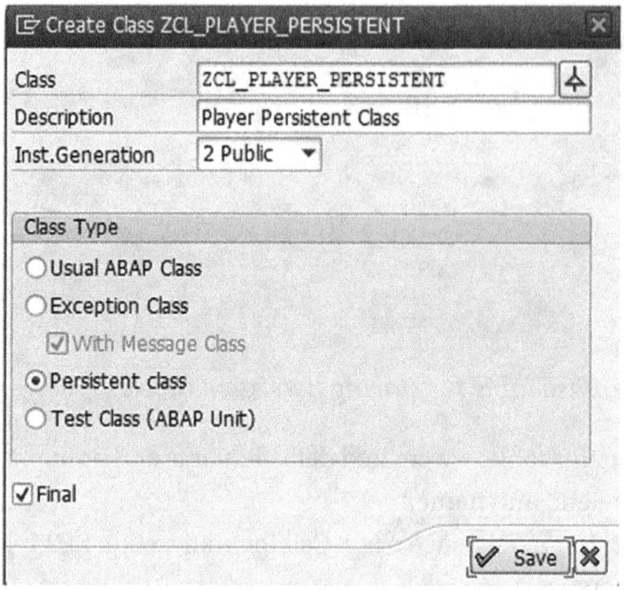

Figure 5-15. *Persistent Class option*

Enter a suitable description and click the Save button.

This will take you to the screen shown in Figure 5-16. As you can see, a number of methods are available in our newly defined persistence class.

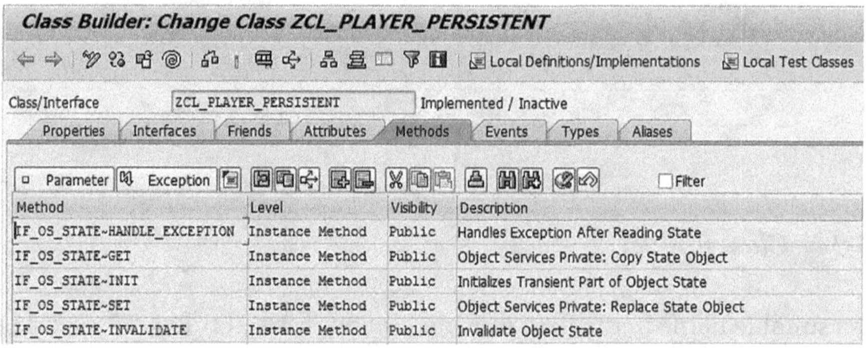

Figure 5-16. *Methods of the persistent class*

As a developer, we can only modify the HANDLE_EXCEPTION and INIT methods. In contrast to other classes, a ⬢ Persistence button appears on the application toolbar. Click the Persistence button to display a popup dialog box, as shown in Figure 5-17.

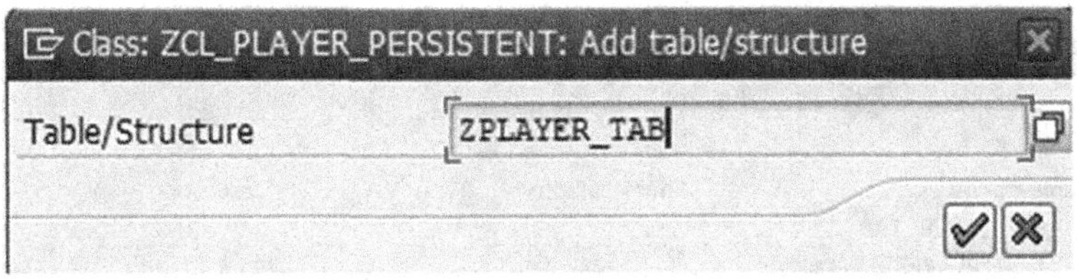

Figure 5-17. *Specifying a table*

Enter the name of the database table (in our case, ZPLAYER_TAB) that you defined earlier. You will then be taken to the mapping editor. The top part of the mapping editor is initially empty (i.e., it contains no fields), as shown in Figure 5-18.

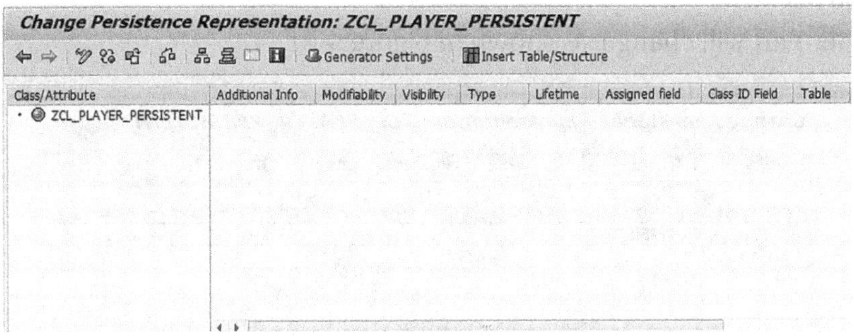

Figure 5-18. *Mapping editor (persistence representation)*

In the lower part of the mapping editor, the table's (that we have added) fields are listed, as shown in Figure 5-19.

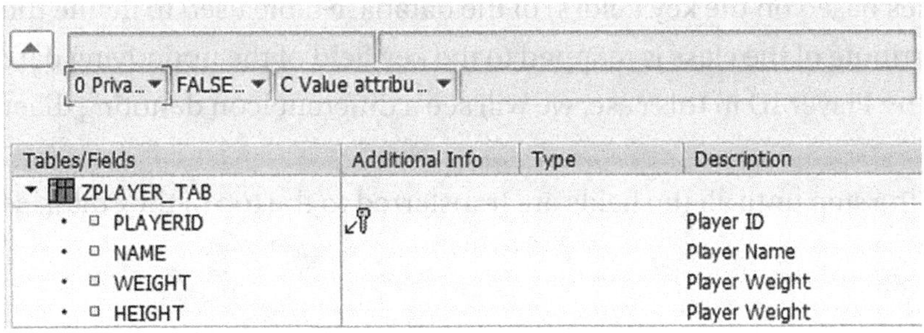

Figure 5-19. *Fields of the table*

We need to specify the fields from the database table that will be included as attributes of the persistence class. For each field of the table, double-click the table field line in the lower part of the screen. The name of the field and other details then appear in the editable fields (shown in Figure 5-20).

157

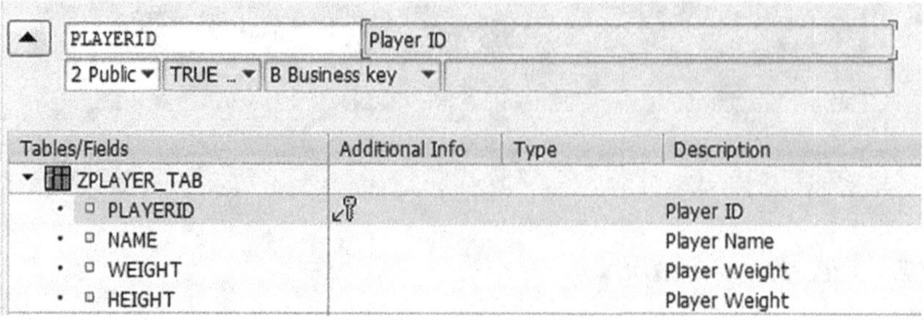

PLAYERID	Player ID		
2 Public ▼	TRUE ... ▼	B Business key ▼	

Tables/Fields	Additional Info	Type	Description
▼ 🎬 ZPLAYER_TAB			
• ☐ PLAYERID	🔑		Player ID
• ☐ NAME			Player Name
• ☐ WEIGHT			Player Weight
• ☐ HEIGHT			Player Weight

Figure 5-20. *Selecting PLAYERID*

Then, click the Set Attribute Values ▲ button to include the field as an attribute of the persistence class.

The upper part will change, as shown in Figure 5-21.

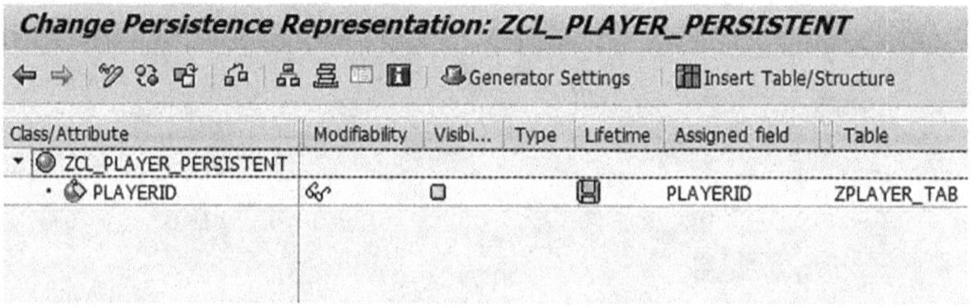

Change Persistence Representation: ZCL_PLAYER_PERSISTENT

⇐ ⇒ | 🖉 ⅋ 🗗 | ⅏ | ⅏ 📇 ⬜ 🗉 | 🖴 Generator Settings | 🎬 Insert Table/Structure

Class/Attribute	Modifiability	Visibi...	Type	Lifetime	Assigned field	Table
▼ ⬤ ZCL_PLAYER_PERSISTENT						
• ◈ PLAYERID	🔑	☐		🖫	PLAYERID	ZPLAYER_TAB

Figure 5-21. *PLAYERID included as a key attribute*

As you can see, we added PLAYERID as an attribute of the persistence class. In this example, we created mapping based on business keys, where the Class Builder generates key attributes based on the key field(s) of the database table used to define the mapping. (The key attribute of the class is mapped to the key field of the underlying database table.) For the Player ID in this case, we will see a different icon denoting that this is the key field.

Repeat the step until all the fields are transferred to the top of the editor, as shown in Figure 5-22.

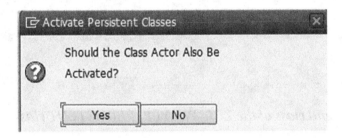

Figure 5-22. *Class/attributes of the persistent class*

The lower area will be blank since all the fields have been transferred to the top portion.

Once this is done, save and activate the class. Upon activation, the system asks whether the class actor should be activated. Click the Yes button to continue (see Figure 5-23).

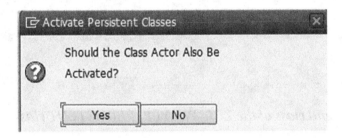

Figure 5-23. *Class actor activation popup*

Three classes are generated once the persistence class is activated. The first is the Zcl_Player_Persistent persistent class that we created. In addition, the system also creates an actor class called ZCA_PLAYER_PERSISTENT. One additional base class called ZCB_PLAYER_PERSISTENT, which is the superclass of the actor, is also created.

The purpose of mapping is to define the relationship between the database table fields and the class attributes. Once mapping is complete, the mapped fields are included in the attributes of the persistence class (see Figure 5-24).

Attribute	Level	Visibility	Read-Only	Persistent	Typing	Associated Type
PLAYERID	Instance Attribute	Public	☑	☑	Type	ZPLAYERID
NAME	Instance Attribute	Public	☐	☑	Type	ZPNAME
WEIGHT	Instance Attribute	Public	☐	☑	Type	ZPWEIGHT
HEIGHT	Instance Attribute	Public	☐	☑	Type	ZPHEIGHT

Class/Interface `ZCL_PLAYER_PERSISTENT`   Implemented / Active
Properties Interfaces Friends Attributes Methods Events Types

Figure 5-24. *Attributes of the persistent class*

The base agent class called ZCB_PLAYER_PERSISTENT is created as a friend of our persistent class ZCL_PLAYER_PERSISTENT, as shown in Figure 5-25.

Class Builder: Change Class ZCL_PLAYER_PERSISTENT

Local Definitions/Implementations

Class/Interface `ZCL_PLAYER_PERSISTENT`   Implemented / Inactive
Properties Interfaces Friends Attributes Methods Events Types Aliases

Friend	Modeled only	Description
ZCB_PLAYER_PERSISTENT	☐	Base agent Player Persistent Class

Figure 5-25. *Friend class of the ZCL_PLAYER_PERSISTENT class*

Our ZCL_PLAYER_PERSISTENT class has a number of methods. There are SET and GET methods for each non-key attribute of the class. For the player ID, no SET method is created since the player ID is the key field. This is because the value of the key field may not be changed once an object is created.

The agent class, in our case ZCA_PLAYER_PERSISTENT, has many important methods for the creation, deletion, and retrieval of object data stored in the database (we will see later how these methods are used).

Storing and Reading Persistent Objects

In this section, we learn how to use simple code in order to store object attributes (of our persistent PLAYER class) in the database, as well as how to read them in your programs. As mentioned, the agent class has important methods, such as CREATE_PERSISTENT and GET_PERSISTENT, that create and read database table records based on the persistent class attributes.

To store persistent objects, we first declare references to our persistence class
ZCL_PLAYER_PERSISTENT and our actor class ZCA_PLAYER_PERSISTENT.

```
data : player type ref to zcl_player_persistent.
data :  agent type ref to zca_player_persistent.
```

We then access the AGENT object using the static attribute AGENT of the actor class
ZCA_PLAYER_PERSISTENT.

```
agent =  zca_player_persistent=>agent.
```

Using the AGENT object, we call the CREATE_PERSISTENT method and pass as
parameters the attribute values for the player ID. The object player is created and the
reference is returned in the parameter PLAYER.

The SET_NAME, SET_HEIGHT, and SET_WEIGHT methods are then called for the PLAYER
object in order to assign appropriate values to NAME, HEIGHT, and WEIGHT, respectively.
Finally, the COMMIT WORK statement is used to store the player attributes in the database
table (in our case, ZPLAYER_TAB). Any exception caught is in the TRY..ENDTRY block using
the CATCH statement.

Once the code is executed, we can see that the corresponding record has been
created in the database (see Figure 5-26).

Data Browser: Table ZPLAYER_TAB Select Entries   1

Table: ZPLAYER_TAB
Displayed Fields: 5 of   5   Fixed Columns:

MANDT	PLAYERID	NAME	WEIGHT	HEIGHT
850	00000002	Oliver Kahn	88	188

Figure 5-26. *Attributes stored in the ZPLAYER_TAB table*

The complete code listing is shown as follows:

```
data : player type ref to zcl_player_persistent.
data :  agent type ref to zca_player_persistent.

agent =  zca_player_persistent=>agent.
try.
    call method agent->create_persistent
```

```
      exporting
        i_playerid = '00000002'
      receiving
        result     = player.

    call method player->set_name
      exporting
        i_name = 'Oliver Kahn'.
    call method player->set_weight
      exporting
        i_weight = '88'.
    call method player->set_height
      exporting
        i_height = '188'.
    commit work.
  catch cx_os_object_existing .
endtry.
```

Once the record is created, we can use a similar code fragment to read the stored data into our programs. Appropriate variables are defined for the NAME and WEIGHT attributes.

The GET_PERSISTENT method of the agent class is used in this case and is supplied with a player ID (in our case, 00000002). We use the GET_NAME and GET_WEIGHT methods for the PLAYER object in order to read the NAME and WEIGHT of the player. The values are then displayed on the user screen.

The code for this is as follows.

```
data : player type ref to zcl_player_persistent.
data : agent type ref to zca_player_persistent.
data : name type zplayer_tab-name.
data : weight type zplayer_tab-weight.

agent =  zca_player_persistent=>agent.
try.
    call method agent->get_persistent
      exporting
        i_playerid = '00000002'
```

```
      receiving
        result      = player.

    name = player->get_name( ).
    weight = player->get_weight( ) .

    write : name, weight.
  catch cx_os_Object_not_found.

endtry.
```

Shared Memory Objects

Using shared memory objects, you can store instances of your classes in the shared memory of the application server. (The attributes of these objects are stored in the application server.) The benefit of this is that all ABAP programs running on the server can access this data.

There are two classes that must be defined in order to use shared memory. These are the area class (defined automatically while creating a shared memory area) and the root class. The root class is the class whose instances (instance's attributes) will be stored in the shared memory. The root class must be created before the area is created.

There are a few steps required to make a shared memory area. Before that, we must create our root class. Call transaction SE24. The screen in Figure 5-27 appears.

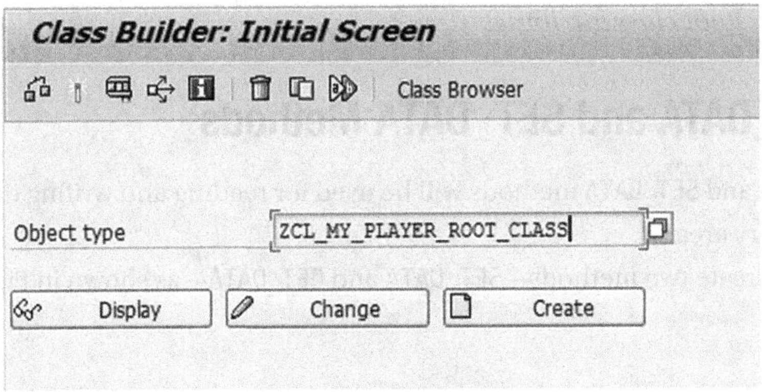

Figure 5-27. *Specifying a root class name*

We need to enter a suitable name for the root class (in our case, we use ZCL_MY_ PLAYER_ROOT_CLASS) in the field provided. Then click the Create button.

Enter a suitable description in the dialog box that appears and click the Save button. Once the class is created, click on the Properties tab. Under General Data, check the Shared Memory-Enabled indicator, as shown in Figure 5-28.

☑ Shared Memory-Enabled   ☑ Fixed point arithmetic
                                 ☑ Unicode checks active

Figure 5-28. *Shared-Memory Enabled property*

On the Attributes tab of our root class, enter the attributes of the PLAYER class. These are the attributes whose values will be stored in the shared memory area on the application server (as shown in Figure 5-29).

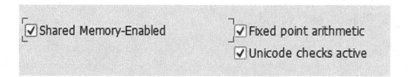

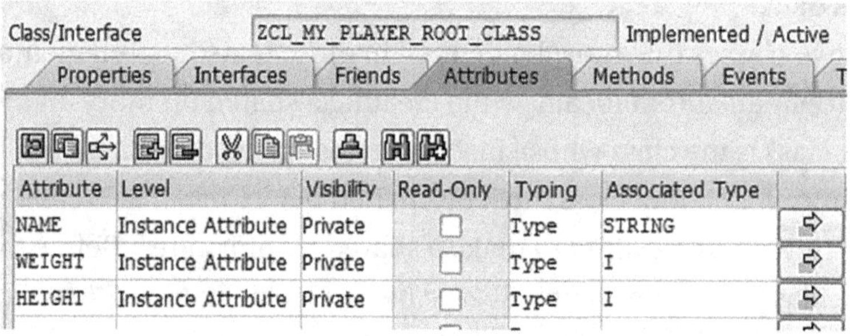

Attribute	Level	Visibility	Read-Only	Typing	Associated Type	
NAME	Instance Attribute	Private	☐	Type	STRING	⇨
WEIGHT	Instance Attribute	Private	☐	Type	I	⇨
HEIGHT	Instance Attribute	Private	☐	Type	I	⇨

Figure 5-29. *Root class attributes*

The GET_DATA and SET_DATA Methods

The GET_DATA and SET_DATA methods will be used for reading and writing data to the shared memory area.

Next, we create two methods—SET_DATA and GET_DATA—as shown in Figure 5-30.

Class/Interface		ZCL_MY_PLAYER_ROOT_CLASS		Implemented / Active

Properties	Interfaces	Friends	Attributes	Methods	Events

□ Parameter Exception 🗐 🗐🗐🗗 🗗🗐 ✂🗐🗐 🖨 🔍🔍

Method	Level	Visibility	Method type	Description
SET_DATA	Instance Method	Public		Setting Player Data
GET_DATA	Instance Method	Public		Reading Player Data

Figure 5-30. *The SET_DATA and GET_DATA methods*

The parameters of SET_DATA are shown in Figure 5-31.

Class/Interface		ZCL_MY_PLAYER_ROOT_CLASS		Implemented / Active

Properties	Interfaces	Friends	Attributes	Methods	Events

Method parameters   SET_DATA

⬅ Methods Exceptions 🗐 🗐 🗗🗐 ✂🗐🗐

Parameter	Type	Pass Value	Optional	Typing ...	Associated Type	
NAME	Importing	☐	☑	Type	STRING	
WEIGHT	Importing	☐	☑	Type	I	
HEIGHT	Importing	☐	☑	Type	I	

Figure 5-31. *Parameters of the SET_DATA method*

There are three importing parameters—NAME, WEIGHT, and HEIGHT—that represent the player. As the name suggests, SET_DATA is used to assign the imported values (NAME, WEIGHT, and HEIGHT) to the corresponding attributes of the PLAYER root class (see Figure 5-32).

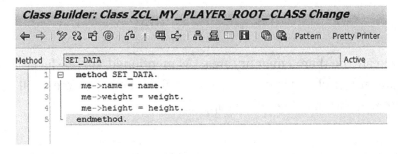

```
Class Builder: Class ZCL_MY_PLAYER_ROOT_CLASS Change

⬅ ➡  🖉 🐾 🖑 ◎  🔓  ┊ 🖳 🖧  🖧 🖳 ▢ 🚯  🖿 🖿  Pattern   Pretty Printer

Method   SET_DATA                                                    Active
    1 ⊟  method SET_DATA.
    2      me->name = name.
    3      me->weight = weight.
    4      me->height = height.
    5 └   endmethod.
```

Figure 5-32. *SET_DATA method code*

Next, we specify the parameters of the GET_DATA method. The method takes as an importing parameter the name of the player. It also has two exporting parameters—HEIGHT and WEIGHT—as shown in Figure 5-33.

Class/Interface		ZCL_MY_PLAYER_ROOT_CLASS			Implemented / Active
Properties	Interfaces	Friends	Attributes	Methods	Events

Method parameters   GET_DATA

Parameter	Type	Pass Value	Optional	Typing ...	Associated Type
NAME	Importing	☐	☐	Type	STRING
WEIGHT	Exporting	☐	☐	Type	I
HEIGHT	Exporting	☐	☐	Type	I
		☐	☐	Type	

Figure 5-33.   *Parameters of the GET_DATA method*

We then write the code in the GET_DATA method. We have an IF statement that checks if the imported name of the player is the same as the attribute name of the object in consideration. If this is true, the WEIGHT and HEIGHT of the object are returned using the appropriate exporting parameters.

```
method GET_DATA.
    if name eq me->name.
     weight = me->weight.
     height = me->height.
     else.
      write 'No data for given player'.
    endif.
 endmethod.
```

Next, we create the shared memory area. (As mentioned, successful creation of the area will create an area class.) In order to create a shared memory area, call transaction SHMA. The screen shown in Figure 5-34 appears.

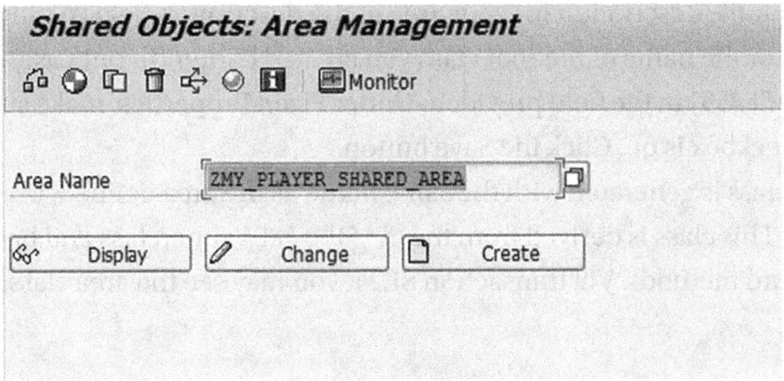

Shared Objects: Area Management

Area Name   ZMY_PLAYER_SHARED_AREA

Display   Change   Create

Figure 5-34. Area creation transaction

Enter a suitable name for the shared memory area into the field provided and click the Create button. This will take you to the screen shown in Figure 5-35, where you must enter the necessary attributes of the shared memory area.

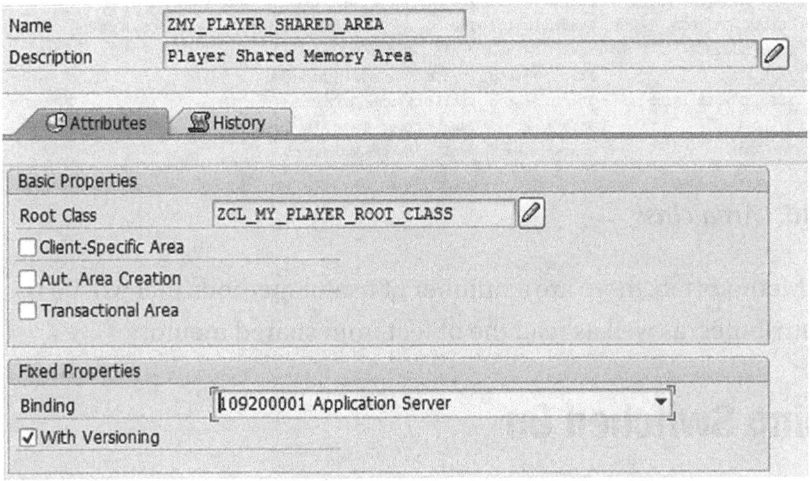

Name   ZMY_PLAYER_SHARED_AREA
Description   Player Shared Memory Area

Attributes   History

Basic Properties
Root Class   ZCL_MY_PLAYER_ROOT_CLASS
☐ Client-Specific Area
☐ Aut. Area Creation
☐ Transactional Area

Fixed Properties
Binding   109200001 Application Server
☑ With Versioning

Figure 5-35. Specifying properties for the shared memory area

Additional Settings

It is also possible to make an area "client-specific" by choosing the appropriate indicator. In addition, if you'll need write changes to the area only when the next database commit occurs, the Transactional Area property must be set.

Enter a suitable description for your area in the description field. Within the Attributes, enter the name of the root class you created earlier (in our case, `ZCL_MY_PLAYER_ROOT_CLASS`) in the field provided. Under Fixed Properties, make sure the With Versioning checkbox is on. Click the Save button.

The area class is generated with the same name as the area defined, i.e. `ZMY_PLAYER_SHARED_AREA`. This class is derived from the `CL_SHM_AREA` superclass and has a number of attributes and methods. Via transaction SE24, you may see the area class. It's shown in Figure 5-36.

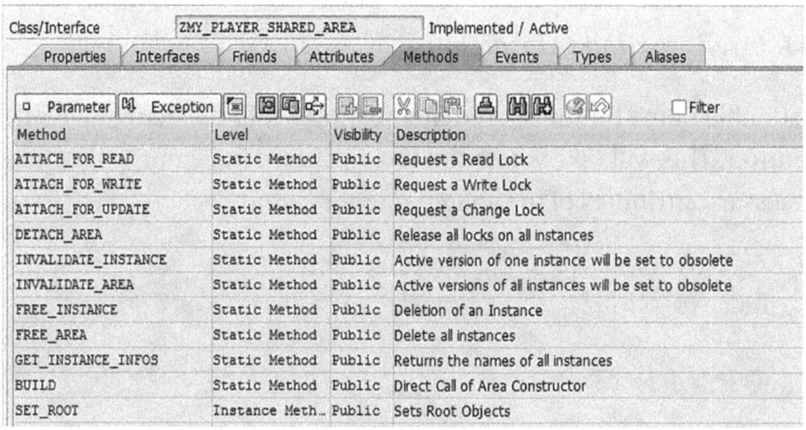

Method	Level	Visibility	Description
ATTACH_FOR_READ	Static Method	Public	Request a Read Lock
ATTACH_FOR_WRITE	Static Method	Public	Request a Write Lock
ATTACH_FOR_UPDATE	Static Method	Public	Request a Change Lock
DETACH_AREA	Static Method	Public	Release all locks on all instances
INVALIDATE_INSTANCE	Static Method	Public	Active version of one instance will be set to obsolete
INVALIDATE_AREA	Static Method	Public	Active versions of all instances will be set to obsolete
FREE_INSTANCE	Static Method	Public	Deletion of an Instance
FREE_AREA	Static Method	Public	Delete all instances
GET_INSTANCE_INFOS	Static Method	Public	Returns the names of all instances
BUILD	Static Method	Public	Direct Call of Area Constructor
SET_ROOT	Instance Meth...	Public	Sets Root Objects

Figure 5-36. *Area class*

On the Methods tab, there are a number of useful methods that will be used to store the object attributes, as well as read the object from shared memory.

Versioning Switched On

A shared memory area may consist of a number of instances. (This is different from the instance of a shared memory enabled class.) There may be multiple versions of an area instance, such as Build, Active, Obsolete, and Expired, when versioning is applicable. When data is first being written on an area instance (or being changed), a Build version is created. When the build process is completed, and the write or update locks are released, the version being built becomes an Active version. There can be only *one* Active version at any given time. In addition, only one change lock may be set on a particular area instance. Any program that tries to read an area instance will automatically impose a read lock on the current active version. While an active version is being read, another new version may be built via a write/change lock. Once the new version build is completed, it is set as Active, and the version being read is set as Obsolete. Any subsequent read locks will be now be set on the new Active version. Once the read on an obsolete version is completed and the read lock is released, the obsolete version is set as Expired, which is later deleted by the system.

Writing and Reading Data Into Shared Memory

In this section, we learn how to write simple code in order to store objects in shared memory.

We will first look at the code for writing into the shared memory area. We must define two variables—AREA_ROOT and PLAYER_HANDLE—based on the area class and the root class created earlier (in our case ZMY_PLAYER_SHARED_AREA and ZCL_MY_PLAYER_ROOT_CLASS).

We then use the static ATTACH_FOR_WRITE method of the shared area class to get a handle on the instance within the area (we named it PLAYER_INST). This sets a write lock to the area instance. We then use CREATE OBJECT to create an instance of the root class PLAYER_ROOT in the area instance pointed to by the handle AREA_HANDLE. The SET_ROOT method is then called to link the root object with the area handle. (This is an important step, as the subsequent SET_DATA method for writing data to the shared area instance will not work.) Next, the SET_DATA method of the PLAYER_ROOT class is called. Finally, the DETACH_COMMIT method is called using the AREA_HANDLE to complete the writing process (to commit the changes to the database) and release the write lock imposed on the area instance PLAYER_INST.

```
data : area_handle type ref to zmy_player_shared_area.
data : player_root type ref to zcl_my_player_root_class.

try .
   area_handle =
   zmy_player_shared_area=>attach_for_write( 'PLAYER_INST').

   create object player_root area handle area_handle.

   area_handle->set_root( player_root ).

   call method player_root->set_data
      exporting
        name   = 'Oliver Kahn'
        weight = '88'
        height = '187'.
      area_handle->detach_commit( ).

   catch cx_shm_attach_error.

endtry.
```

Once the program is executed, we can see the shared memory area (in our case ZMY_
SHARED_PLAYER_AREA) using the transaction SHMM, as shown in Figure 5-37.

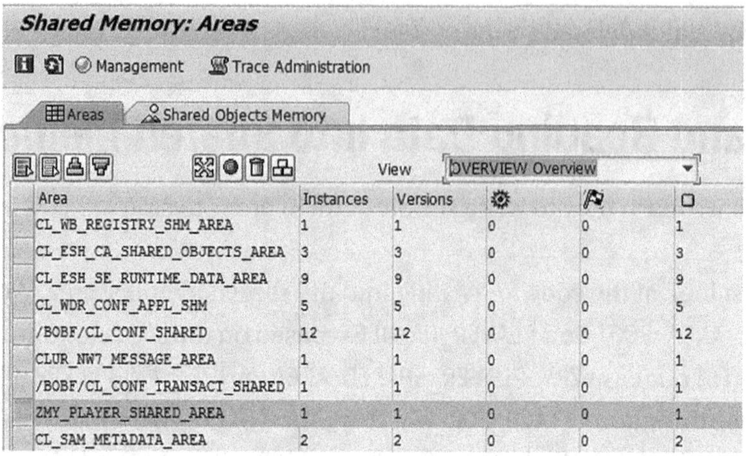

Figure 5-37.   *Shared memory areas and SHMM*

This area has one instance of which one version exists—the Active version (denoted
by the green square icon in the right-most column).

Double-clicking the row will take you to the details shown in Figure 5-38.

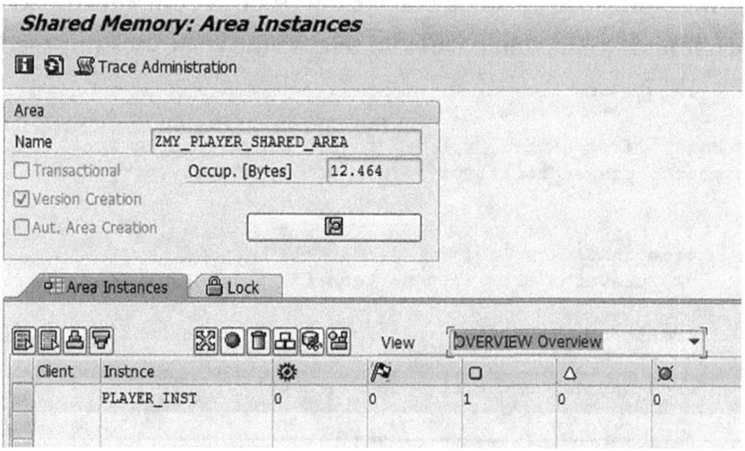

Figure 5-38.   *Area instances*

The name of the instance we created is PLAYER_INST and it's shown along with the
versions and the occupied size in bytes.

In addition to writing data to memory, it is also possible to read data from the shared memory area instance into your program. The code pertaining to our PLAYER_INST example is as follows.

```
data : area_handle type ref to
       zmy_player_shared_area.
data : weight type i.
data : height type i.

try.
    call method
    zmy_player_shared_area=>attach_for_read
      exporting
        inst_name = 'PLAYER_INST'
      receiving
        handle    = area_handle.

    call method area_handle->root->get_data
      exporting
        name    = 'Oliver Kahn'
      importing
        weight = weight
        height = height.

    call method area_handle->detach( ).
    write : 'Oliver Kahn' , weight, height.
  catch cx_shm_attach_error.
 write : 'Error While Reading '.
endtry.
```

We first declare appropriate variables for WEIGHT and HEIGHT, which will be read from the shared area. The static method ATTACH_FOR_READ of the area class ZMY_PLAYER_SHARED_AREA is called to impose a read lock on the area instance PLAYER_INST and return an area handle. Using this handle, the GET_DATA method of the root is then called in order to read the weight and height of the player whose name is specified via parameter NAME. After this, the DETACH method is called and the read lock set on the area instance is released.

The data read from the shared memory area is then displayed on the screen, as shown in Figure 5-39.

```
Oliver Kahn          88          187
```

Figure 5-39. *Output of player weight and height*

Summary

We saw the basics of exception and exception handling as applied to ABAP Objects, along with a fully working demo. We covered how we can create persistent objects in object-oriented ABAP. Finally, we learn about the theory and saw real working code of shared objects.

CHAPTER 6

More Topics in Object-Oriented ABAP

In this chapter, we cover many diverse and useful object-oriented topics. The lessons have been designed to build on each other, with each one progressing and layering the information and skills.

I start with a discussion of the NEW operator (introduced in NetWeaver 7.40) used to create objects. I will then discuss using an ALV object model to create reports. We discuss the various ALV classes and methods along with a practical coding demo. Next, you will see how chaining methods enables you to write compact code. An example of ALV-related code written in conjunction with chaining methods is included. I then cover object-oriented transactions followed by the Refactoring Assistant tool in the Class Builder. A detailed discussion of the various ways a class can be enhanced is also included. At the end of the chapter, you will learn about a number of constructs and statements in detail that are not allowed in the ABAP Objects arena.

Using the New Operator to Create an Object

Starting with NetWeaver 7.4, ABAP allows creation of objects via the NEW operator. This operator provides an alternate to the CREATE OBJECT statement. There are a number of ways in which it may be used for object instantiation. The NEW operator may be used to create instances of local and global classes.

173

© Rehan Zaidi 2019
R. Zaidi, *SAP ABAP Objects*, https://doi.org/10.1007/978-1-4842-4964-2_6

Before we look at the actual coding, let's go through the general syntax for the NEW operator. For object creation, the NEW operator may be used in the following two ways:

1. *Used in conjunction with a class name.* The construct for this is:

```
DATA MYOBJ TYPE REF TO MYCLASS.
MYOBJ =  NEW myclass( param1 = val1
                      param2 = val2
                      ...
                      paramN = valN).
```

Using the inline declaration supported by ABAP 7.40, the above form may be written in one single statement, as shown here:

```
DATA(MYOBJ) =  NEW myclass(
                      param1 =   val1
                      param2 = val2
                          ...
                      paramN = valN).
```

In both cases, the NEW operator is used in conjunction with the class name. This will create an instance of class MYCLASS and assign to the reference variable MYOBJ. In the latter case, there is an implicit declaration of MYOBJ based on class MYCLASS (where the type of MYOBJ is derived from the content of the right side of the assignment). If the constructor of the class has mandatory importing parameters, the corresponding data must be passed to the instance constructor within the parentheses shown.

2. *Used with # character.* Another form is via usage of the NEW operator with the # character. The syntax form is shown as follows:

```
DATA MYOBJ TYPE REF TO MYCLASS.
MYOBJ = NEW #( param1 = val1
               param2 = val2
                  ...
               paramN = valN).
```

We declare a MYOBJ variable referred to the MYCLASS class. Since we have already declared a reference variable based on the class in question, there is no need to specify the class again with the NEW operator. Instead of the class name, the # character can be used. Any non-optional parameters are provided in parentheses, as shown earlier.

To better understand how to use the two forms of the NEW operator, let's look at a few examples. We will use the global football player class called ZST6_FOOTBALL_PLAYER_CLASS that we defined earlier in the book.

Consider the following code block (this is a pre-ABAP 7.40 version):

```
DATA FOOTBALL_PLAYER
            TYPE REF TO ZST6_FOOTBALL_PLAYER_CLASS.

CREATE OBJECT FOOTBALL_PLAYER

" Without NEW Operator

  EXPORTING
    NAME   = 'Oliver Kahn'
    WEIGHT = '88'
    HEIGHT = '178'
    FOOTBALL_CLUB = 'Bayern Munich'.
FOOTBALL_PLAYER->DISPLAY_PLAYER_DETAILS( ).
```

We created an object of the global class using the CREATE OBJECT statement. The DISPLAY_PLAYER_DETAILS method was then called in order to print the details of the created football player. This block of code was earlier used to create a football player object.

We will now see two ways that we can instantiate the object using the NEW operator (and not the CREATE OBJECT statement). The block of code shown in the previous listing may be replaced with the following:

```
DATA(FOOTBALL_PLAYER) =
NEW ZST6_FOOTBALL_PLAYER_CLASS( NAME = 'Oliver Kahn'
                                WEIGHT = '88'
                                HEIGHT = '178'
                        FOOTBALL_CLUB = 'Bayern Munich' ).
FOOTBALL_PLAYER->DISPLAY_PLAYER_DETAILS( ).
```

We used the inline declaration of FOOTBALL_PLAYER along with the NEW operator in a single statement. This involves the implicit definition of FOOTBALL_PLAYER as a reference of the ZST6_FOOTBALL_PLAYER_CLASS class. In this case, we did not have to declare a variable based on a separate statement. An object for the given class is created and the reference variable FOOTBALL_PLAYER may then be used to display the player details.

Let's look at another piece of code that uses the NEW operator in conjunction with the # character. The corresponding code is shown here:

```
DATA: FOOTBALL_PLAYER
      TYPE REF TO ZST6_FOOTBALL_PLAYER_CLASS.
FOOTBALL_PLAYER = NEW #( NAME = 'Oliver Kahn'
                        WEIGHT = '88'
                        HEIGHT = '178'
                        FOOTBALL_CLUB = 'Bayern Munich' ).
FOOTBALL_PLAYER->DISPLAY_PLAYER_DETAILS( ).
```

In this form, we declare a reference variable FOOTBALL_PLAYER for the ZST6_FOOTBALL_PLAYER_CLASS class. We use the NEW operator to create an object of the given class. Instead of specifying the name of the class, we used the # character. The reference to the newly created object is assigned to the FOOTBALL_PLAYER variable. The values for the various importing parameters are supplied as shown earlier. The complete class name is not required, as the system automatically detects it from the type of the variable to which the created object's reference is assigned (in our case, FOOTBALL_PLAYER).

The following block of code pertaining to our requirement will be unacceptable, as the class whose object is to be created is unknown:

```
DATA(FOOTBALL_PLAYER) =
                NEW #( NAME = 'Oliver Kahn'
                      WEIGHT = '88'
                      HEIGHT = '178'
                      FOOTBALL_CLUB = 'Bayern Munich' ).
""""""   NOT ALLOWED
FOOTBALL_PLAYER->DISPLAY_PLAYER_DETAILS( ).
```

In this code, the error appears, as shown in Figure 6-1. An error results since the type (class name) of the football player object cannot be determined.

```
10
11    DATA(FOOTBALL_PLAYER) =
12                     NEW #( NAME = 'Oliver Kahn'
13                            WEIGHT = '88'
14                            HEIGHT = '178'
15                            FOOTBALL_CLUB = 'Bayern Munich' ).
16    """"""  NOT ALLOWED
17    FOOTBALL_PLAYER->DISPLAY_PLAYER_DETAILS( ).
```

Syntax error		
Description	Row	Type
Program ZNEW_OPERATOR_DEMO	12	⊘◯◯
No type can be derived from the context for the operator "NEW".		

Figure 6-1. *Syntax error using the NEW operator*

ALV Object Model

In this section, we look at one of the most popular and commonly used applications of ABAP Objects in everyday usage.

For reporting, I recommended that you do not use list creation techniques via WRITE statements. Rather, you should use the ALV or the ABAP/SAP List Viewer to output data to the user. ALV provides a number of advantages, including:

- It provides a number of functions. The programmer does not have to program these functions. These functions include sorting, filtering, etc.

- The user may also save layouts.

There are three major standard classes used for ALV display. However, in this section, we will use the CL_SALV_TABLE – Table display class to fulfill a simple requirement.

Along with the global CL_SALV_TABLE class, there are a number of other classes that are used in order to generate the output. The important methods of these classes are shown in Table 6-1.

Table 6-1. *Methods for ALV-Related Classes*

Class	Methods
CL_SALV_TABLE	FACTORY
	DISPLAY
	GET_COLUMNS
	GET_FUNCTIONS
CL_SALV_FUNCTIONS	SET_ALL
CL_SALV_COLUMNS	SET_OPTIMIZE
CL_SALV_COLUMN_TABLE	SET_MEDIUM_TEXT
	SET_SHORT_TEXT
	SET_LONG_TEXT
	SET_OUTPUT_LENGTH

We will take a detailed look at the other classes (and the methods) used in conjunction with CL_SALV_TABLE to create the solution.

We will create a report based on the ALV format. The report will display, for a number of players, information such as name, weight, and height.

We assume that the data is outputted to an ALV format and stored in the IT_PLAYER table, as shown here:

```
TYPES : BEGIN OF TY_PLAYER,
        NAME TYPE CHAR20,
        HEIGHT TYPE I ,
        WEIGHT TYPE I,
        END OF TY_PLAYER.

DATA : WA_PLAYER TYPE TY_PLAYER,
       IT_PLAYER TYPE STANDARD TABLE OF TY_PLAYER.
```

We then define references to the ALV object, the ALV function object, and the columns objects. The CL_SALV_TABLE, CL_SALV_FUNCTIONS, and CL_SALV_COLUMNS_TABLE classes are involved. The variables defined are ALV, FUNCTIONS, and COLUMNS, respectively.

```
DATA :   ALV TYPE REF TO CL_SALV_TABLE,
         FUNCTIONS TYPE REF TO CL_SALV_FUNCTIONS,
         COLUMNS TYPE REF TO CL_SALV_COLUMNS_TABLE.
```

Next, we use the static factory method of the CL_SALV_TABLE class to create the ALV object. The internal table IT_PLAYER is passed as a parameter to this method. The reference to the newly created ALV object is then returned in the variable ALV (this was defined in the previous step).

```
CALL METHOD CL_SALV_TABLE=>FACTORY
  IMPORTING
    R_SALV_TABLE = ALV
  CHANGING
    T_TABLE = IT_PLAYER.
```

We then call the GET_COLUMNS method of the CL_SALV_TABLE to get the columns object for the ALV object. This is then returned to the variable define earlier. We then use the SET_OPTIMIZE method provided by the standard CL_SALV_COLUMNS_TABLE class. This is used to optimize the width of the various columns included in the display.

```
COLUMNS = ALV->GET_COLUMNS( ).
COLUMNS->SET_OPTIMIZE( ).
```

Similarly, the GET_FUNCTIONS of the CL_SALV_TABLE are called. The returned parameter is assigned to the FUNCTIONS variable declared earlier. We then call SET_ALL of the CL_SALV_FUNCTIONS class to enable the standard toolbar functions of the ALV:

```
FUNCTIONS = ALV->GET_FUNCTIONS( ).
FUNCTIONS->SET_ALL( ).
```

Since everything is done, we just need to display the ALV on the user screen. The method DISPLAY of the CL_SALV_TABLE class is used to display the data:

```
ALV->DISPLAY( ).
```

The output of the ALV is shown in Figure 6-2.

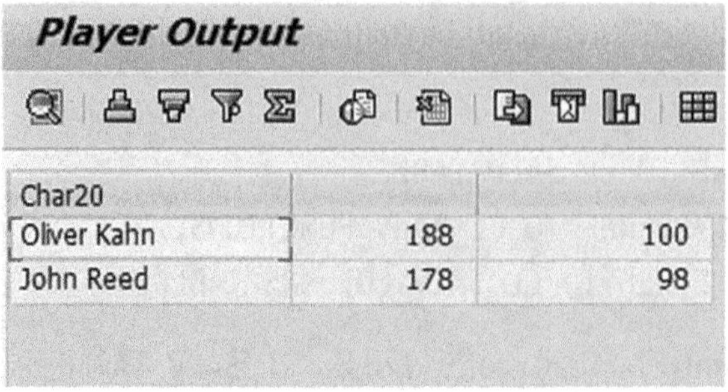

Figure 6-2. *ALV output*

The output does not have proper column headers. In the next subsection, we add column header texts for the three displayed columns-player, weight, and height.

Adding Header Texts to ALV Columns

In this subsection, we will now add header text to the columns of our ALV output, i.e., the three created columns—Name, Weight, and Height. The SET_LONG_TEXT, SET_MEDIUM_TEXT, and SET_SHORT_TEXT methods of CL_SALV_COLUMN_TABLE are used for this purpose.

We first declare a COLUMN variable based on the CL_SALV_COLUMN_TABLE class. The COLUMNS object is then used along with the GET_COLUMN method of the CL_SALV_COLUMNS_TABLE class. The result of this method is stored in the COLUMN variable. The SET_MEDIUM_TEXT, SET_LONG_TEXT, and SET_SHORT_TEXT methods are then called to specify the column headers in the ALV output. The (?=) operator is used for this purpose.

The code for this is shown here:

```
DATA : COLUMN TYPE REF TO CL_SALV_COLUMN_TABLE.
....
    COLUMNS = ALV->GET_COLUMNS( ).

    COLUMN ?=  COLUMNS->GET_COLUMN( 'NAME').
    COLUMN->SET_MEDIUM_TEXT('Player Name').
    COLUMN->SET_SHORT_TEXT('Pl. Name').
    COLUMN->SET_LONG_TEXT('Player Name').
    COLUMN->SET_OUTPUT_LENGTH('25').
```

```
COLUMN ?= COLUMNS->GET_COLUMN( 'WEIGHT' ).
COLUMN->SET_MEDIUM_TEXT(").
COLUMN->SET_SHORT_TEXT(").
COLUMN->SET_LONG_TEXT('Weight').

COLUMN ?= COLUMNS->GET_COLUMN( 'HEIGHT' ).
COLUMN->SET_MEDIUM_TEXT(").
COLUMN->SET_SHORT_TEXT(").
COLUMN->SET_LONG_TEXT('Height').
```

Note   For simplicity's sake, separate blocks of statements for each column are shown. You can modularized the code in order to avoid repetition of the similar statements.

Once this is done, the program code will look like this:

```
types : begin of ty_player,
          name   type char20,
          height type i,
          weight type i,
        end of ty_player.

data : wa_player type ty_player,
       it_player type standard table of ty_player.

data : alv       type ref to cl_salv_table,
       functions type ref to cl_salv_functions,
       columns   type ref to cl_salv_columns_table.

data : column type ref to cl_salv_column_table.
"" Internal Table IT_PLAYER population part not shown
""

try.
    call method cl_salv_table=>factory
      importing
        r_salv_table = alv
```

```abap
       changing
         t_table        = it_player.

    functions = alv->get_functions( ).
    functions->set_all( ).

    columns = alv->get_columns( ).
    column ?= columns->get_column( 'NAME').
    column->set_medium_text('Player Name').
    column->set_short_text('Pl. Name').
    column->set_long_text('Player Name').
    column->set_output_length('25').

    column ?= columns->get_column( 'WEIGHT').
    column->set_medium_text(").
    column->set_short_text(").
    column->set_long_text('Weight').

    column ?= columns->get_column( 'HEIGHT').
    column->set_medium_text(").
    column->set_short_text(").
    column->set_long_text('Height').

    alv->display( ).

  catch cx_salv_msg.
    write: / 'Problem while generating ALV Output'.
endtry.
```

After adding the column headers, the output of the program (along with the data) is shown in Figure 6-3.

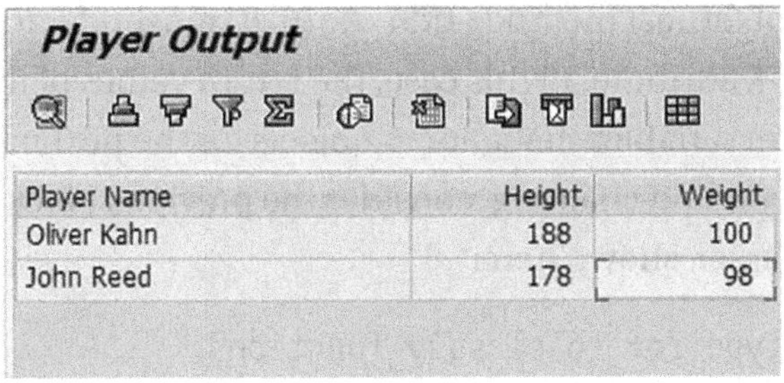

Figure 6-3. *Final player output*

Method Chaining

A newer concept that has evolved is *method chaining.* This involves combining calls of functional methods (i.e., methods that have one returning value as output). The chaining of methods makes the code more compact and allows requirements to be met without the need for additional reference variables. There are two types of chaining possible: chained method access and chained method call. (The primary emphasis of this section is on chained method access.) Let's take a look at what each means.

In chained method access, there could be two forms, as shown here:

```
obj_ref->inst_meth_a(..)->inst_meth_b(..)->inst_meth(..).

class=>static_meth_a(..)->inst_meth_b(..)->inst_meth(..).
```

The return value of one functional method is a reference to an object that is used to call the next method in the chain. The returning value of the last method is used as an operand.

In this case, the first use may be a class component selector (=>) or an object component selector (->). After that, all the methods are called using the component. Or, in other words, the first method may be a static or an instance method; other than that, you must have all functional instance methods.

Chained attribute access, on the other hand, is similar to chained method calls. In this case, the instance attribute is used as an operand.

The chained attribute access may be one of the following forms:

```
obj_ref->inst_meth_a(..)->inst_meth_b(..)->inst_attr.

class=>static_meth_a(..)->inst_meth_b(..)->inst_attr.
```

The return value of the last method (INST_METH_B) must refer to the object that contains the INST_ATTR attribute. In this case, the return values of the previous functional methods are variables that refer to objects for the next method.

As an example of method chaining, consider the previous block of code that we used in our ALV example earlier, shown here:

```
 data : functions type ref to cl_salv_functions.

        functions = alv->get_functions( ).
        functions->set_all( ).
```

Method chaining can be applied in this case. These three lines can be replaced with a single line of code, as shown here:

```
alv->get_functions( )->set_all( ).
```

There is also no need to define the FUNCTIONS variable, and the coding is very compact.

Let's look at one more example of method chaining. Going back to our football example involving the NEW operator:

```
DATA: FOOTBALL_PLAYER TYPE REF TO ZST6_FOOTBALL_PLAYER_CLASS.
FOOTBALL_PLAYER = NEW #( NAME = 'Oliver Kahn'
                        WEIGHT = '88'
                        HEIGHT = '178'
                        FOOTBALL_CLUB = 'Bayern Munich' ).

FOOTBALL_PLAYER->DISPLAY_PLAYER_DETAILS( ).
```

We can combine the NEW operator shown earlier and method chaining. The previous block of code can be written more compactly, as shown here:

```
NEW ZST6_FOOTBALL_PLAYER_CLASS(
        NAME = 'Oliver Kahn'
        WEIGHT = '88'
        HEIGHT = '178'
FOOTBALL_CLUB = 'Bayern Munich')->DISPLAY_PLAYER_DETAILS( ).
```

Object-Oriented Transactions

An *object-oriented transaction* is a transaction (defined via SE93) that may be linked to a method of a class. When the transaction is called, the method gets executed automatically. The transaction may be linked to a global or a local class residing in your SAP system. The method used may be both static and instance. If the underlying method is an instance method, the object of the class is instantiated within the internal session in which the transaction is run.

In this section, we learn how to create an object-oriented transaction.

We will create an object-oriented transaction called ZPLAYER that will be used to create and display instances of a local PLAYER class (defined in Chapter 1).

Before actually creating the transaction via SE93, we will carry out some prerequisite steps. This is to ensure that a callable method exists for our transaction.

We will create a copy of the program shown in Chapter 1. We will name the copy program ZOOTRANSACTION_DEMO. In this program, we will add a class creator with definition and implementation shown here:

```
class creator definition.
  public section.
    class-methods create_display_players.
endclass.

class creator implementation.
  method create_display_players.
    data : player1 type ref to player.
    data : player2 type ref to player.

    create object player1
      exporting
        name    = 'John Mann'
        country = 'Germany'
        club    = 'Bayern Munich'.

    create object player2
      exporting
        name    = 'Paul Goldberg'
```

```
        country = 'Britain'
        club    = 'Liverpool'.

    player=>display_list_of_players( ) .

  endmethod.
endclass.
```

We have defined a new class called CREATOR with a static method called CREATE_
DISPLAY_PLAYERS that will be used to instantiate two instances of the local class PLAYER
using the CREATE OBJECT statements. Finally, within the method, we will call the static
method DISPLAY_LIST_OF_PLAYERS to display the players on the user screen.

We will modify the DISPLAY_LIST_OF_PLAYERS method in order to display the list in
ALV format instead of using traditional WRITE statements (for simplicity's sake, this code
is not shown but may be easily written using the concept shown earlier in this chapter).

Since we have completed all the prerequisite steps, let's now create the transaction.
To define an object-oriented transaction, call transaction SE93. The screen shown in
Figure 6-4 appears.

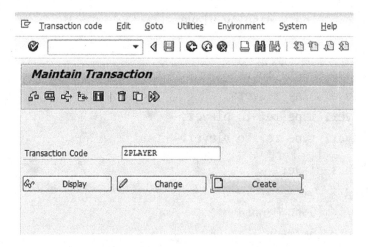

Figure 6-4. *Entering the transaction code*

Then click the Create button. This will display the dialog box shown in Figure 6-5.

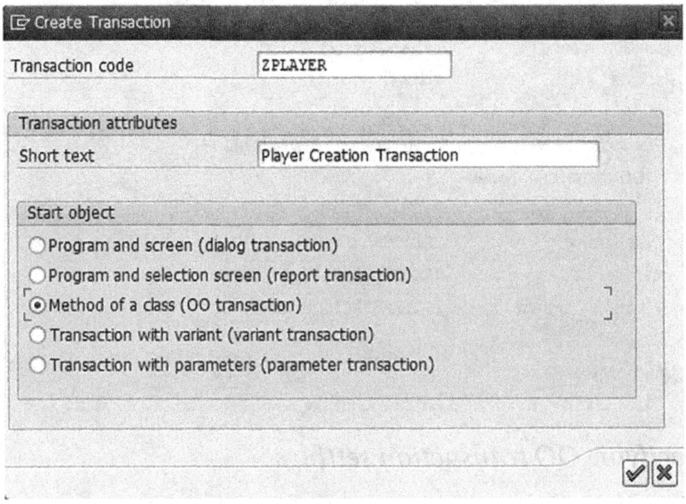

Figure 6-5. *Choosing the OO Transaction option*

Enter a suitable description for the transaction. Make sure that the third option (Method of a Class OO Transaction) is selected. Then click the Continue button.

This will take you to the screen shown in Figure 6-6.

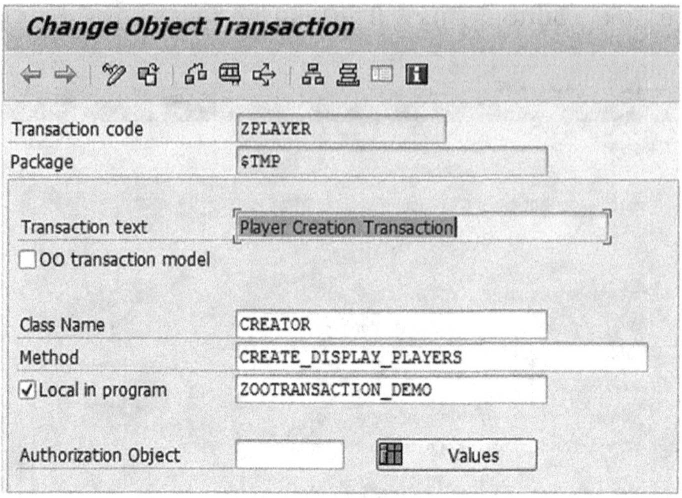

Figure 6-6. *Specifying OO transaction settings*

Enter a suitable name for the transaction in the Transaction Text field. Make sure to uncheck the OO Transaction Model checkbox. Since we will be using a local class defined in the program, check the Local in Program checkbox. Fill in the Class Name and Method Name fields as well (refer to Figure 6-6 again).

Once all the settings are done, save your newly created transaction.

When we execute the transaction, the output is generated, as shown in Figure 6-7.

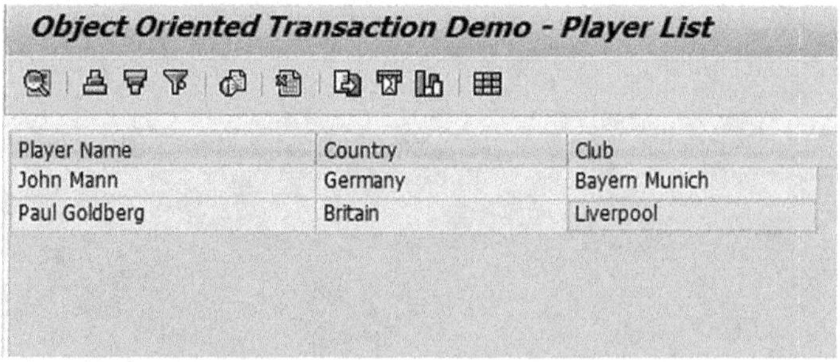

Figure 6-7. *Output of the OO transaction*

When the transaction in ZPLAYER is executed, the static method CREATE_DISPLAY_ METHOD of the CREATOR class is automatically called. The method creates two objects of the PLAYER class by the names PLAYER1 and PLAYER2. For each object, the NAME, COUNTRY, and CLUB attributes are assigned values via the corresponding parameters of the constructor.

Finally, the static method DISPLAY_LIST_OF_PLAYERS of the PLAYER class is called in order to display the created players in ALV format on the screen.

The complete code listing is shown in Listing 6-1.

Listing 6-1. Complete Program Listing

```
report zootransaction_demo.

class player definition deferred.
types: ty_player type ref to player.

class player definition.
  public section.
    methods write_player_details.
    methods constructor importing name type string
                                  country type string
                                  club    type string.
    class-methods display_list_of_players.

  private section.
    data name type string.
    data country type string.
    data club type string.

  class-data: players_list type standard
              table of ty_player.
endclass.

class player implementation .
  method write_player_details.
    skip.
    write :/ 'Name    :', me->name.
    write :/ 'Country :', me->country.
    write :/ 'Club    :', me->club.
  endmethod.

  method constructor.
    me->name =  name.
    me->country = country.
```

```abap
    me->club = club.
    append me to players_list.
  endmethod.

  method display_list_of_players.
    types : begin of ty_player,
                name      type char20,
                country type char20,
                club      type char20,
              end of ty_player.
    data :  wa_player type ty_player,
        it_player type standard table of ty_player.
    data :   alv        type ref to cl_salv_table,
            functions type ref to cl_salv_functions,
        columns    type ref to cl_salv_columns_table.
    data : temp_player type ref to player.

    loop at players_list into temp_player.
      wa_player-name = temp_player->name.
      wa_player-country = temp_player->country.
      wa_player-club = temp_player->club.
      append wa_player to it_player.
    endloop.
    try.
        call method cl_salv_table=>factory
          importing
            r_salv_table = alv
          changing
            t_table       = it_player.
        functions = alv->get_functions( ).
        functions->set_all( ).
        """"""""""""""""" adding column headers
    data : column type ref to cl_salv_column_table.
        columns = alv->get_columns( ).

      column ?= columns->get_column( 'NAME').
      column->set_medium_text('Player Name').
```

```
          column->set_short_text('Pl. Name').
          column->set_long_text('Player Name').
          column->set_output_length('25').

          column ?= columns->get_column( 'COUNTRY').
          column->set_medium_text(").
          column->set_short_text(").
          column->set_long_text('Country').

          column ?= columns->get_column( 'CLUB').
          column->set_medium_text(").
          column->set_short_text(").
          column->set_long_text('Club').
            alv->display( ).
          catch cx_salv_msg.
        endtry.
      endmethod.
endclass.

class creator definition.
  public section.
    class-methods create_display_players.
endclass.

class creator implementation.
  method create_display_players.
    data : player1 type ref to player.
    data : player2 type ref to player.

    create object player1
      exporting
        name    = 'John Mann'
        country = 'Germany'
        club    = 'Bayern Munich'.

    create object player2
      exporting
        name    = 'Paul Goldberg'
```

```
        country = 'Britain'
        club    = 'Liverpool'.
    player=>display_list_of_players( ) .
  endmethod.
endclass.
```

Refactoring Assistant

In the ABAP Objects arena, *refactoring* involves changing (improving) the structure of a class (or classes) without changing its functionality. For this purpose, the Refactoring Assistant is available in the ABAP workbench tool from the Class Builder, ABAP Editor, and the Function Builder. The primary emphasis of this will be on refactoring classes via transaction SE24.

The Refactoring Assistant provides the following advantages to developers:

- It enables developers to change the structure (components) of classes in the least possible time without any inconsistencies.

- It has an easy graphical tool that lets developers move components from classes to interfaces/classes and vice versa via simply dragging and dropping. This relieves the developer from the burden of manually editing the classes.

Some examples of refactoring include:

- Moving components from a subclass to a superclass
- Moving components from a superclass to a subclass
- Moving components from an interface to a class
- Moving components from a class to an interface

Likewise, we may also move a class' components to another class (provided an association exists between them). In case of nested interfaces, we can also move components from one interface to another.

From the display mode, the Refactoring Assistant is not available. While in the change mode within the class (in transaction SE24), choose Utilities ➤ Refactoring ➤ Refactoring Assistant.

Note   Refactoring is only possible in Edit mode. The Refactoring Assistant is not available in the Display mode of the Class Builder.

Alternately, you can also use the F7 key. This will show the Refactoring Assistant for the given class or interface. For example, if we have the ZST6_PLAYER_CLASS class defined earlier, the Refactoring Assistant will look like Figure 6-8.

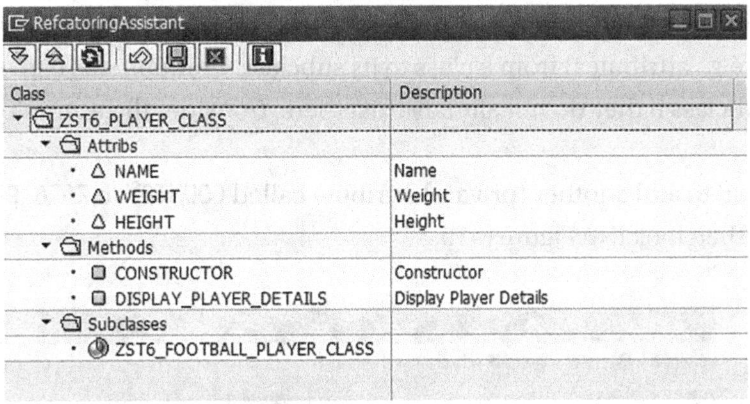

Figure 6-8. *Refactoring Assistant*

As you can see, this shows the class has three attributes—NAME, WEIGHT, and HEIGHT. In addition, the methods of the class and the subclass that has been derived from the given class are also displayed. The Refactoring Assistant displays the colors according to the visibility of the components. The private components are shown in red, public components are in green, and components that are protected are shown in yellow.

It must also be noted that refactoring is not supported for classes that have been enhanced. If you try to run the Refactoring Assistant on these, the following message appears (Figure 6-9).

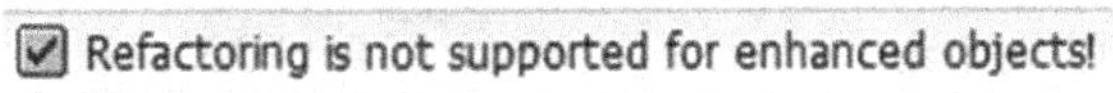

Figure 6-9. *"Not supported" message*

If a component with the same name already exists in the target class, an error will be displayed and no transfer will be made.

Once we know how to switch on the Refactoring Assistant, we will see a few examples applicable to refactoring classes.

Moving Components from a Class to its Direct Subclass

As mentioned, the Refactoring Assistant allows you to move the various attributes from the one class (or interface) to another. In this subsection, we see how we can move components (e.g., attributes) from a class to its subclass. Components can only be moved to a subclass if they do not already exist there. Consider the example shown in Listing 6-1.

Say we need to add another (private) attribute called COUNTRY to ZST6_PLAYER_CLASS. The class will then look like Figure 6-10.

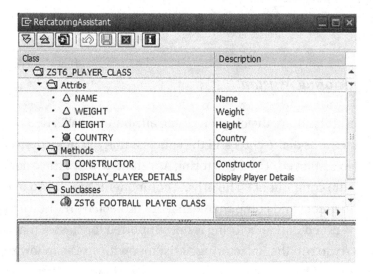

Figure 6-10. *Refactoring Assistant*

To move the COUNTRY attribute to the subclass ZST6_FOOTBALL_PLAYER_CLASS, simply drag the COUNTRY node and drop it on the subclass name node. After the change, the class will look like Figure 6-11.

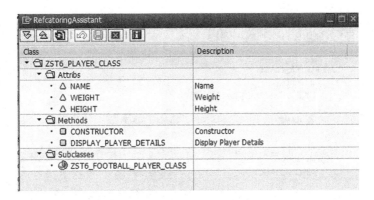

Figure 6-11. *ZST6_PLAYER_CLASS*

A message will appear at the bottom of the Refactoring Assistant dialog, as shown in Figure 6-12.

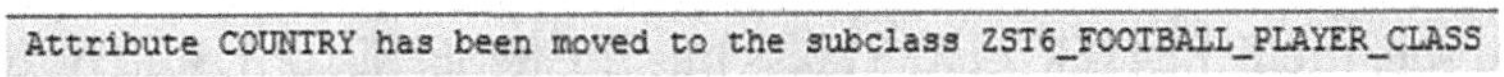

Attribute COUNTRY has been moved to the subclass ZST6_FOOTBALL_PLAYER_CLASS

Figure 6-12. *Attribute COUNTRY moved to subclass*

You may use the Undo ↺ button on the Assistant toolbar to return the class to its original form. If you want to go ahead with the change, click the 💾 Save button.

In our case, when the changes are saved, we can see that the COUNTRY attribute does not exist in the superclass, but has been created (also as a private attribute) in the subclass. You may now activate both classes.

Moving Components from a Class to an Implemented Interface

Let's consider another example. As mentioned, the components of a class may be moved to an implementing interface. Take an example of a class Z_PLAYER_CLASS that implements an interface Z_INTERFACE_DISPLAY. The class within the Refactoring Assistant is shown in Figure 6-13.

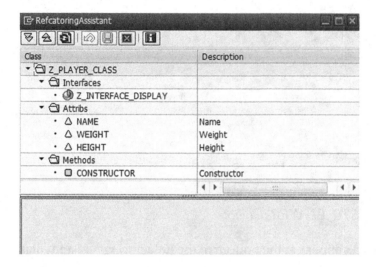

Figure 6-13. *Interface used in class*

As you can see, the Z_PLAYER_CLASS class has the NAME, WEIGHT, and HEIGHT attributes and implements Z_INTERFACE_DISPLAY. It must be noted that the components within the Z_INTERFACE_DISPLAY interface are not shown.

Suppose we need to move the HEIGHT attribute to the Z_INTERFACE_DISPLAY interface. Simply move the attribute by dragging and dropping it to the interface. A message appears saying that the attribute has been moved, as shown in Figure 6-14.

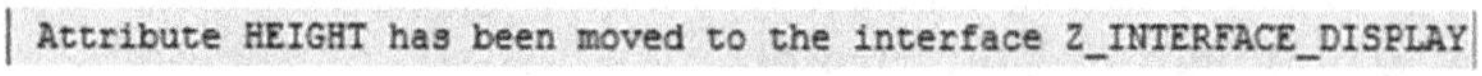

```
Attribute HEIGHT has been moved to the interface Z_INTERFACE_DISPLAY
```

Figure 6-14. *The HEIGHT attribute has moved*

Save your refactoring using the Save button. You will see that the HEIGHT attribute has been moved to the Z_INTERFACE_DISPLAY interface. You may now go to transaction SE24 and activate the interface.

The Refactoring Assistant dialog is shown in Figure 6-15.

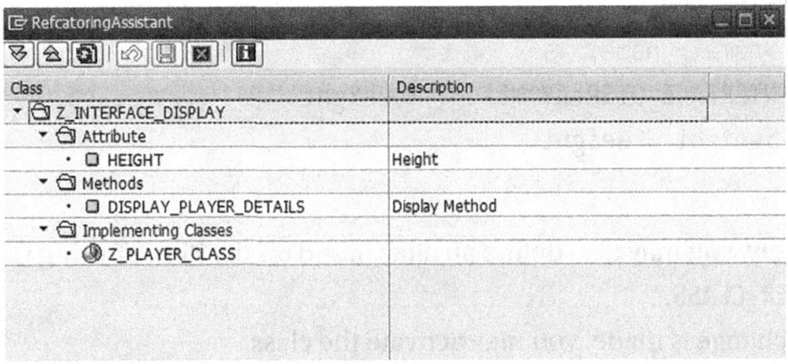

Figure 6-15. *Refactoring Assistant*

Since all of the components of an interface have public visibility, once the private attribute HEIGHT of the Z_PLAYER_CLASS is transferred to the class, its visibility becomes public (denoted in green).

Within the Z_PLAYER_CLASS, this may be seen but we cannot change its visibility (see Figure 6-16).

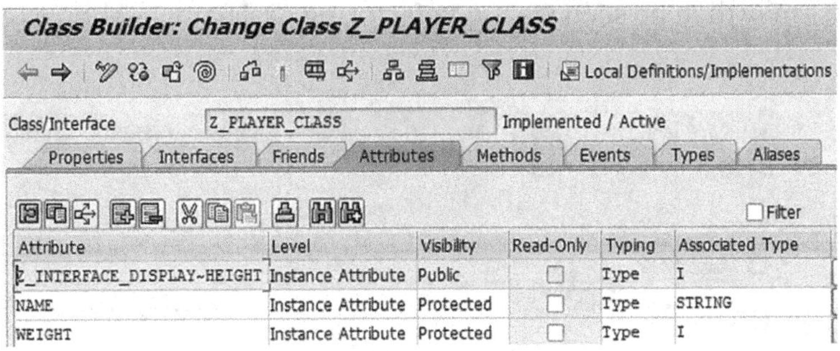

Figure 6-16. *HEIGHT attribute*

After activating the interface, when you try to activate the Z_PLAYER_CLASS class, the class will give a syntax error. This is because the constructor addresses the HEIGHT attribute using ME->HEIGHT, as shown here:

```
method CONSTRUCTOR.
        me->name = name.
        me->height = height.  ""ERROR
        me->weight = weight.
endmethod.
```

The constructor must be changed, as shown here:

```
method CONSTRUCTOR.
      me->name = name.
      Z_INTERFACE_DISPLAY~HEIGHT = height.
      me->weight = weight.
endmethod.
```

Alternatively, you may also define an alias based on the HEIGHT using the ALIAS tab of the Z_PLAYER_CLASS.

Once the change is made, you may activate the class.

Moving Components from a Class to an Associated Class

Another scenario in which the Refactoring Assistant may be used is when associations exist between classes. This means that within a class another class has been referenced as an attribute using TYPE REF TO.

Consider the example where we have an empty class called ZST_ASSOC_CLASS that has been referenced in an attribute residing in the class. Once this association exists, the associated class may then be seen via the Refactoring Assistant, as shown in Figure 6-17.

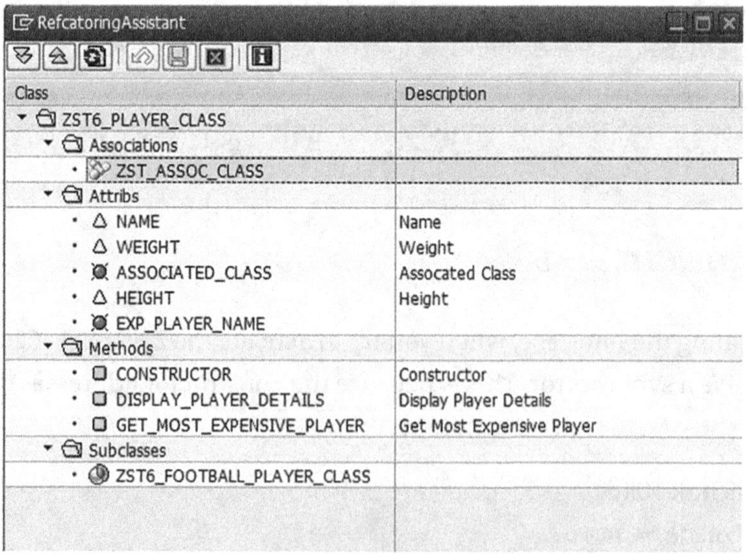

Figure 6-17. *ZST6_PLAYER_CLASS class in the Refactoring Assistant*

Suppose in our ZST6_PLAYER_CLASS class, we have the EXP_PLAYER_NAME (attribute) and GET_MOST_EXPENSIVE (method) components. You may now drag and drop these two components to the associated class.

Once the transfer is done successfully, a message appears, as shown in Figure 6-18.

```
Method GET_MOST_EXPENSIVE_PLAYER has been moved to the class ZST_ASSOC_CLASS
Attribute EXP_PLAYER_NAME has been moved to the class ZST_ASSOC_CLASS
```

Figure 6-18. *Method and attributes transferred*

You may then adjust the code within the ZST6_PLAYER_CLASS class in order to address the components of the associated class.

Enhancement of Classes

SAP allows you to define enhancement (exits) for methods. This allows you to enhance the behavior of standard methods. In addition, using the enhancement concept, you may add new methods to the original class and call them in the defined exits. There are three possibilities, as listed here:

- **PreExit**. This method is called before the method in question is executed. Any code that you want to be executed before the actual method must be placed here. The code run may be used, for example, to supply additional data to the original method or to display an information message.

- **PostExit**. This method is executed after execution of the method under consideration. If there is any activity that you want to happen after, it should be placed within the PostExit method. Any activity that you want to happen after execution of the method must be placed here.

- **Overwrite-Exit**. This is used for overwriting (replacing) the original method. Once the Overwrite-Exit is defined, any program that calls the original method executes the overwrite method code and not the original method. For the Overwrite-Exit to be running without any errors, make sure that the PostExit and PreExit methods do not exist.

These can be used for enhancing methods residing in the standard SAP classes. However, for the sake of this illustration, we will enhance the global class ZST6_PLAYER_CLASS that we created earlier.

Now let's look at how we can modify the behavior of an already-defined global class. Two examples will be shown. Before we do that, we will first see the actual (original) output of the method. A simple block of code that uses the DISPLAY_PLAYER_DETAILS method is shown here:

```
NEW ZST6_FOOTBALL_PLAYER_CLASS(
        NAME = 'Oliver Kahn'
        WEIGHT = '88'
        HEIGHT = '178'
FOOTBALL_CLUB = 'Bayern Munich' )->DISPLAY_PLAYER_DETAILS( ).
```

The original output of the method (as in the code) is shown in Figure 6-19.

```
Player Name:  Oliver Kahn
Height    :   178
Weight    :   88
Club Name :   Bayern Munich
```

Figure 6-19. *Original method output*

Example 1. PreExit and PostExit Methods

The first example will be based on PreExit and PostExit methods for the DISPLAY_PLAYER_DETAILS method of the ZST6_FOOTBALL_PLAYER_CLASS. We will now use both of these exits to change the output of the DISPLAY_PLAYER_DETAILS method.

Call transaction SE24, enter the name of the class that is to be enhanced (in our case ZST6_PLAYER_CLASS) in the field provided, and click the Display button. Initially, the enhancement menu options will be disabled, as shown in Figure 6-20.

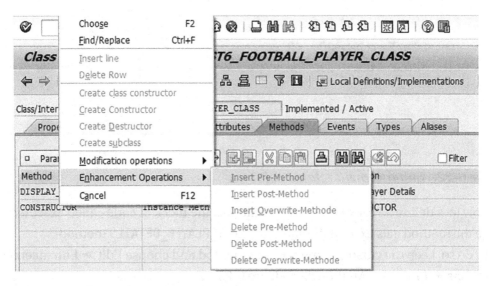

Figure 6-20. *Enhancement Operations menu*

From the screen that appears, click the  button from the application toolbar. This will display the dialog box shown in Figure 6-21.

Figure 6-21. *Enhancement implementation creation*

Enter the name of the enhancement and the short text in the fields provided and then click the Continue button.

This will enable the enhancement menu options. In addition, on the Methods tab for each method, three columns (PreExit, PostExit, and Overwrite-Exit) will also be displayed. See Figure 6-22.

Description	PreExit	PostExit	Overwrite-Exit
Display Player Details			
CONSTRUCTOR			

Figure 6-22. *Enhancement related columns*

Now let's define a PreExit method PreExit (i.e., the block of code called executed before the method gets executed) for our DISPLAY_PLAYER_DETAILS method.

To do so, keep the cursor on the relevant method and choose Edit ➤ Enhancement Operations ➤ Insert Pre-Method. See Figure 6-23.

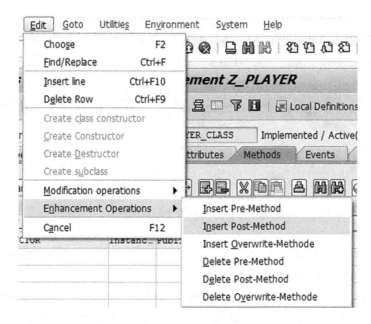

Figure 6-23. *Enhancement Operations menu path*

This will create a PreExit method. A button will now appear for the respective method under the column PreExit method, as shown in Figure 6-24.

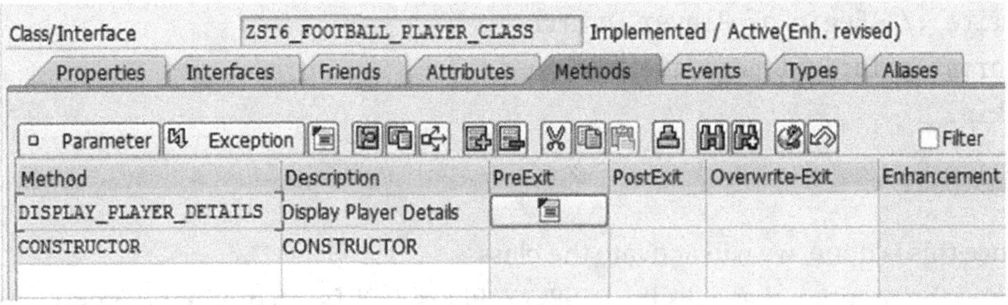

Figure 6-24. *PreExit column shown with a new button*

Click the   button to go to the source code editor, as shown in Figure 6-25.

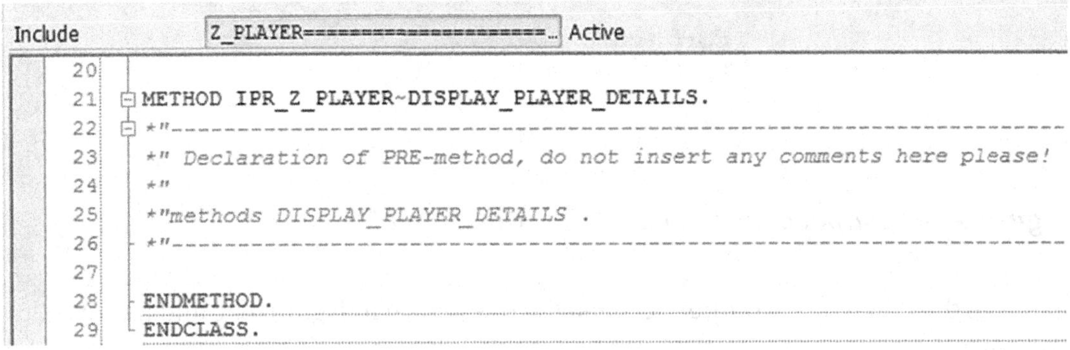

Figure 6-25. *PreExit method editor*

As you can see when the PreExit method is created, an interface by the name IPR followed by the enhancement we create (Z_PLAYER) has been generated. Within this exists the DISPLAY_PLAYER_DETAILS method. For our example, we will write simple code to add the heading Begin of Player Details displayed in red. The code is shown as follows:

```
method ipr_z_player~display_player_details.
*"------------------------------------------------------------*
*" Declaration of PRE-method, do not insert any comments here please!
*"
*"methods DISPLAY_PLAYER_DETAILS
```

```
*"------------------------------------------------------------*
    skip.
    format color col_negative on.
    write :/ 'Begin of Player Details'.
    format color col_negative off.
    skip.

  endmethod.
```

Once this is done, we will activate the class.

When the program that calls the DISPLAY_PLAYER_DETAILS original method of the ZST6_FOOTBALL_PLAYER_CLASS is executed, the PreExit method is automatically invoked. The output of the method call is displayed as shown in Figure 6-26.

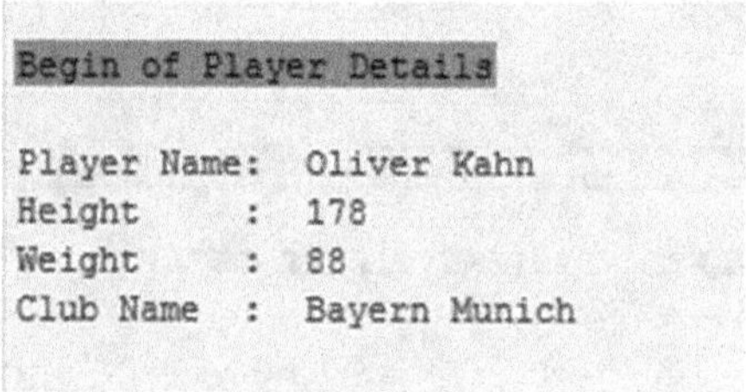

Figure 6-26. *Output of method with PreExit method*

Note the difference in output between the one shown in Figure 6-20 and this one (Figure 6-26).

Now let's define the PostExit method for our DISPLAY_PLAYER_DETAILS method. This will be executed after the original method has executed. We will follow the similar steps shown earlier. In this case, however, we will use Enhancement Operations ➤ Insert Post-Exit. Simply place the cursor on the method and then choose the given menu path. This will now enable the [🖿   ] button in the PostExit column. We may then click the button to go to the editor and write the code for the PostExit method.

```
method ipo_z_player~display_player_details.
*"------------------------------------------------------------*
*" Declaration of POST-method, do not insert any comments here please!
*"
*"methods DISPLAY_PLAYER_DETAILS .
*"------------------------------------------------------------*
```

```
*"------------------------------------------------------------*
    skip.
    format color COL_POSITIVE on.
    write :/ 'End of Player Details'.
    format color COL_POSITIVE off.
    skip.

  endmethod.
ENDCLASS.
```

In this case, we see that the PostExit is a method residing in the interface having the name beginning with IPO followed by our enhancement option Z_PLAYER. Enter the code that you like to run after the DISPLAY_PLAYER_DETAILS method has executed. We will insert a single line of code to print the message End of player Details. Save and activate your class.

Once the original method is executed, the final output (of the PreExit, Original Method, and the PostExit) is shown in Figure 6-27.

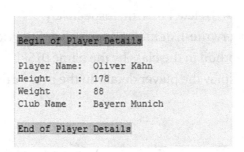

Figure 6-27. *New output of method execution*

After the PreExit method, the DISPLAY_METHOD_DETAILS original method is executed. After completion of DISPLAY_METHOD_DETAILS, the PostExit method is called. Figure 6-28 shows the sequence of execution of the three methods in our example.

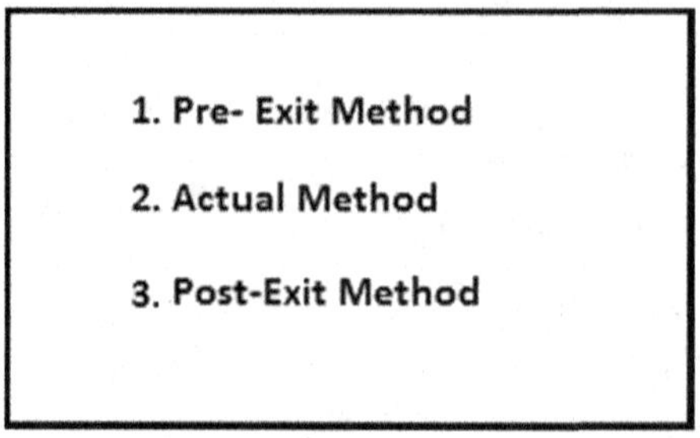

> 1. Pre- Exit Method
>
> 2. Actual Method
>
> 3. Post-Exit Method

Figure 6-28. *Method execution sequence*

Example 2. Overwrite Method

We will now use the Overwrite-Exit (only) to change the output of the DISPLAY_PLAYER_
DETAILS method. The final output will be the same as the one shown earlier, achieved via
the Pre- and PostExit methods.

As a prerequisite of the step required in creating the overwrite method, we need to
delete the Pre- and PostExit methods, if they exist. Make sure that enhancement mode
is on. Then choose Edit ➤ Enhancement Operations ➤ Delete PreExit and Edit ➤
Enhancement Operations ➤ Delete PostExit, respectively.

Before creating the Overwrite-Exit method, we will define, via enhancement
implementation, a new method in the class by the name DISPLAY_PLAYER_DETAILS_NEW
(see Figure 6-29). It will display the player details in the new format. We will then call this
method in Overwrite-Exit.

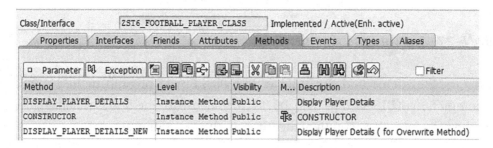

Figure 6-29. *The DISPLAY_PLAYER_DETAILS_NEW method*

The code of the new method is shown in Figure 6-30.

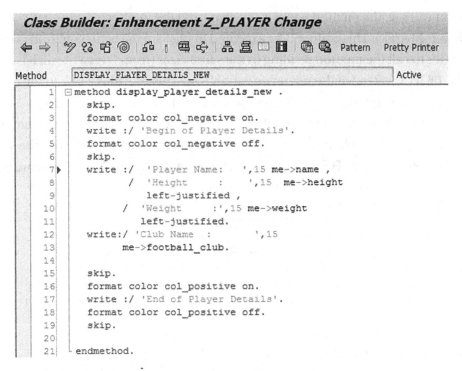

```
Class Builder: Enhancement Z_PLAYER Change

⇐ ⇒  ⍺ ⅋ ⊞ ◎   ⌂    ⊟ ⇨   ⊞ ⊟ ▢ ⓘ   ⅏ ⅏   Pattern   Pretty Printer

Method    DISPLAY_PLAYER_DETAILS_NEW                              Active

 1  ⊟ method display_player_details_new .
 2      skip.
 3      format color col_negative on.
 4      write :/ 'Begin of Player Details'.
 5      format color col_negative off.
 6      skip.
 7▶     write :/  'Player Name:    ',15 me->name ,
 8              /  'Height     :    ',15  me->height
 9                 left-justified ,
10              /  'Weight       :',15 me->weight
11                 left-justified.
12      write:/ 'Club Name   :       ',15
13                me->football_club.
14
15      skip.
16      format color col_positive on.
17      write :/ 'End of Player Details'.
18      format color col_positive off.
19      skip.
20
21  └ endmethod.
```

Figure 6-30. *Code of the DISPLAY_PLAYER_DETAILS_NEW method*

In addition to the main block of player details printing, we added a header and footer in red and green, respectively. Save and activate your method.

Next, we create the overwrite method. To create the overwrite method, we use Edit ➤ Enhancement Operations ➤ Overwrite-Exit. This will enable the [   ] button in the Overwrite column.

We then use the [   ] button to go to the Overwrite-Exit editor. We enter the following code there.

```
method iow_z_player~display_player_details.
*"------------------------------------------------------------*
*" Declaration of Overwrite-method, do not insert any comments here please!
*"
*"methods DISPLAY_PLAYER_DETAILS .
*"------------------------------------------------------------*
  core_object->display_player_details_new( ).
endmethod.
```

As you will see, the method name is the same and the interface begins with OVR (and then Z_PLAYER). This code will be executed in place of the actual method code.

In order to call the method residing in the same class (from Overwrite-Exit), use the CORE_OBJECT instead of the reference variable me. This provides a link to the current object in question. You cannot use the me variable in Overwrite-Exit.

Once the method is activated and the entire class activated, all programs that refer to the DISPLAY_PLAYER_DETAILS original method will now be calling the Overwrite-Exit and the DISPLAY_PLAYER_DETAILS_NEW method. The output of this is shown in Figure 6-31.

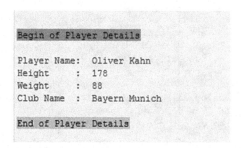

Figure 6-31. *Final overwrite output*

Statements/Constructs Not Allowed in Object-Oriented ABAP

Code within ABAP Objects has a number of restrictions. Many statements (or variants of statements), for example, may not be allowed in the method of classes. These may not give any errors when used outside ABAP Objects.

In this final section of this chapter, I look into a few statements (or constructs) that are not allowed in the context of ABAP Objects. These constructs will return a syntax error when used in local and global classes. They are explained in the following subsections.

Naming Variables

Within ABAP Objects, variable names can only contain letters ranging from A to Z and numbers 0 to 9, as well as an underscore (-). In addition, variable names cannot begin with a number (such as 1_abc).

Any attempt to break these guidelines will raise a syntax error. A typical example of this is shown here:

```
data : 1_abc(1) type c .
"" not allowed
```

The following is not permissible since FIELD-1 contains a dash, as shown here:

```
data : field-1 type i .
"" not allowed
```

Using Logical Operators

In ABAP Objects, using logical operators ><, =<, and => is prohibited. This includes use of IF statements as well as the WHERE clause used in open SQL statements, and the WHERE or LOOP statements executed on internal tables.

```
    if name >< 'Adrian'.    "" not allowed
...
    endif.
```

If you try to use any of these, the code will give the syntax error shown in Figure 6-32.

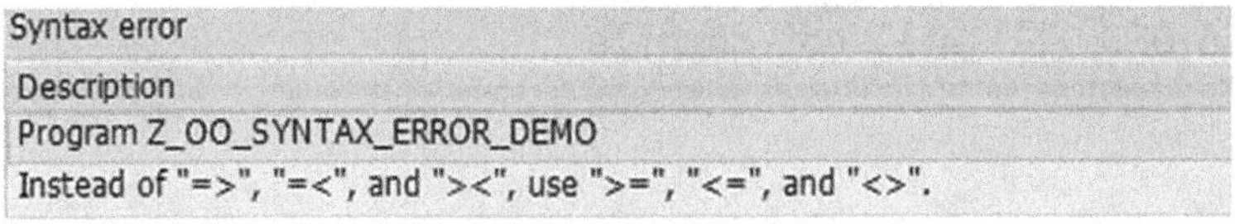

Syntax error
Description
Program Z_OO_SYNTAX_ERROR_DEMO
Instead of "=>", "=<", and "><", use ">=", "<=", and "<>".

Figure 6-32. *Syntax error*

Instead of the operators mentioned, use <>, <=, and >= (or their equivalents NE, LE, and GE, respectively).

CASE Statement Usage

A CASE..ENDCASE block should be semantically equivalent to an IF..ELSEIF
control structure. No statement (or statements) must be placed before the first WHEN in a
CASE... ENDCASE control structure. In ABAP Objects, this is not permitted. Consider the
following block of code:

```
CASE INT.
   A = 2.   " statement gives error
  WHEN 1.
     WRITE INT.
  WHEN OTHERS.
     WRITE 'OTHERS'.
ENDCASE.
```

Using ON CHANGE OF

The ON CHANGE OF statement is not allowed within ABAP Objects. This will give a syntax
error when used in the code of a class method. For example, consider the following:

```
METHOD MY_PLAYERS.
  LOOP AT.
    ON CHANGE OF.   """ will not compile
    ENDON
   ENDLOOP.
ENDMETHOD.
```

Instead of the ON CHANGE OF construct, use temporary variables that store values and
then check for the change in their values using an IF statement.

Restrictions to Using the TYPES Statement

While defining types within a method via the TYPES statement, you must specify the type
of character types. For example, the following is unacceptable:

```
TYPES TY_C.   """ error
```

The correct form of this is shown here:

```
TYPES: TY_C TYPE c length 1.
```

In addition, the length of TYPES based on the elementary types P, N, and X must also be specified.

In the case of P types, specifying the number of decimal places is also important. For example, the following code will give an error:

```
TYPES TY_2 TYPE p length 8. ""Error
```

The correct form is shown here:

```
TYPES TY_2 TYPE p length 8 DECIMALS 0.
```

It must be also noted that for these data types—T(Time), D(Date), I(Integer), and F(Floating)—length may not be specified. This is because these data types have predefined lengths that cannot be changed.

Restrictions to Using DATA Declarations and Constants

Within ABAP Objects, it is not possible to specify a length for the definition of variables, or constants that are based on the elementary data types T(Time), D(Date), I(Integer), or F(Floating). These data types have predefined lengths that cannot be changed. Consider the following examples:

```
DATA DATE1(10) TYPE d.  "" syntax error
DATA INT1(10) TYPE i.   "" syntax error
```

Both these statements will issue syntax errors.

Untyped Field-Symbols

In an OO context, the TYPE addition must always be used while declaring FIELD-SYMBOLS. If the type is not specified, at least the TYPE ANY addition must be used. For example, the following declaration is not allowed and will result in a syntax error:

```
FIELD-SYMBOLS <field1>.  """"not allowed
```

Internal Table-Related Statements

As with other syntax issues, a number of things must be kept in mind while programing with internal tables in ABAP Objects. Let's review them them one by one.

One major restriction is that no code must be written that creates a header line internal table with a header line. Internal tables with headers are not supported within the OO context. Consider for example the following block of code:

```
data : begin of itab occurs 0,
   "" not allowed
     field_1,
   end of itab.
```

This code will give a syntax error. In addition, you are not allowed to read an internal table without a work area with a READ TABLE statement. The following form is not permissible:

```
READ TABLE MYITAB.
```

Looping on an internal table using LOOP AT ITAB (without a work area) is not allowed. This is shown here:

```
loop at itab.
  ...
endloop.
```

In addition, we may not even use the CLEAR ITAB statement within a LOOP as shown here:

```
LOOP AT ITAB INTO WA_ITAB.
  CLEAR ITAB.  """ syntax error
ENDLOOP.
```

Some other constructs that are not allowed while programming with internal tables in object-oriented context are shown here:

```
INSERT TABLE itab.
COLLECT itab.
MODIFY TABLE itab ...
MODIFY itab ... WHERE ...
```

Database Table-Related Statements

The database-related statements also have some restrictions within the realm of ABAP Objects. Let's look at a few examples.

The TABLES statement may not be used in a method, for example. This may result in a syntax error, as shown in the following line of code:

```
tables: lfa1 .
```

While using SELECT statements, it is absolutely mandatory to use an INTO clause. (Even when using Dynamic Open SQL, the INTO clause must never be omitted.) Consider the following block of code:

```
SELECT * FROM LFA1."""  NOT ALLOWED
ENDSELECT.
```

In ABAP Objects, the following statements are not allowed and will result in an error message:

```
SELECT ... FROM DBTABLENAME ...
```

```
INSERT DBTABLENAME.
```

```
UPDATE DBTABLENAME.
```

```
DELETE DBTABLENAME.
```

A few correct and acceptable form of statements are shown here:

```
DATA MYWA TYPE DBTABLENAME.
SELECT ... FROM DBTABLENAME INTO MYWA.
```

```
INSERT DBTABLENAME FROM MYWA.
```

```
INSERT INTO DBTABLENAME VALUES MYWA.
```

Untyped Method Parameters

Within ABAP Objects, the TYPE addition is necessary for all parameters of methods. The following form of definition is not allowed:

```
METHODS MYMETHOD IMPORTING param1
                 EXPORTING param2. ""ERROR
```

This is not acceptable and will result in a syntax error. An acceptable form is shown here:

```
METHODS meth IMPORTING p1 TYPE I
                EXPORTING p2 TYPE I.
```

If you are not sure of the type to which the parameters belong, you may keep them as generic. In this case, TYPE ANY must be specified. An acceptable form is shown here:

```
METHODS mymethod IMPORTING p1 TYPE ANY        EXPORTING p2 TYPE ANY.
```

In addition, while specifying the types of formal parameters of a method, the STRUCTURE addition should not be used. The following statement, for example, will cause a syntax error:

```
    METHODS mymethod
  IMPORTING param1 STRUCTURE struct1.
```

An acceptable form of this is shown here:

```
  METHODS mymethod
  IMPORTING param1 TYPE struct1.
```

Summary

In this chapter, we discussed the NEW operator, which is used to create objects, and the ALV object model, which is used to create reports. We also covered various ALV classes and methods along with a practical code demo. Then, we discussed how method chaining is possible and enables you to write compact code. An example of ALV-related code written in conjunction with method chaining was discussed. We also covered object-oriented transactions, followed by the Refactoring Assistant tool in the Class Builder. A detailed discussion on the various ways a class can be enhanced was included. Finally, we went over a number of constructs and statements in detail that are not allowed in the ABAP Objects arena.

CHAPTER 7

ABAP Unit Test-Driven Development

An important topic that remains to be discussed is testing the methods and code that we write. SAP provides the unit test framework embedded in ABAP. In this chapter, we learn in detail about the following topics:

- Unit testing advantages

- Defining unit classes

- Exception handling in unit testing

- Using the unit test browser

We will start with a brief explanation of testing and its various types. We will then see what unit testing and test-driven development are. We will also cover the advantages of unit testing. We will then cover creation of the unit test method and classes in detail and the relevant coding and class and methods involved. Finally, we will see a full-fledged programming demo.

We cover how to execute the unit test and check results with and without the Code Inspector. We end the chapter with a note on the unit test browser that is available for searching and displaying unit test classes residing in the ABAP system.

Testing Need and Phases

Before going into the details of unit testing, let's first see why the need for testing arises in program development.

© Rehan Zaidi 2019
R. Zaidi, *SAP ABAP Objects*, https://doi.org/10.1007/978-1-4842-4964-2_7

Within a project's development lifecycle, there may be a number of stages and phases. There is a need to test programs or products in both the development and integration stages.

Testing products is a necessary activity and has a number of advantages:

- There is less chance of bugs and problems arising in the product. Testing allows us to make a more accurate and better quality product for our customers.

- Good testing done in the early stages is more cost effective than later testing.

- Testing improves customers' confidence in the products.

Before moving forward, let's discuss the various levels of testing. There are a number of levels in software testing:

1. **Unit testing.** This is the initial testing level. Basic (individual) units of codes are checked in order to ensure they work as required. Each code portion is subjected to a set of test scenarios or cases. Unit testing may be done manually or be automated. However, developers usually perform automated tests.

2. **Integration component testing.** As the name indicates, this checks the integration testing of different units (or modules) that have been unit tested. These are grouped in a number of ways to confirm the correctness of integration and communication.

3. **System/UI testing.** This emphasizes the UI (User Interface) and can be done manually or via automated tools. It confirms the characteristics and state of the user interface elements. This may be done by sets of test cases.

4. **Acceptance testing.** This is based on the Quality **Assurance** (QA) approach and determines which features of an application work (or do not work). The team has the option to discover and test the applications(s) in real-time. Usually, test cases are not made in advance. While testing, the team decides which application is next to be tested and how many days are to be given to a feature during the testing phase.

Note   Other than unit testing, the internal details of an application are visible as a "black box" to the test team during the testing stage.

Basics of ABAP Unit Test Driven Development

The unit test ABAP unit framework provides an automated mechanism within the ABAP programming language for carrying out test driven development. In test-based development, we first write a code block carrying the production code. We then write tests to check the correctness, by comparing the Expected Value and the Actual value returned. Finally, we refactor code so that it passes the test. All this may occur in cycles, i.e. our code may go through many cycles and iterations, such as test writing, changing production code, and then test execution (see Figure 7-1).

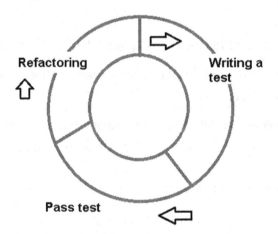

Figure 7-1. *Test driven development cycle*

While writing the test code, we must keep in mind several aspects pertaining to the requirements, code test, and production methods. These aspects include definition of the attributes and the method parameters.

As mentioned, there are two separate methods—test methods and production methods. The production methods are also called the *methods under test*, whereas the class where the production code resides is known as the *class under test*.

Every time we want to check a small unit and its functioning is working as normal, we use unit testing. A unit is simply termed the smallest testable part of an application. This can be a class or a method, which can be separated from the other code while being checked if it functions correctly.

You should also consider and manually compute the expected result corresponding to the respective inputs. For example, if you have a method for doubling a number, we can first expected value $(2 * X)$. We can then compare this with the actual value computed by the program code.

We specify the *Risk Level* and *Duration* test properties while designing the test. Risk level, as the name indicates, is the risk of the test.

While running the tests, SAP checks the risk level with the level that's predefined within the client setting. If our test has a bigger risk level, the ABAP framework will not run the test in question. For risk levels, one of the three following values may be set:

- **Harmless.** As the name indicates, executing this test will not affect a process and will not make any changes to the database. This is the default.

- **Dangerous/alarming.** Such tests change data in the database.

- **Critical.** These are the critical tests and changes that customize the database/persistent data.

As far as Duration goes, the ABAP unit framework does not run tests with a higher duration than that specified in the client level configuration in the `SAUNIT_CLIENT_SETUP` transaction.

The Duration may have the following values:

- **Short.** Refers to tests that run very quickly (default setting at the client level). Typically, this is less than 60 seconds.

- **Medium.** Refers to tests running slightly longer than short values. These lie in the range of 60 to 600 seconds.

- **Long.** These tests take a considerable amount of time to execute; more than 600 seconds.

The unit test class definition has the following form.

```
CLASS Abap_Unit_Testclass DEFINITION FOR TESTING
    "#AU Duration Short
    "#AU Risk_Level Harmless
.
```

As of Release 702 (Release 7.0 Enhancement Pack 2), the unit class definition has the following form:

```
CLASS Abap_Unit_Testclass DEFINITION FOR TESTING
    DURATION SHORT
    RISK LEVEL HARMLESS
```

Unit Test Benefits

Unit tests have a number of advantages. Unit tests:

- Are very fast in execution. Many thousands of tests can be executed per second.

- Emphasize small portions of the product.

- Are written separately from the production code.

Unit tests cover 75 to 85 percent of the code. They are fast and accurate. Unit tests help point to the exact location where the code is buggy. Consistent unit test repetition helps make an application more stable and perform better.

In contrast to the other tests mentioned earlier, when using unit testing you need to have a good knowledge of system architecture. Unit testing is referred to gray box (or white box) testing and are defined by the ABAP developer.

Like other programming languages, ABAP has a unit testing framework. Within the framework, the processes needed for testing are embedded into the IDE. This allows developers to run unit tests in each compilation of the test program.

Unit tests do not interact with external coding or external systems. They are executed in a secluded environment. Unit tests are typically run on test methods, which reside in test classes.

As a developer you should make sure that you program in a manner that makes it fast and easy for you to create unit tests.

- Unit testing is applicable in situations where carrying out tests serves a definite purpose or meaning. Usually, the business layer is good for executing tests and is where unit testing mainly focuses.

- You must code automated tests as well as testable code. After executing the unit tests, you can amend the source code in order to fix bugs and bring the code to a testable state.

- You have to ensure that when a correction is done in one unit that no other code units are affected.

A test method can have a number of input (importing) parameters and usually a single output parameter. You can use transactions SE38 and SE80 to create an ABAP unit. You also have another option for doing unit testing in the ABAP Unit Framework, which is via the Eclipse IDE. This is contained in the ABAP Development Tools (ADT), so you need to only install the respective add-on in Eclipse. We discuss unit test using Eclipse in Chapter 8.

Within the "then" portion of the test method, the resulting value is checked by comparing the expected value with the actual value the method under test returns. If the two results differ, the ABAP Test Framework issues an error. Say we have a class called CL_AUNIT_ASSERT, which provides a number of utility methods. For comparison purposes, we use the ASSERT_EQUALS method of the CL_AUNIT_ASSERT class.

The main challenge is to figure out the cases to cover during testing. Unit tests are made by the developer, since the developer who coded the product is the best person to know how the functionality can be tested. When we do ample testing of the small parts of our product, there will be less time and effort needed in debugging and fixing issues later on.

Demo Example

As mentioned earlier, the ABAP Unit Framework allows developers to test program coding at the unit level, i.e., check each unit code independently and separately without worrying about the entire solution. Checking these smaller units ensures that when they are all put together into a bigger solution, they will function without error. This unit framework allows us to use what is called the *test-driven development* approach.

Now let's look at a simple example of a requirement in which we will use the unit test framework. Consider this simple code:

```
class my_class definition .
  public section.
    methods square importing int1         type i
                   returning value(sq_in) type i .
endclass.

class my_class implementation.
  method square.
    sq_in = int1 * int1.
  endmethod.
endclass.
```

Our code has a class called my_class and has a method called SQUARE. The purpose of the method is to square the number it imports and return the square as a parameter. The square method is called the *production method,* whereas my_class is referred to as the *production class* in the Unit Test Framework.

We will now code a class to act as a test class. We call this mytestclass. In order to code it, we need to add FOR TESTING to the method definition. Likewise, we add the keyword FOR TESTING to our CHECK_SQUARE method to designate it as a test method. These additions separate the class from the productive code.

We also add pseudo comments #AU Risk_Level and #AU Duration:

```
CLASS mytestclass DEFINITION FOR TESTING
  Risk Level Harmless
  Duration   Short
.

  PUBLIC SECTION.
    METHODS check_square FOR TESTING.
ENDCLASS.
```

Note   Before ABAP 7.02, pseudo comments allowed the framework to learn about the ABAP unit class. From 7.02 onward, we use addition RISK LEVEL and DURATION in the class definition.

Recall that the risk level can be critical, dangerous, or harmless and the duration can be short, medium, and long.

Now that we have our test class ready, let's implement the test method. For testing the code, we need to:

1. Create an object of my_class.

2. Call the SQUARE method of this class. A value will be supplied to the method and the result will be calculated in the method and returned (if we supplied 10, we would expect a squared value of 100 to be returned).

3. Compare the actual value returned from the square method to our expected result.

    If these two match, no error is present.

    On the other hand, if actual and expected result do not match, we need to inform the ABAP Unit Framework of this erroneous state.

4. For this, we use methods of the standard class CL_AUNIT_ASSERT. In our example we will use the ASSERT_EQUALS method of this class.

All this is shown in the following code:

```
CLASS mytestclass IMPLEMENTATION.
  METHOD check_square .
    DATA:  obj TYPE REF TO my_class.
    DATA:  square TYPE i.

    CREATE OBJECT obj.
    square  = obj->square( 10 ).

    cl_aunit_assert=>assert_equals(
        EXP               = 100
        act               = square
        msg               = 'Wrong Result'
           ).
  ENDMETHOD.

ENDCLASS.
```

As you can see, we called the `square` method. We then call the `ASSERT_EQUALS` method. This method has three parameters—expected (`EXP`), actual (`AC`), and message (`MSG`). We supply the expected value 100 to the method, the actual value of the square computed by the test method `square`, and the message to be displayed if the values do not match.

Note   It is not mandatory for a test method to have this pattern. We show this style for consistency and better understanding

---

The complete code for our requirements is as follows.

```
class my_class definition .
  public section.
    methods square importing int1         type i
                    returning value(sq_in) type i .
endclass.

class my_class implementation.
  method square.
    sq_in = int1 * int1.
  endmethod.
endclass.

CLASS mytestclass DEFINITION FOR TESTING
  Risk Level Harmless
  Duration   Short
.

  PUBLIC SECTION.
    METHODS check_square FOR TESTING.
ENDCLASS.

CLASS mytestclass IMPLEMENTATION.
  METHOD check_square .
    DATA:  obj TYPE REF TO my_class.
    DATA:  square TYPE i.

    CREATE OBJECT obj.
```

```
    square  = obj->square( 10 ).

    cl_aunit_assert=>assert_equals(
        EXP                  = 100
        act                  = square
        msg                  = 'Wrong Result'
            ).
  ENDMETHOD.

ENDCLASS.
```

Executing a Unit Test

Now that the code is complete, we will execute the unit test and check the results.

Before going into details, it is a good idea to look at the menu options within the ABAP transactions (class editor, program editor, and function module editor) that pertain to unit tests. Transactions SE37, SE80, and SE24 have separate menu options for executing unit tests:

- For Class Builder, use Class ➤ Unit Test.

- For programs using SE38, use Program ➤ Execute ➤ Unit Tests.

- For the Function Module (transaction SE37), use Function Module ➤ Test ➤ Unit Test.

For our code example shown in the last section, we would use the relevant menu option Program ➤ Execute ➤ Unit Tests. In our case, the expected and actual results are the same, so no error messages appear. Only one message will be displayed on the status bar, as shown in Figure 7-2.

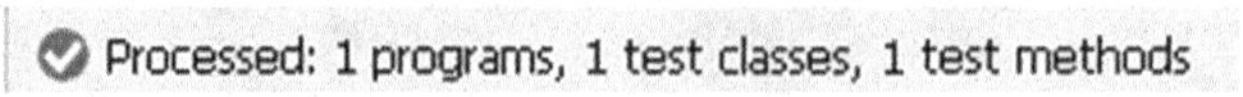

Figure 7-2. *Status message*

You may also choose Execute ➤ Unit Tests With ➤ Coverage in order to view the details. This is shown in Figure 7-3.

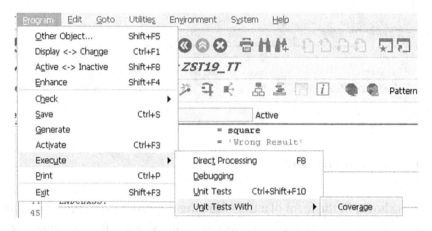

Figure 7-3. *Unit test menu option*

This will display results, as shown in Figure 7-4.

ABAP Unit: Result Display

ABAP Unit Results	Coverage Metrics

Task/Program/Class/Method	Status	Failed assertion	Exception error	Runtime abortion	Warning
✔ Test task: STUDENT01920190410200519	■	0	0	0	0
✔ ○ ZST19_TT	■	0	0	0	0
✔ ● MYTESTCLASS	■	0	0	0	0
• ⚙ CHECK_SQUARE (< 0.01 s)	■	0	0	0	0

Figure 7-4. *Coverage*

Now let's complicate things a little. As you see in our code, we have correctly used the square function. I will now purposely create an error by using addition instead of multiplication:

```
class my_class implementation.
  method square.
    sq_in = int1 + int1. ""   wrong should be *  and not +
  endmethod.
endclass.
```

If we rerun the unit test result, we will now get messages denoting something went wrong. These error messages are shown in Figure 7-5.

ABAP Unit: Result Display

Task/Program/Class/Method	Status	Failed assertion	Exception error	Runtime abortion	Warning
˅ Test task: STUDENT01920190410201023	●	1	0	0	0
˅ ○ ZST19_TT	●	1	0	0	0
˅ ● MYTESTCLASS	●	1	0	0	0
• ⓒ CHECK_SQUARE (< 0.01 s)	●	1	0	0	0

***Figure 7-5.** Unit result display*

The task is shown in the form of a tree showing the program name, class name, and method name. We also see the test class and method in which the problem has occurred. Here, we are also shown the number of failed assertion(s).

On the right-bottom part of screen (see Figure 7-6), we can see the actual and expected values shown as 20 and 100, respectively. This clearly shows the developer that the production method implementation is not correct. We also can display the line number where the error occurred. By simply double-clicking the line number, we can go to the exact line within the source code.

We also see the actual error message. Note the text Wrong Result was specified by us via the ASSERT_EQUALS method call (see Figure 7-6).

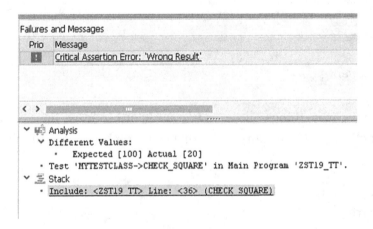

***Figure 7-6.** Failures and Messages window*

As mentioned earlier, there is a mistake in the implementation of the production method. Instead of multiplication. we used addition. Once we correct the method and rerun the test, the results will not show any error messages.

Methods in CL_ABAP_UNIT_ASSERT for Testing

The CL_ABAP_UNIT_ASSERT class has several methods, known as *assertion methods*. They are used to pass messages to the ABAP Unit engine.

Before moving forward, it is a good idea to understand the main methods provided by the the CL_ABAP_UNIT_ASSERT class. These methods are shown in Figure 7-7.

Class/Interface	CL_ABAP_UNIT_ASSERT		Implemented / Active				
Properties	Interfaces	Friends	Attributes	Methods	Events	Types	Aliases

Method	Level	Visibility	M...	Description
ABORT	Static Method	Public		Abort test execution due to missing context
ASSERT_BOUND	Static Method	Public		Ensure the validity of the reference
ASSERT_CHAR_CP	Static Method	Public		Ensure that character string fits to simple pattern
ASSERT_CHAR_NP	Static Method	Public		Ensure that character string does not fit to simple pattern
ASSERT_DIFFERS	Static Method	Public		
ASSERT_EQUALS	Static Method	Public		Ensure equality of two data objects
ASSERT_EQUALS_FLOAT	Static Method	Public		Ensure approximate consistency of 2 floating point numbers
ASSERT_FALSE	Static Method	Public		Ensure that boolean equals ABAP_FALSE
ASSERT_INITIAL	Static Method	Public		Ensure that data object value is initial
ASSERT_NOT_BOUND	Static Method	Public		Ensure invalidity of the reference of a reference variable
ASSERT_NOT_INITIAL	Static Method	Public		Ensure that value of data object is not initial
ASSERT_NUMBER_BETWEEN	Static Method	Public		Ensure that number is in given range
ASSERT_SUBRC	Static Method	Public		Ensure specific value of return code
ASSERT_TABLE_CONTAINS	Static Method	Public		Ensure that data is contained as line within internal table
ASSERT_TABLE_NOT_CONTAINS	Static Method	Public		Ensure that data is not contained as line in internal table

Figure 7-7. *Class methods*

Some of the more useful and commonly used methods are shown:

- ASSERT_EQUALS
- ASSERT_DIFFERS
- ASSERT_BOUND
- ASSERT_NOT_BOUND
- ASSERT_INITIAL
- ASSERT_NOT_INITIAL

- ASSERT_CHAR_CP

- ASSERT_CHAR_NP

- ASSERT_EQUALS_F

- FAIL

- ABORT

Let's look at the purpose of these methods:

- ASSERT_EQUALS. Checks if two data objects are equal.

- ASSERT_DIFFERS. Checks if two data objects are different.

- ASSERT_BOUND. Checks if the reference variable is pointing to a valid reference.

- ASSERT_NOT_BOUND. Checks for the invalidity (initial) of the reference of a reference variable.

- ASSERT_NOT_INITIAL. Determines whether a data object is storing its initial value.

- ASSERT_SUBRC. Determines whether the return code variable SY-SUBRC has a specific value.

Of special importance is the ASSERT_EQUALS method. It is the most commonly used method and is shown in Figure 7-8.

Class/Interface	CL_ABAP_UNIT_ASSERT				Implemented / Active			
Properties	Interfaces	Friends	Attributes	Methods	Events	Types	Aliases	

Parameters of Method				ASSERT_EQUALS			▲ ▼
← Methods	⚡	Exceptions	Sourcecode	Properties			

Parameter	Type	Pass ...	O...	Typing Method	Associated Type	D	Description
ACT	Importing	✓	☐	Type	ANY		Data object with current value
EXP	Importing	✓	☐	Type	ANY		Data object with expected type
IGNORE_HASH_SEQUENCE	Importing	☐	✓	Type	ABAP_BOOL	...	Ignore sequence in hash tables
TOL	Importing	☐	✓	Type	F		Tolerance Range (for directly passed f..
MSG	Importing	☐	✓	Type	CSEQUENCE		Description
LEVEL	Importing	☐	✓	Type	INT1	I..	Severity (TOLERABLE, CRITICAL, FAT..
QUIT	Importing	☐	✓	Type	INT1	I..	Alter control flow/ quit test (NO, >M..
ASSERTION_FAILED	Returning	✓	☐	Type	ABAP_BOOL		Condition was not met (and QUIT = ..

Figure 7-8. *Method parameters*

As mentioned earlier, it checks the equality of two variables. The parameters of the method are as follows:

- ACT. Actual result

- EXP. Expected result

- MSG. Message to be displayed

- LEVEL. Error level (tolerable/critical/fatal)

- Quit. Defines how the flow level is controlled when the test fails. Possible values of Quit include:

    - No (0). No action taken. The execution of the current test method continues.

    - Method (1). The test method is interrupted.

    - Class (2). The test class is interrupted.

    - Program (3). All test classes in the tested program are stopped.

- Level. Has the following values:

    - Tolerable

    - Critical

    - Fatal

- TOL. Tolerance

If the given tolerance is exceeded, an error is displayed. Let's see this with an example. Suppose we have the following values:

Actual result: 99

Expected result: 100

Tolerance specified as 0.9999

Difference = Expected Result - Actual Result

In this case, the difference is 100 – 99 = 1. Since 1 is greater than the tolerance limit (.9999), this is above the tolerance limit. Hence, an error would be displayed.

There are certain private methods employed within test classes that are provided by the Unit Test Framework. They include the test as well as the links required for running the tests. These methods are:

- SETUP( ). An instance method run prior to each test or execution of a test method.

- TEARDOWN( ). An instance method run after execution of a test method.

- CLASS_SETUP( ). A static method run once prior to all the tests of a given class. This is used for initializing variables that will be used in the tests.

- CLASS_TEARDOWN( ). A static method that is run after all tests of the class have been run. This is used for clearing any data variables used.

These optional methods are also known as *fixture methods*. These names are predefined so they can be recognized at execution time.

ABAP Unit Results in Code Inspector

We also can see the ABAP unit test results using the Code Inspector. Within the variant, we need to check the ABAP unit test within the Dynamic Tests category. Let's see how this is done.

First, we call transaction SCI. The screen shown in Figure 7-9 will appear.

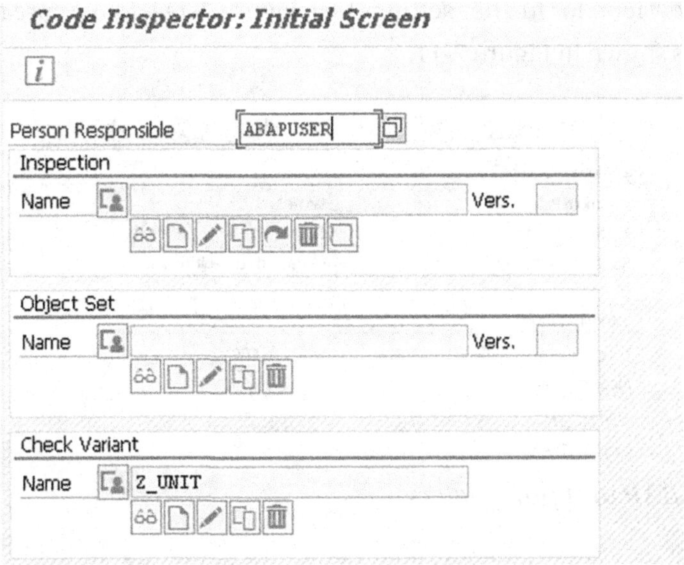

Figure 7-9. *SCI transaction*

Enter a suitable name for the check variant (in our case, it is Z_UNIT) and click the
Create button under the field provided. The screen shown in Figure 7-10 appears.

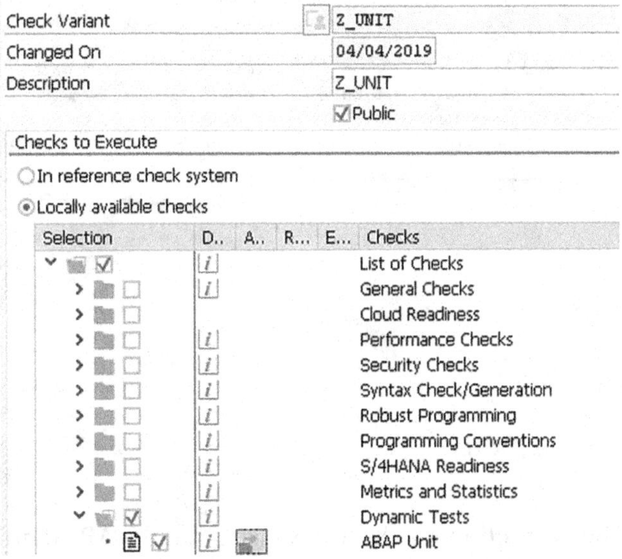

Figure 7-10. *Check variant*

Click the arrow icon for further settings (see Figure 7-11). Make sure to check the ABAP unit test as shown in Figure 7-11.

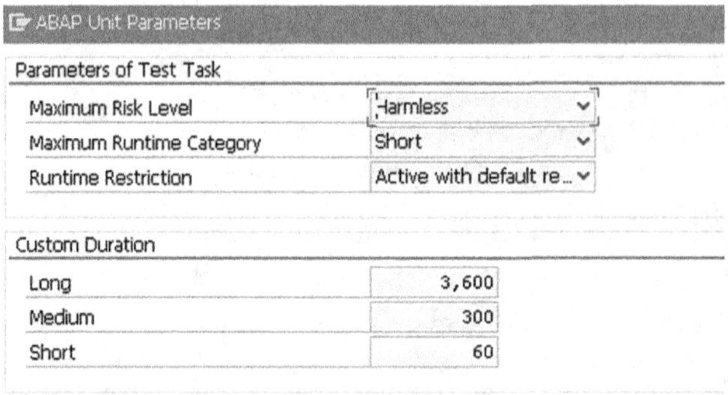

Figure 7-11. *ABAP unit parameters*

Once this is done, we can use this variant in our code inspections.

We will now create a code inspection ZS_1. For this code inspection, we assume that the object set ZS_2 already exists. The checks will be executed against that object set. We create an inspection using our variant Z_UNIT, as shown in Figure 7-12.

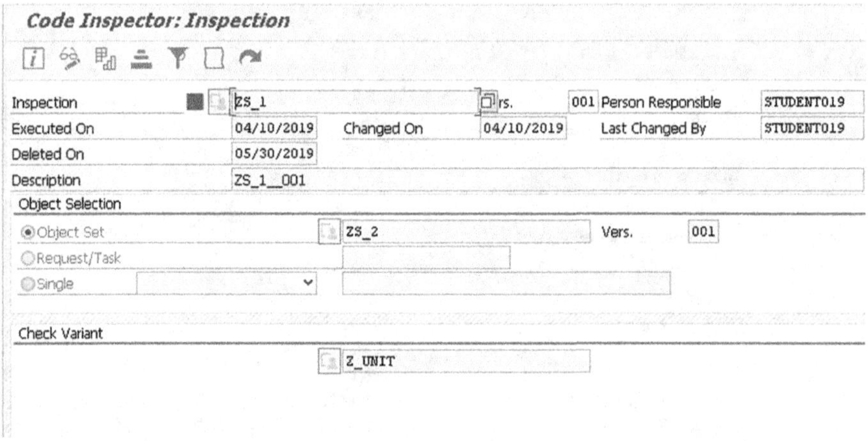

Figure 7-12. *Inspection ZS_1*

When we view the inspection results, we can see that the ABAP unit related errors, warnings, and other messages. This is shown in the Code Inspector results (see Figure 7-13).

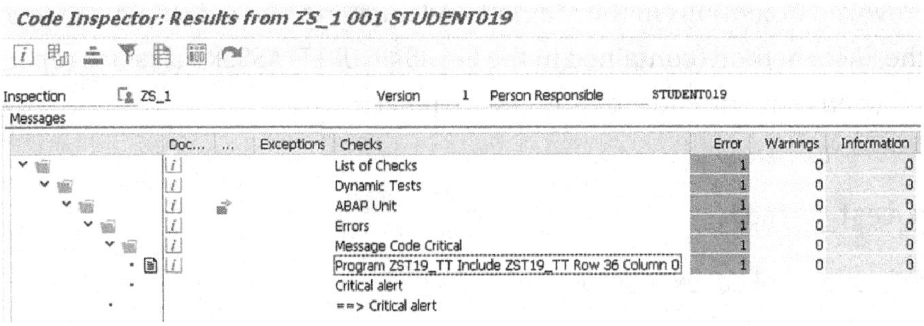

Figure 7-13. *Code Inspector results*

As an example, we have executed this inspection on the program we earlier created in the chapter involving squares. Clicking the message will take us to the exact location where the error occurred.

Exceptions in ABAP Unit Tests

As with classes in general, exceptions may occur in unit test classes as well. If an exception occurs with a method, the unit test fails. The exception may be reported as the reason for the failure. If the method declares and includes the exception in the signature, the test exception may be propagated to the ABAP runtime.

A preferred approach is that the test method declares the exception in a signature in order to clarify the functioning of the method. However, the exception should be caught in the test method.

```
METHODS m_test_method FOR TESTING
  RAISING cx_sy_zerodivide.
...
METHOD m_test_method.
  obj->division( num = 10 ).
...
ENDMETHOD.
```

For provoked exceptions in the method under testing, the developer can include a call to the FAIL method (contained in the CL_ABAP_UNIT_ASSERT class) to report the failure of a given test. The code for this is shown here:

```
...
METHOD m_test_method.

* catching a provoked exception
TRY.
  obj->division( num = 10 ).
...
  CATCH cx_sy_zerodivide.
ENDTRY.

cl_abap_unit_assert=>fail(
  msg = 'exception not raised'
  level = if_aunit_constants=>critical ).

ENDMETHOD.
```

Enabling and Executing ABAP Unit Browser

SAP provides an ABAP unit browser for searching and viewing unit test classes residing within the system. The ABAP unit browser is embedded in transaction SE80. By default, the ABAP unit browser is switched off, and should be first switched on in order to be used.

In this section, we learn how to enable the unit test browser and how to run it in order to view the various unit classes defined in our system. Follow these steps:

- Call transaction SE80. By default, the screen on the left side will appear, as shown in Figure 7-14.

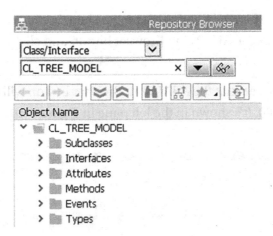

Figure 7-14. *SE80 transaction*

As you will see, there is only a Repository Browser button on
the top. We want to include a second button by the name Unit
Browser over here.

- Choose Utilities ➤ Settings. This will open the dialog box shown in
  Figure 7-15.

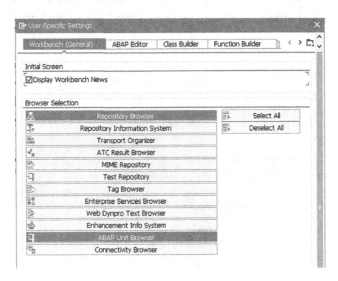

Figure 7-15. *User-specific settings*

- Click the Workbench (General) Settings. Then, in the browser selection, click the ABAP Unit Browser button and click the Continue button.

- Next, you will see that the ABAP Unit Browser button will appear, as shown in SE80. It's shown in the left pane in Figure 7-16.

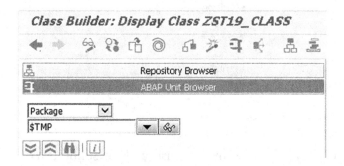

Figure 7-16. *ABAP unit browser*

- Now click the ABAP Unit Browser button and choose Package in the first list box. Enter $tmp in the field provided (see Figure 7-17). We will then click the Display button. (As an example, we will browse through local objects, so we have used $tmp.) Then, click the Display button.

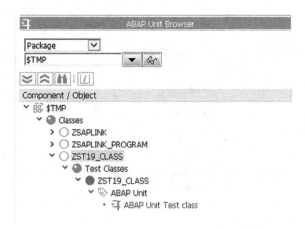

Figure 7-17. *ABAP unit browser*

- You will see that the various unit test classes appear, as shown in Figure 7-18. As a matter of example, we had earlier created a global test class by the name ZSt19_class.

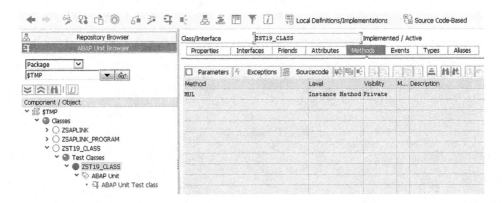

Figure 7-18. *ABAP unit test classes*

Double-clicking the unit class name in the left pane will show details of the class in the right pane.

Summary

In this chapter, we covered various types of testing. We learned what unit testing and test-driven development are and covered the advantages of unit testing. Finally, we saw a full-fledged programming demo. We also executed a unit test and checked the results with and without the Code Inspector. We ended the chapter with a note on the unit test browser, which is available for searching and displaying unit test classes residing in the ABAP system.

CHAPTER 8

Creating ABAP Classes Using Eclipse

In recent releases, SAP allows you to develop ABAP programs and classes using the popular Eclipse IDE. Eclipse provides a number of useful features. We can work with a number of systems using Eclipse. Eclipse also provides a number of useful templates that can be modified according to our needs. It also includes code completion features in order to work faster. In this chapter, we look at all these features in detail.

One of the main reasons we use Eclipse instead of the ABAP Editor is the ease of code completion and shortcuts that are not provided in the ABAP Editor. These allow developers to code programs faster.

Here are some of the topics this chapter addresses:

- Configuring the ABAP development environment with ABAP Development Tools (ADT) in Eclipse

- Creating your first ABAP project

- Using Eclipse to code unit test classes

- Using the Quick Fix feature of Eclipse with ABAP Objects

Installing Eclipse and Loading ABAP Perspective

In this section, we see how to install Eclipse and the ABAP Development tools (ADT) in order to develop ABAP classes and methods. Eclipse allows you to create programs (and local classes) as well as global classes (and unit test classes).

Before working with Eclipse, you need to download and install Eclipse from `www.eclipse.org`. Once Eclipse is installed, launch it using the desktop shortcut or via the Program list.

239

© Rehan Zaidi 2019
R. Zaidi, *SAP ABAP Objects*, https://doi.org/10.1007/978-1-4842-4964-2_8

We can now install the ABAP Development Tools for SAP NetWeaver. From the menu bar, choose Help ➤ Install New Software. The dialog box in Figure 8-1 will appear.

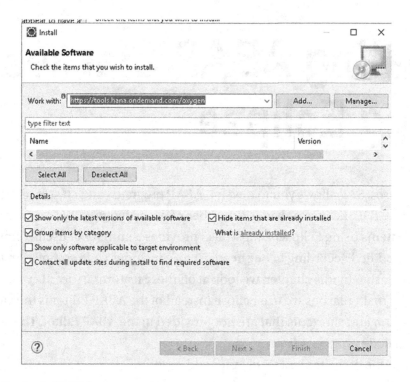

Figure 8-1. *Install dialog*

Within the dialog box that appears, place the URL relevant to the current version. For example, you use https://tools.hana.ondemand.com/oxygen for Eclipse Oxygen. Then press Enter in order to see the available options.

Select ABAP Development Tools for SAP NetWeaver and choose Next. On the next screen, you will be shown the features that will be installed. Choose Next. Accept the license agreement and click Finish in order to start the installation. This will install ABAP Development tools (ADT) on Eclipse.

Once ADT is installed, we need to open the ABAP perspective. Follow these steps to do so:

1. Close any Welcome page that appears. Choose the menu path Window ➤ Open Perspective ➤ Other. Alternately, you may click the ▦ button on the top-right corner, as shown in Figure 8-2.

Figure 8-2. *Open perspective*

This will display the dialog box shown in Figure 8-3.

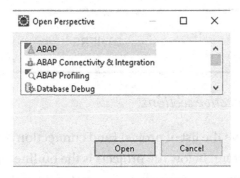

Figure 8-3. *Perspective lists*

2. Choose ABAP from the list and click Open. This will load the
   ABAP perspective.

   It is a good idea to familiarize yourself with the layout of the tools
   within the Eclipse IDE. The ABAP perspective has various tools
   that are arranged in order for you to work easily. You are free to
   change positions of views in order to suit your liking.

3. Go to the Project Explorer. The various sections in the Eclipse IDE
   (for the ABAP perspective) are shown in Figure 8-4.

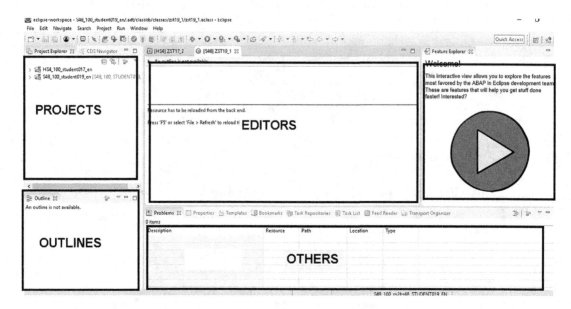

Figure 8-4. *ABAP perspective sections*

On the top-left, we have the list of project (and connection) nodes that list the various objects in that system. Below the projects is the outline window (showing the main structure and elements) of the selected object. On the right are the main editors for writing code for classes and programs, and under Editors is the window showing miscellaneous messages such as errors, warnings, and the program output in some cases.

Creating an ABAP Project in Eclipse

Within Eclipse, we need to have an ABAP project corresponding to SAP systems connections. Follow these steps:

Choose the menu path File ➤ New ➤ ABAP Project. The dialog box shown in Figure 8-5 will appear.

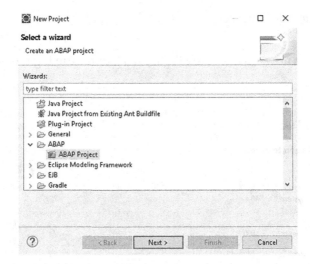

Figure 8-5. *Backend systems*

Choose the ABAP project under the ABAP node and click Next. The screen shown in Figure 8-6 appears.

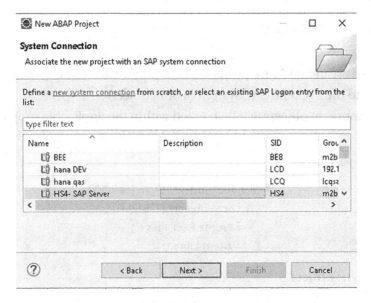

Figure 8-6. *System connection list*

Here you can either create a new system connection or select an existing one from the list. We assume that the connection is already there on our SAP Logon pad. From the list of backend systems, select the system you want to connect to and choose Next. The connection settings will appear.

On the Connection Settings screen, accept the default settings and click the Next button.

On the screen that now appears (see Figure 8-7), enter the login credentials and click the Finish button.

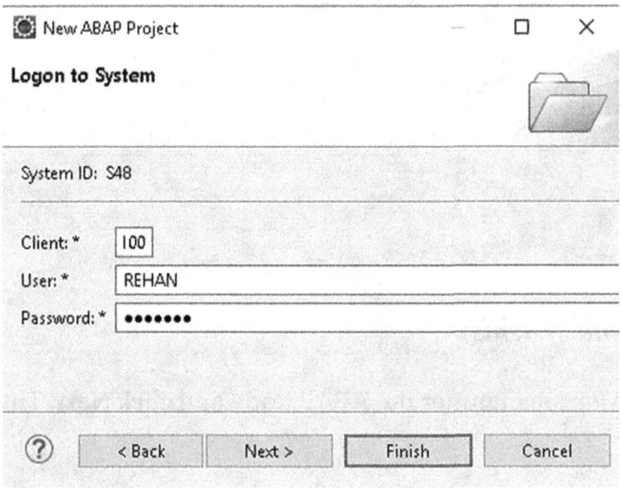

Figure 8-7. *Logon credentials*

This will then create the ABAP project, which is in the left pane. (It now corresponds to a connection to the backend SAP system of our choice.)

All our development objects will be created within the applicable projects. See Figure 8-8.

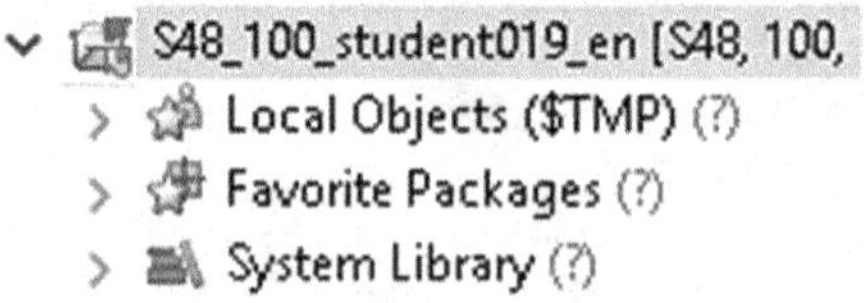

Figure 8-8. *ABAP project*

Creating a Global Class in Eclipse

In this section, we learn how to create a global class using Eclipse (same as the SE24 transaction). The required steps are described next.

First we select the project node we created earlier. Right-click to display the context menu. From the menu, choose the New ➤ ABAP class option. The dialog box in Figure 8-9 appears.

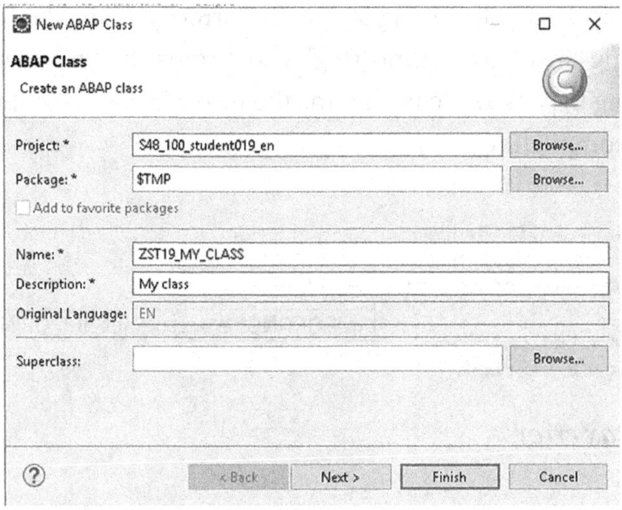

Figure 8-9.   *Dialog for the new ABAP class*

Enter a suitable name and description for the class and superclass (if applicable). Then click Next. On the next screen, click the Finish button.

This will generate the basic coding of the global class, as shown in Figure 8-10.

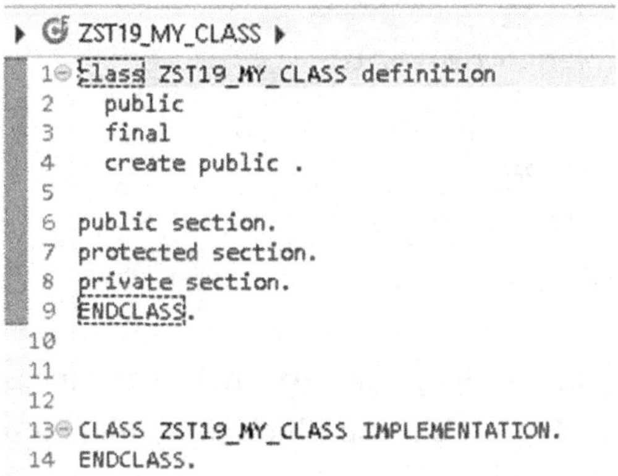

Figure 8-10.   *Basic generated code*

Here we can write the additional code we need to specify within the class. These may include public or private (or protected) methods, attributes, and events. We will add a private attribute called NUM with a type of integer. We will also add an instance constructor method along with an instance method called DISP_NUM.

Eclipse provides syntax help when you type incorrectly. Consider for example if we typed "imporing" instead of "importing". The error is shown as a red cross (see Figure 8-11). Keeping the cursor on it explains the error. These errors are shown during typing (i.e., before compilation).

```
 6  public section.
 7    methods disp_num .
 8    methods constructor imporing
 9                        "IMPORTING" expected, not "IMPORING".
10  protected section.
11  private section.
```

***Figure 8-11.** Syntax error*

Moreover, Eclipse makes it easy and quick to work with attributes and methods by providing autocomplete features. For example, consider a situation where we are in the code of a class constructor. If we type the self-referencing variable me followed by the -> operator, the popup appears, as shown in Figure 8-12.

```
17  CLASS ZST19_MY_CLASS IMPLEMENTATION.
18    method disp_num.
19        write : num .
20    endmethod.
21    method constructor.
22        me->|
                    □ num
   *Global Class    ● disp_num
```

***Figure 8-12.** Help popup*

Here we see the components of the class we are in. (In our case it is the NUM attribute and the DISP_NUM method.) We can choose which component is used by double-clicking the relevant item in the list.

Another useful feature is the outline window, where the structure of the class is shown. For the class that we are developing, the outline shows the attribute NUM, and the methods constructor and DISP_NUM, as shown in Figure 8-13.

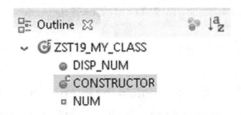

Figure 8-13. *Class outline*

The complete code that we wrote for our example is shown here. This code is written in the code editor for the global class.

```
class ZST19_MY_CLASS definition public final create public.

 public section.
  methods disp_num .
  methods constructor importing num type i.
 protected section.
 private section.
  data num type i.
ENDCLASS.

CLASS ZST19_MY_CLASS IMPLEMENTATION.
  method disp_num.
    write : num .
  endmethod.

  method constructor.
    me->num = num.
  endmethod.
ENDCLASS.
```

Once you have created your class, click the 🐞 button on the toolbar. This will activate the class and a message will appear, as shown in Figure 8-14.

ℹ Activation for ZST19_MY_CLASS successful

Figure 8-14. *Activation message*

We created a simple class that will contain the NUM private attribute with an `integer` type. This can be viewed using the transaction SE24 via SAP GUI, as shown in Figure 8-15.

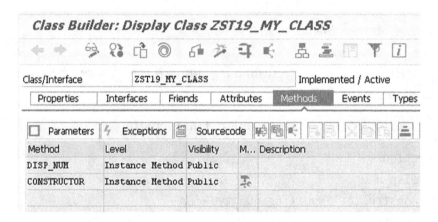

Figure 8-15. *SE24 transaction*

This class may be used globally by all classes in the system and may also be tested via transaction code SE24.

In addition to the global class, a number of other useful tabs exist within the Eclipse IDE at the bottom of the screen. These include the class-relevant local types, local types, test classes, and macros (see Figure 8-16).

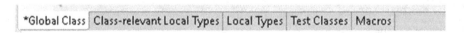

Figure 8-16. *Class-relevant tabs*

We may click the relevant tab in order to display the code editor at the top part of the screen and insert the appropriate code. Since we have used the global classes editor for our current example, these tabs have not been used.

Creating a Local Class in Eclipse

To create a local class, we need to first create an ABAP program within which the local class will be created. This will create local classes as programs created via transaction SE38 using SAP GUI. Follow these steps to create a local class:

- Right-click your project and choose New ➤ ABAP Program. This will create an ABAP program.

- You can then type the definition and implementation code of the given class into the program (see Figure 8-17).

```
▶ Ⓟ ZS_10 ▶ Ⓖ MYCLASS ▶
 1  program zs_10.
 2⊖ class myclass definition .
 3
 4     private section.
 5       methods:
 6         first_test .
 7  endclass.
 8
 9
10⊖ class myclass implementation.
11
12⊖   method first_test.
13
14     endmethod.
15  |
16  endclass.
```

Figure 8-17. *Local class code*

A number of features are available for coding with local classes in Eclipse, especially for working with methods. In order to see the options that are available for a particular method, place the cursor on the method name and press CTRL+1. The options are shown in Figure 8-18.

```
      private section.
        methods:
          first_test .
     endclass.          ┌─────────────────────────────────────┐
                        │ ⌶ Rename first_test  (Ctrl+2, R)     │
                        │ ◇ Make first_test protected          │
     ⊝class myclass     │ ● Make first_test public             │
                        │ ✖ Delete first_test                  │
     ⊝  method first    │ @ Add ABAP Doc                       │
                        └─────────────────────────────────────┘
       endmethod.

       endclass.

     ‹
```

roblems ▥ Proper ──────────────────────────────────────
                        Press 'Ctrl+Shift+1' to show in Quick Assist View

Figure 8-18. *Options*

If you need to rename a method, simply choose the Rename first_test option. This will put the method name in a box (see Figure 8-19). As you change the name in the definition, you will see that the name changes accordingly in the implementation.

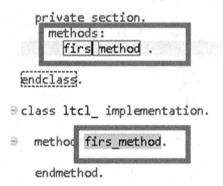

Figure 8-19. *Renaming a method*

Both the definition and implementation parts are automatically adjusted.

We can also make the first_test method protected or public, using the appropriate options. Currently it is private, so the private option is not shown. We can also delete the method. This will delete it from the definition and implementation.

Suppose we have a method called second_method, which only exists in the definition and has not yet been implemented. Place the cursor on the method name in the definition part and press CTRL+1. The options will now appear as shown in Figure 8-20.

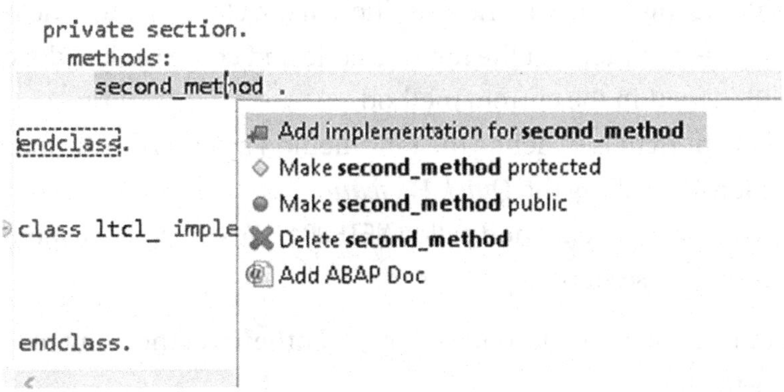

```
    private section.
      methods:
        second_method .

endclass.        Add implementation for second_method
                 ◇ Make second_method protected
                 ● Make second_method public
 class ltcl_ imple ✖ Delete second_method
                 @ Add ABAP Doc

    endclass.
    <
```

Figure 8-20. *Add implementation option*

Note that a new option has been added called Add Implementation.

Choosing this option will add an implementation to the class in which we add our method code (see Figure 8-21).

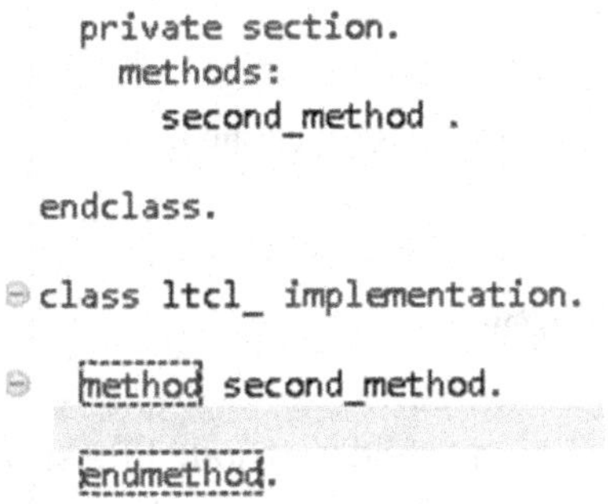

```
    private section.
      methods:
        second_method .

    endclass.

 class ltcl_ implementation.

   method second_method.

     endmethod.
```

Figure 8-21. *Second method implementation*

The cursor will jump inside the newly created method, and we can start writing code immediately.

Method Wizard in Eclipse

We have an embedded form-based wizard within the Eclipse editor for quick creation of class methods along with its signature. In this section, we see how this tool may be used.

Suppose you are in the editor and have already created an ABAP class and are currently within a class method. You now need to define another method that will be called from the method you are currently in.

One way of doing this is to go to the definition of the class and add the new method and its signature. Then implement the method code and come back to the calling point (of the new method) within the current method.

Another quick shortcut is to define the new method by entering the name of the new method in the code and calling the *Quick Fix feature*.

In the example, we have a method called METHOD1. We can create a method called METHOD2 by following these steps:

1. Enter the name METHOD2 followed by parentheses at the point of calling the new method.

2. Press CTRL+1 upon placing the cursor on the method name. This will display the popup shown in Figure 8-22.

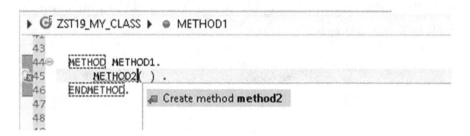

Figure 8-22. *Quick Fix in Eclipse*

3. Double-click the Create method method2 line shown in the popup. A Method Signature popup will appear, as shown in Figure 8-23.

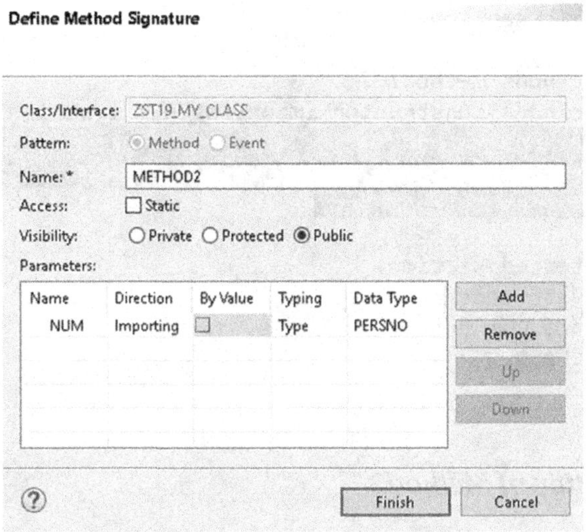

Figure 8-23.   *Defining method signature*

4.   This will display a wizard that defines the signature of the new method we like to define. Here we specify the method details, such as visibility, access, and name.

5.   We also specify the method parameters using the table control provided. We can add and remove method parameters using the Add and Remove buttons, respectively. We specify if we need importing, exporting, changing, or returning parameters. The type of the relevant parameters can be specified using the given value help.

6.   When you are done, click the Finish button. You will see that the wizard automatically generates the new method's declaration along with the necessary parameters (see Figure 8-24).

```
 6  public section.
 7
 8     methods method1 .
 9     methods constructor importing num type i.
10     methods method2
11       importing
12         num type persno.
13
14  protected section.
15  private section.
16    data num type i.
17  ENDCLASS.
18
19
```

Figure 8-24. *Definition of Method2*

Moreover, the call of Method2 within Method1 is also added with the parameters we specified from the Method Creation wizard (see Figure 8-25).

```
30     method method1.
31       method2(
32         num1  =
33         num2 =  )
```

Figure 8-25. *Method call*

An empty implementation of Method2 will also be created. We can now proceed within the code of the new method in the implementation.

Unit Test Templates Using Eclipse

Eclipse offers several useful templates for fast and easy code completion. Using and being aware of such templates is essential for ABAP developers. These are also applicable to unit test programming and are very easy for practicing Test Driven Development (TDD). We can code tests and then design global classes by generating blank methods via the CTRL+1 Quick Fix feature from the test class.

Let's see an example where we have an ABAP program in which we want to create a local unit test class. Within the program, we need to type test or testClass and then call the template for Quick Fix.

- Simply place the cursor on test in the program and press CTRL+SPACE. This will display the popup shown in Figure 8-26.

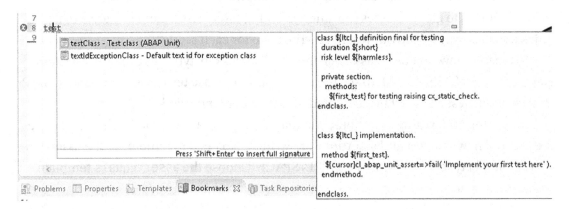

Figure 8-26. *Quick Fix for testClass*

Double-click the **test** class (ABAP unit) option. You will see that the code for the unit class is inserted automatically, as shown in Figure 8-27.

```
 5  *&------------------------------------------------------------------------*
 6  REPORT zst19_test111.
 7
 8⊝ class ltcl_ definition final for testing
 9    duration short
10    risk level harmless.
11
12    private section.
13      methods:
14        first_test for testing raising cx_static_check.
15  endclass.
16
17
18⊝ class ltcl_ implementation.
19
20⊝   method first_test.
21      cl_abap_unit_assert=>fail( 'Implement your first test here' ).
22    endmethod.
23
24  endclass.|
```

Figure 8-27. *Inserted unit class code*

As you see, Eclipse has inserted the basic coding for our test class. The template for the ABAP test class has been used. It contains a class definition having the "for testing" addition. By default, the risk level is harmless, and the duration is specified as short. The name is ltcl_ and the developer can change it. It contains a FIRST_TEST method, which calls the fail method of the CL_ABAP_UNIT_ASSERT class.

For global classes, things are even better. As mentioned, when editing global classes within Eclipse, we have a number of tabs at the bottom of screen. This is very useful when used in context of unit tests. These tabs allow the developer to easily see which section belongs to global classes (production code), test classes, etc. They are a really quick and easy way to find out where to write code for each section.

To create a new unit test class, click the Test Classes tab, type `test` in the Test Class view, and press CTRL+SPACE to see the suggestions. Choose testClass – Test class (ABAP Unit), and the test class will be generated. It can be later modified.

For testing and writing assertions, you may simply initialize variables and then code the method in which test and assertions are written. No need to remember the assertion syntax. Simply type `assert` and use CTRL+SPACE. Choose the `assertEquals` template shown on display.

Modifying Templates

As mentioned earlier in this chapter, Eclipse provides a number of templates for code completion. Templates are very powerful and make the coding process very fast. The shortcuts CTRL+SPACE and CTRL+1 for code generation make coding faster than when using SE80.

You may create new templates or change existing ones.

Note   Templates can be used for any ABAP development and not only in development related to ABAP classes.

To change templates, follow the menu path Window ➤ Preferences.

The dialog box shown in Figure 8-28 appears.

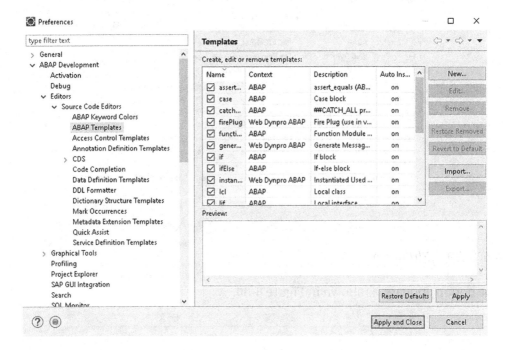

Figure 8-28. *Templates*

Under the node ABAP development on the left pane, choose Source -> Templates. On the right side, you will see the various templates available. There are buttons for editing an existing template and the New button to create a new template.

Each template is denoted by a name, which may be called from within a program.

These templates belong to the General, ABAP, ABAP Objects, or Web Dynpro categories (or contexts). The existing ABAP object-related templates are `assertEquals`, `lif`, `lcl`, and `testClass`.

When you are coding the program, simply type the entire name of the template or part of it. Then use the code completion technique CTRL+SPACE or the CRL+1 shortcut to see proposals with code completion.

You can also change the existing templates. For example, by default, the assertion is written on one line, but you can update the template to have each parameter shown on a new line. Simply select the template and click the Edit button, as shown in Figure 8-29.

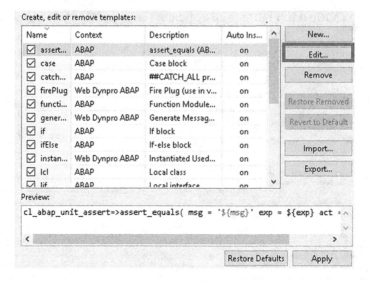

Figure 8-29. *Edit option*

The popup appears, as shown in Figure 8-30.

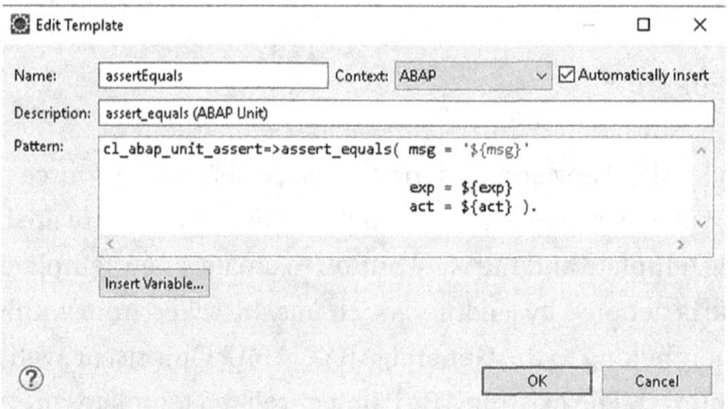

Figure 8-30. *Editing method call*

Here, we change the pattern of the code for the assertEquals method. Then click OK. This will take us back to the previous screen. Make sure to click the Apply button.

Once this is done, the CTRL+SPACE option will show us the method call, as shown in Figure 8-31.

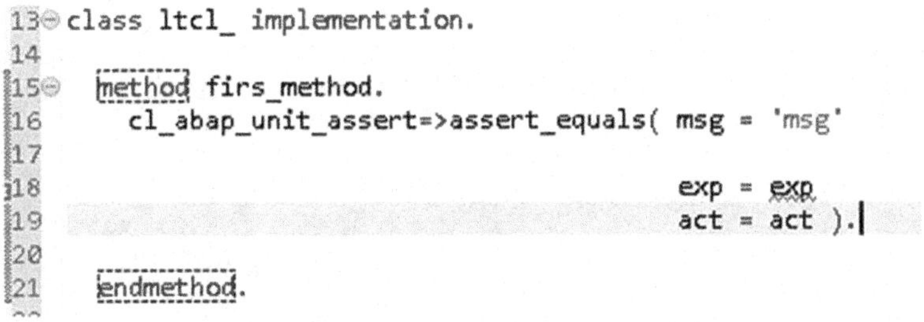

```
13⊖ class ltcl_ implementation.
14
15⊖    method firs_method.
16        cl_abap_unit_assert=>assert_equals( msg = 'msg'
17
18                                             exp = exp
19                                             act = act ).|
20
21    endmethod.
```

Figure 8-31. *Method call*

Summary

In this chapter, you configured the ABAP development environment with ABAP Development Tools (ADT) in Eclipse, created your first ABAP project, used Eclipse to code unit test classes, and saw Eclipse's Quick Fix feature used in conjunction with ABAP Objects.

Index

A, B

ABAP Project in Eclipse
    backend systems, 243
    development objects, 244
    logon credentials, 244
    system connection list, 243
ABAP unit browser
    button, 236
    SE80 transaction, 235
    steps, 234
    test classes, 237
    user-specific settings, 235
Abstract classes, 94–96
ALV Object Model
    add header text, 180–183
    advantages, 177
    CL_SALV_COLUMNS_TABLE class, 179
    CL_SALV_FUNCTIONS class, 179
    CL_SALV_TABLE class, 178, 179
    output, 180
ASSERT_EQUALS method, 220, 222, 223, 226, 228
ATTACH_FOR_WRITE method, 169

C

Casting and polymorphism, 73
    CREATE OBJECT statements, 76
    DISPLAY_PLAYER_DETAILS method, 75
    downcasting, 73

    GET_COLUMN method, 74
    program output, 77–80
    upcasting, 73
CL_ABAP_UNIT_ASSERT class
    ASSERT_EQUALS method, 228
    fixture methods, 227, 228, 230
    parameters, 228, 229
    values, 229
Class builder, 101, 104
    buttons on SE24 tab, 112, 113
    class browser, 113, 114
        screen, 114
        testing classes in SE24, 114
        testing static method, 115–119
    features, 104, 105
    instance methods, testing, 119
        account attributes, 122
        Attributes tab, 120
        calculation code, 121
        class methods, 123
        constructor method, 120
        cube class, 119
        cubic value, 122
        debit amount method, 125
        Instance screen, 121
        method deposit balance, 123
        NEW_BALANCE method, 124
        object testing, 125
        parameters tab, 120
        setting new balance, 126–128

© Rehan Zaidi 2019
R. Zaidi, *SAP ABAP Objects*, https://doi.org/10.1007/978-1-4842-4964-2

Printed in the United States
By Bookmasters

Printed in the United States
By Bookmasters